ISBN 978-1-330-76228-8
PIBN 10102156

1 MONTH OF
FREE
READING

at

www.ForgottenBooks.com

By purchasing this book you are eligible for one month membership to ForgottenBooks.com, giving you unlimited access to our entire collection of over 700,000 titles via our web site and mobile apps.

To claim your free month visit:

www.forgottenbooks.com/free102156

English
Français
Deutsche
Italiano
Español
Português

www.forgottenbooks.com

Mythology Photography **Fiction**
Fishing Christianity **Art** Cooking
Essays Buddhism Freemasonry
Medicine **Biology** Music **Ancient
Egypt** Evolution Carpentry Physics
Dance Geology **Mathematics** Fitness
Shakespeare **Folklore** Yoga Marketing
Confidence Immortality Biographies
Poetry **Psychology** Witchcraft
Electronics Chemistry History **Law**
Accounting **Philosophy** Anthropology
Alchemy Drama Quantum Mechanics
Atheism Sexual Health **Ancient History**
Entrepreneurship Languages Sport
Paleontology Needlework Islam
Metaphysics Investment Archaeology
Parenting Statistics Criminology
Motivational

American Teachers' Series

The Teaching of Latin and Greek in the Secondary School

BY

CHARLES E. BENNETT, A.B.

AND

GEORGE P. BRISTOL, A.M.

PROFESSORS IN CORNELL UNIVERSITY

NEW EDITION

LONGMANS, GREEN, AND CO.

FOURTH AVENUE & 30TH STREET, NEW YORK

LONDON, BOMBAY AND CALCUTTA

1911

UNIVERSITY PRESS · JOHN WILSON
AND SON · CAMBRIDGE, U.S.A.

Editor's Preface

SECONDARY education is no new thing. Human society has always granted commanding positions to men who were qualified by natural ability and special training to lead their fellows. With advancing civilization the need of specially trained leaders became increasingly apparent; schools were eventually established to meet this need. Such institutions, however rudimentary their course of instruction, were essentially secondary schools. Thus the schools of the grammarians and rhetoricians were calculated to develop leadership in the forum at a time when oratory was a recognized power in the political life of Greece and Rome. Later in the Middle Age the Church became the dominant social force, and gave rise to cathedral and monastic schools for the education of the clergy. With the founding of universities, however, the secondary schools took over the ·preparation of promising youths for professional study in the interests of Church and State. And this function has continued to be the chief characteristic of secondary education until the present time.

The modern elementary school, on the other hand, is of comparatively recent growth. In a certain sense every man is educated, but historically the education of

the masses comes for the most part through custom
and tradition and the ordinary experiences of life.
Schools for the people and formal instruction are not
required until there is universal recognition of individual worth, such as the worth of the human soul which
inspired Luther to found the elementary schools of
Germany, or the worth of the citizen and his political
rights under a representative government which led
to the public schools of America and England. The
recognition of such rights by a democratic society obviously leads to a complete school system in which the
line of demarcation between its various divisions, as elementary, secondary, and higher, is arbitrarily drawn.

The ideals which determine the growth of educational
systems never remain long fixed; they change from age
to age to conform to the development of the political,
economic, and spiritual life of a people. The mediæval
school system was quickly overthrown in Protestant
countries by the combined influence of the humanists
and the reformers. And the Protestant schools, in
turn, held undisputed sway only so long as their religious ideals found popular support. Within the last
hundred years another transformation has been effected
in the educational ideals of the western world, and new
school systems have been evolved under the direction
of the State for the purpose of promoting civil order
and social stability. The social mind has come to
recognize the fact that the Church is no longer able to
shape society as it once did; and it also recognizes
that each generation is under moral obligations to im-
prove its cultural inheritance and transmit it unentailed.

Hence the resort to the strongest force in modern society for the accomplishment of this purpose. The process of socializing the individual — of making him an efficient, intelligent, loyal member of society — has no mean significance. The end in view is one of the greatest of human needs; and it is equally the concern of every parent and every citizen.

School reform, however, never amounts to complete revolution. The organization and administration of school systems may be revolutionized by ministerial rescript, as in Prussia during the Napoleonic wars, or by act of Parliament, as in England within the past thirty years, or by the adoption of a constitution, as in many American states, but the instruction of children cannot be reached by legal enactment or popular vote. The average teacher will consistently conform to the letter of the law and as persistently violate its spirit. The result is that long after new ideas are distinctly enunciated, even after they are generally accepted by intelligent persons, the strangest confusion often pervades the class-room. Teachers are naturally conservative; they can teach only what they themselves have learned, and the traditions of the profession combined with their own acquired habits incline them to teach as they themselves have been taught. Thus the prevailing means and methods of instruction do not always conform to the accepted standards of education, and reform is halted midway in its course.

Great progress has been made in recent years, but the results which show up so well on paper are not in all respects satisfactory. We have state school systems well organized and thoroughly equipped; we have, too, institutions in great variety serving ends of their own choosing. The growth has been in two directions, from the top downward and from the bottom upward. The colleges have dipped down into the lower strata and given rise to preparatory schools largely patronized by the favored classes of society; the common schools, imbued with more democratic sympathies, have expanded into public high schools in which social distinctions have no place. The preparatory school aims to send its pupils to college; the ways and means of best attaining this purpose are conditioned by what the college wants and what it will accept. The American high school, in its effort to serve all classes, purports to be a school preparatory both for college and the ordinary avocations of life. One class in the community expects it to complete the educational structure begun in the common schools; another class expects it to lay a substantial foundation for further academic training. Thus the confusion resulting from the natural conservatism of the teacher is worse confounded by conflicting social interests.

In all the field of education there are no problems more difficult to solve than those pertaining to the work of the secondary school. What is the aim of secondary education? What is its function in modern society? What knowledge is of most worth? What means and methods produce the best results? Such questions as these come to every secondary teacher and demand an answer. The most encouraging sign of the times is the growth of a teaching profession pledged to study these problems intelligently and to find some rational solution of them.

The "American Teachers Series," the first volume of which is herewith presented, will review the principal subjects of the secondary school curriculum. The purpose is to discuss the educational value of each subject, the reasons for including it in the curriculum, the selection and arrangement of materials in the course, the essential features of class instruction and the various helps which are available for teachers' use. These books are not intended to correct the faults of ignorant teaching; they are not put forth as manuals of infallible methods. They are merely contributions to the professional knowledge necessary in secondary education. They are addressed to teachers of liberal culture and special scholarship who are seeking to make their knowledge more useful to their pupils and their pupils more useful to the State.

JAMES E. RUSSELL.

TEACHERS COLLEGE,
Columbia University.

Contents

THE TEACHING OF LATIN IN THE SECONDARY SCHOOL

THE TEACHING OF GREEK IN THE SECONDARY SCHOOL

THE TEACHING OF LATIN IN THE SECONDARY SCHOOL

BY

CHARLES E. BENNETT, A.B.

PROFESSOR OF LATIN IN CORNELL UNIVERSITY

The Teaching of Latin in the Secondary School

INTRODUCTION

HISTORICAL POSITION OF THE STUDY OF LATIN IN MODERN EDUCATION

BIBLIOGRAPHY.

Paulsen, F. Geschichte des gelehrten Unterrichts auf den deutschen Schulen und Universitäten vom Ausgang des Mittelalters bis zur Gegenwart. Leipzig. 1885. Second ed., 1897.

Dettweiler, P., in Baumeister, A., Handbuch der Erziehungs- und Unterrichtslehre für höhere Schulen. Vol. iii. Didaktik und Methodik der einzelnen Lehrfächer, Erste Hälfte, III. Lateinisch, p. 7 ff., 'Die geschichtliche Entwickelung des lateinischen Unterrichts.'

. IT[1] is a sufficiently familiar fact that, whatever considerations now determine the retention of Latin as an instrument of the higher education, its place was not originally secured as the result of conscious deliberation and choice, but *Position of Latin in the Middle Ages.* purely as the result of irresistible historical circumstances. The political, ecclesiastical, and literary conditions of the Middle Ages made the study of Latin indispensable to every person of station. Latin was the language of the Church, of the State, of law, of scholars, of the professions. It was studied therefore in the monastic schools with the object of ac-

---

[1] In this introductory chapter I have drawn largely upon the treatment of Dettweiler above cited.

quiring a practical mastery of the spoken idiom for actual use. Pupils were trained in the preparation of letters and such other documents as the necessities of the political and ecclesiastical life of the day demanded. Latin was not only the medium of instruction in the schools, but was also the medium of all conversation. The Latin authors read served merely the purpose of increasing and improving the pupil's knowledge of the language and his facility in its employment. The *content* of the Latin writers was practically disregarded throughout the entire period of the Middle Ages. This conception of the function of Latin naturally determined the method pursued in teaching. As the Latin vocabulary was confessedly inadequate for the needs of the day, it became necessary to add new words, coined to cover new conceptions. These were incorporated in special vocabularies, which pupils committed to memory. Mechanical oral reading was also extensively practised, — often before the pupils were capable of understanding what was read. Intended to serve merely mechanical purposes, Latin was studied exclusively in a mechanical way. Yet, irrational as the method seems to us, we can hardly deny that it was entirely consistent with the purposes which the study was at that time intended to subserve. Nor can we feel surprise that, with this conception of the function of Latin, there should have prevailed a low and almost barbarous standard in the employment of the spoken and written idiom.

With the humanistic revival of the fourteenth and fifteenth centuries there manifested itself an altered and **The Human-** a loftier conception of Latin study. This new **istic Revival.** conception was a natural and inevitable result of the fundamental spirit of the humanistic movement. While throughout the Middle Ages all intellectual life

had culminated in the ecclesiastical ideals of the scholastic philosophy, the new movement placed man, human
capacities, human achievements, and human aspirations
in the foreground. The great works of classical antiquity were recognised as of vital importance in under
standing and solving the new problems.

This conception of Latin as an instrument of education speedily wrought a revolution in methods of teaching. Hitherto both form and content of the Latin
masterpieces had been neglected. Now both began to
meet recognition. The great Latin classics were read
and studied for their vital bearings on the intellectual
life and aspirations of the new era. They were no
longer primarily a means of acquiring a familiarity with
the *disjecta membra* of the barbarous idiom which had till
recently prevailed.

Along with this appreciation of the substance of
Roman thought went an appreciation for the form in
which it was expressed. The spirit of the day was
anti-barbarous to a degree. Correctness and elegance
of diction came to be a passion with the Latinists of
the time. This tendency naturally went too far, and
we notice the beginning of an arbitrary exaltation of
the Ciceronian manner of speech as the sole example
worthy of imitation, — an attitude which unfortunately,
despite frequent and vigorous protest, is still widely
prevalent to-day.

It is essentially this humanistic conception of Latin
study which has prevailed in modern education since the
Renaissance. The special details of devel- Latin in
opment for Germany may be found pre- Recent Times.
sented by a master hand in the work of Paulsen above
cited. So far as I know, no such presentation of the
historical stages of Latin study in any other European
country is yet available. Probably in no other would

such a history have the interest or the historical and pedagogical significance afforded by the experience of the German schools.

In the United States, Latin, as a study of the secondary education, naturally started with purely English **In the United** traditions. These traditions fortunately were **States.** humanistic in the best sense. Still, for a long time Latin was thought to be peculiarly a study for boys who were preparing for college. In the earlier history of this country this meant that Latin was thought to have educative importance primarily for those looking forward to activity in the church, in letters, in the law, in medicine, or in teaching. During the last generation in particular a different attitude seems to be manifesting itself. The number of students of Latin in our secondary schools has in recent years been increasing out of all proportion to the number of students who go to college. Unless this phenomenon be attributed to an unaccountable infatuation, it admits to my mind of but a single interpretation: Latin is now recognised as an important element of secondary education for the average pupil, whether he be intending to go to college or not. It is perhaps unfortunate that the present tendency towards a larger study of Latin in our schools cannot be traced to any recent sober discussions of the value of Latin; in fact it is not a little surprising that this rapidly increased recognition has occurred in the face of the most vigorous assaults upon the classics which this country has ever witnessed. Yet experience is the great teacher, more convincing than all the arguments of the academicians. Is it too bold to say that the experience of those who have studied Latin and of those who have seen the positive results of the study upon others, is after all the ultimate reason which is at present so potent in winning increased recognition

for Latin? Whatever the cause of the existing conditions, they are with us. That they may be permanent
is to be hoped. That there is abundant justification
for their permanence, it will be the aim of the following
chapter to show.

CHAPTER I

THE JUSTIFICATION OF LATIN AS AN INSTRUMENT OF SECONDARY EDUCATION

BIBLIOGRAPHY.[1]

Laurie, S. S. Lectures on Language and Linguistic Method. Cambridge University Press. 1890. Chapter i. and particularly Chapter vii. Chapters on the Aims and Practice of Teaching, edited by Frederic Spencer. Cambridge University Press. 1897. Chapter ii., Latin, by W. L. Paton.

Fouillée, Alfred. Education from a National Standpoint. London, Arnold. New York, Appleton. 1892.

Handbuch der Erziehungs- und Unterrichtslehre für höhere Schulen, herausgegeben von A. Baumeister. Munich. C. H. Beck'sche Verlagsbuchhandlung. 1898. Didaktik und Methodik der einzelnen Lehrfächer. III. Lateinisch, von P. Dettweiler.

Boyesen, H. H.; Brandt, H. C. G.; Sachs, Julius; Mackenzie, James C.; and others, in Proceedings of the First Annual Convention (1893) of the Association of Colleges and Preparatory Schools in the Middle States and Maryland. Published for the Association. Philadelphia. 1894. pp. 38–64.

Paulsen, Friedrich. Geschichte des gelehrten Unterrichts auf den deutschen Schulen und Universitäten. Leipzig. 1885. Veit & Comp. Particularly " Schlussbetrachtung." pp. 755–784.

Harris, W. T. On the Function of the Study of Latin and Greek in Education. Journal of Social Science. 1885.

Harris, W. T. A Brief for Latin. EDUCATIONAL REVIEW. April, 1899.

Peck, Tracy. Discussion in SCHOOL REVIEW. 1893. pp. 593 ff.

Shorey, Paul. Discipline vs. Dissipation. SCHOOL REVIEW. 1897. pp. 217 ff.

Collar, W. C.; Burgess, Isaac; Manny, Frank. Proceedings of the National Educational Association. 1896. pp. 563 ff.

Bennett, C. E. Latin in the Secondary School. SCHOOL REVIEW. May, 1893.

Spencer, Herbert. Education, Intellectual, Moral, and Physical. London, Williams & Norgate. New York, D. Appleton & Co. 1861.

---

[1] Only the more important recent literature is here cited.

Bain, Alexander. Education as a Science. London, Kegan Paul & Co. New York, D. Appleton & Co. 1881.

Planck, H. Das Recht des Lateinischen als wissenschaftlichen Bildungsmittel. Stuttgart. Schulprogramm. 1888.

Schmeding. Die klassische Bildung in der Gegenwart. Berlin. 1885.

Frary, R. La Question du Latin. Paris. 1890.

James, Professor Edmund J. The Classical Question in Germany. POPULAR SCIENCE MONTHLY. January, 1884.

Barnett, P. A. Common Sense in Education and Teaching. Chapter viii. London and New York. Longmans, Green, & Co. 1899.

Jebb, R. C. Humanism in Education. (Romanes Lecture for 1899.) London. Macmillan & Co. 1899.

Eliot, C. W. American Contributions to Civilization. New York. The Century Co. 1897.

Sidgwick, Henry. Theory of Classical Education, in his Miscellaneous Essays and Addresses. London. 1904.

THE question as to the educational worth of any study must always be a pertinent one. This is particularly true in the case of Latin, which has not only The Question for generations occupied a commanding place before us. in the curriculum of American secondary education, but in recent years has even been winning enormously increased favour among us. Despite the extensive literature on the subject, it has seemed necessary, at the beginning of this volume on the teaching of Latin in the secondary school, to examine afresh the title of Latin to the present respect it enjoys, and to state anew the reasons why it is of value in secondary education. Lest there be any misconception as to the subject of the chapter, it is desirable to emphasize at the outset that the value of Latin as a college study does not here enter into consideration. That question, interesting and important as it is, seems to me entirely distinct from the question as to the value of Latin in the secondary school.

The fundamental importance of the examination proposed hardly needs to be urged. For obviously the general method of instruction to be followed in teaching Latin must depend largely upon the results that the study is capable of achieving, and the teacher who fails clearly to apprehend the goal to be attained must necessarily pursue but a groping course in imparting instruction. The recent increase, too, in the number of pupils studying Latin in our secondary schools makes it of increasing importance to get clearly before our minds the functions and purpose of the study. The Statistics of the Commissioner of Education for the United States show that in the eight years prior to 1898 the number of pupils studying Latin in our secondary schools had increased 174 per cent, while the total enrolment of pupils in the secondary schools for the same period had increased but 84 per cent. In the eight years from 1898–1906 also the increase in the number of Latin students more than kept pace with the increase in school attendance. No thoughtful person can fail to be impressed by these figures. If Latin is not of basal importance in the secondary curriculum, then large numbers of students are making a prodigious error in pursuing the subject; and the sooner we understand this, the better. If, on the other hand, the increase is the result of wise choice or even of wise instinct, we must, while rejoicing at the greater recognition Latin is securing, at the same time admit our own vastly increased responsibility for its wise direction and promotion.

Before considering the special reasons that exist in favor of studying Latin, let us first consider the function of language in general as an instrument of education.

Educational Function of Language in General.

The function of education is confessedly to prepare pupils to be useful members of society. To make them such, it is essential that they be taught to understand as fully as possible the nature and character of the national life — social, civil, political, religious — in which they are born or in which their lot is cast. To a certain extent, also, it is essential that they learn to apprehend the nature and character of the larger life of the race.

What now is the instrument best adapted to the attainment of this end? It is language. As pointed out by Laurie (*Lectures on Language and Linguistic Method*, chapter i.), language is the supreme instrument in education, *i. e.* the higher education, because of its universal nature. It promotes intellectual discipline and brings intellectual power, because the study of language brings us at every turn face to face, as nothing else does, with subjects and questions of intellectual concern and intellectual interest. Language deals with ideas, it touches perpetually on problems of the relations of man to man, of man to society, of man to the State. Its analysis demands refinement and nicety of thinking. So long then as ideas are important, and so long as the underlying conceptions which reflect the national life of a people are important, the supreme value of the mastery of these through language study will continue to be recognised.

By the study of language is meant the study of one's own language; but, as will be pointed out later in this chapter, this study of one's own language is achieved incomparably better by the indirect method of studying another language. Only so can the necessary processes of comparison be effectively instituted. To this it has often been objected that the Greeks, so con- Significance spicuous for their brilliant civilization and of the Neglect their permanent contributions to the intel- Study by lectual life of subsequent ages, studied no the Greeks. language but their own. An excited partisan,[1] in the heat of discussion, once went so far as to assert, " Grant-

---

[1] Professor E. L. Youmans in the POPULAR SCIENCE MONTHLY for December, 1883, p. 270, b.

ing the unapproachable perfection of Greek literature, and that the Greeks surpassed the world in philosophical acuteness, the invincible fact remains that they expended no effort in the study of foreign languages, *and common sense declares it was because of it.*" Obviously, if " common sense " declared anything so absurd, it should explain to us why the Hottentots or the Eskimos or the hordes of other barbarians who likewise know no language but their own, have not been similarly eminent for their contributions to human thought.

As to the Greeks, it will probably always be impossible to account for the achievements of that wonderful people on the basis of their system of education. What they accomplished seems rather the result of an inexplicable national endowment. Their fine æsthetic sense, their keen speculative capacity, are as difficult to account for as the unique genius of the Romans for political organization, for government, and for law, or the profound sense of moral obligation to a higher power so impressively formulated by the Hebrews, — as difficult to explain as the rise of a Charlemagne in the eighth century or an Alfred in the ninth. Great as the Greeks were by endowment, they certainly were not great for their attainments. With all their highly developed æsthetic sense and their subtle speculative acumen, they were manifestly deficient in the capacities which it is the function of modern education to develop, namely, a just understanding of the problems of society, an understanding which shall secure and promote the stability of the social and political organism. Had the Greeks been as well educated as they were highly gifted, it is likely that their own national life would have run a longer and a more glorious course, and that their great legacy to posterity would thus have been immensely increased.

At all events, the fact that the Greeks, despite their neglect of language study, nevertheless attained a certain national greatness in some directions, cannot be · cited as disproving the educative value of such study for us to-day.

What, now, are the reasons for studying Latin in the secondary school? What are the effects of the study upon the pupil that are at present so potent Reasons for not merely in maintaining its status but in Studying extending its vogue? These reasons are Latin. several, and I shall enumerate them in what seems to me the order of their importance.

First and foremost, I should say Latin is of value because it confers a mastery over the resources of one's mother tongue.[1] This mastery comes as the direct and necessary result of careful daily translation, — a process involving on the one hand a careful consid- Training eration and analysis of the thought of the in the author read, and on the other a severe and Vernacular. laborious comparison of the value of alternative English words, phrases, and sentences, with the consequent attainment of skill in making the same effective as vehicles of expression. No one, I think, will undertake to deny that the results here claimed are actual; and it actual, it can hardly be denied that they constitute an important justification for the study of Latin.

Training in English, then, as the result of careful translation from Latin is here set down as the first and most important reason for studying Latin. To my own mind this reason weighs more than all others combined,

---

[1] This is not meant in the narrow sense of a mere understanding of the *meanings* of words; it is the mastery of *ideas* of which words are but the symbols, and the assimilation of these into one's own intellectual life, that I have in mind.

though several other excellent reasons for the study of Latin will be discussed later.   Let us examine more in

Analysis of the Process. detail how translation from Latin gives such admirable training in English.   Translation is a severe exercise.   The lexicon or vocabulary tells the meanings of words, and the grammar states the force of inflected forms; but it is only after the pupil, provided with this equipment, has attacked his Latin sentence with a view to translation that the real struggle begins.   His vocabulary may have given him a dozen or even twenty meanings under a single verb or noun, and the pupil must reflect and nicely discriminate before he can choose the right word, the one just suited to the context.   Further, his Latin sentence may be long, complex, and periodic, entirely different in structure from anything we know in English; such a sentence must be broken up and so arranged as to conform to our English mode of expression; or the Latin sentence may have one of those Protean ablative absolutes, — an idiom that our English style practically abhors.   Every such ablative absolute has to be examined with care prior to an English rendering.   It may express time, cause, concession, condition, attendant circumstance, means, or what not, and must be rendered accordingly. Again the Latin sentence may secure by its arrangement of words certain effects of emphasis which English can bring out only by the employment of very different resources.

For the purpose of further illustration, let us take the opening lines of Nepos's life of Miltiades, and note the problems that suggest themselves to the pupil's mind as he endeavours to secure a passable translation for the Latin.   The text runs as follows: *Miltiades, Cimonis filius, Atheniensis, cum et antiquitate generis et gloria majorum et sua modestia unus omnium maxime floreret,*

*eaque esset aetate ut non jam solum de eo bene sperare,
sed etiam confidere cives possent sui talem eum futurum
qualem cognitum judicarunt, accidit ut Athenienses Cher-
sonesum colonos vellent mittere.*

Probably the first stumbling-block to the pupil will
be the proper rendering for *modestia*. The vocabulary
gives ' moderation,' ' modesty,' ' temperance,' ' humility,'
' discretion,' and the question is, which one of these
represents the idea that Nepos is trying to convey.
The pupil has to pause and consider. Reflection shows
that ' humility ' will not do, and ' modesty ' is no better.
These qualities hardly constitute a title to eminence.
The pupil, therefore, turns to ' moderation ' or ' temperance.' The latter of these will hardly answer his
purpose; it has an unfortunate acquired connotation
suggesting predominantly an abstinence from strong
drink. Nor will ' moderation' satisfy the pupil's sense of
the demands of his native tongue, for we hardly speak of
a man eminent for his moderation. Of the five words
given for *modestia*, therefore, the last only, ' discretion,'
will answer in the present passage. The pupil then
passes to the following words: *unus omnium maxime.*
Their literal translation is easy, ' alone of all especially;'
but this is jargon, and clearly must be bettered in some
way. By reflection, the pupil comes to see that ' alone
of all ' may be rendered by our ' beyond all others,' or
some other equally idiomatic phrase. But here a new
problem presents itself, how to join ' especially ' with
' beyond all others.' Possibly after a few trials the boy
hits upon the device of rendering ' far beyond all others.'
Whether this phrase or another be chosen, however,
may depend somewhat upon the rendering selected for
floreret; in fact at each point in a translation the rendering .must be regarded as possibly only temporary;
one's selection of words and phrases will often require

modification as a result of the rendering chosen for other parts of the same sentence. The pupil meets no further special difficulty until he comes to *qualem cognitum judicarunt*. Literally, 'such as they judged him known.' In and of itself, the participle may mean 'if known,' 'though known,' 'when known,' 'since known.' All these possibilities, however, must be weighed before a safe decision can be reached as to the actual meaning here.

But I need not dwell further on the details of the process we are considering. Every teacher knows what it is; he knows that it is serious work, often slow work, but he knows what it means to the pupil who submits to it. He knows that such a pupil is gaining a mastery over the resources of his mother tongue. Positive knowledge, except to a very limited degree, he is not gaining; but he is learning what words mean; he is learning to differentiate related concepts; he is acquiring sense for form and style, and if he be so fortunate as to be endowed with any native gifts of thought himself when he reaches maturer years, he has that indispensable equipment of the educated man, — the capacity to say what he says with directness, clearness, precision, and effect.

There has been a great outcry in recent years about the importance of English, and it has been one with which I think the body of thoughtful men have in large measure sympathized. All have cheerfully acknowledged the great importance of an ability to use one's native idiom with skill and power. It is because I sympathize so heartily with this sentiment that I enter this defence of translation. It is because translation from Latin to English seems to me such a stimulating, vitalizing exercise, and so helpful to the student who would attain mastery of his own language, — it is because of this that I find full justification for the study of Latin.

Perhaps I approach this subject with prejudice, but I can never forget the inspiration of my own early Latin training, nor ever fail in gratitude to the teacher who first suggested to me the boundless resources of our own language, who by his own happy and faithful renderings of Cicero and Virgil stimulated a little class of us to do our best to make our own translations show truth, and strength, and literary form. Can we afford to underrate the value of such discipline? How many a lad has felt his heart kindle and his ambition rise at some happy rendering by mate or teacher? And with what persistence these little niceties of phrase cling to us and influence us? Language is subtle. We cannot explain its charm by any philosophy. But it is the key to literature, and our own language must ever be the best key to our own literature.

How finely Barrie has put this in his story of Tommy! Who that has read that unique description of the essay-contest can have done so without feeling the profound truth it contains? You remember the scene in the old Scotch school-house, — how Tommy and young McLauchlan had been given paper and pen and set to work to write on " A Day in Church " in competition for the Blackadder Prize, and how at the end of the time allotted Tommy had brought himself to scorn for the lack of a word. " What word? " they asked him testily; but even now he could not tell. He had wanted a Scotch word that would signify how many people were in church and it was on the tip of his tongue, but would come no farther " Puckle " was nearly the word, but it did not mean so many people as he meant. The hour had gone by like winking; he had forgotten all about time while searching his mind for the word.

Then the friends who had been waiting in confident

expectation of Tommy's victory begin their reproaches. His teacher, Cathro, is the first. " What ailed you at 'manzy'? " he cries, "or" ·—. " I thought of 'manzy,'" replied Tommy, wofully, for he was ashamed of himself, "but — but a manzy's a swarm. It would mean that the folk in the kirk were buzzing thegither like bees, instead of sitting still."

" Even if it does mean that," says another friend, " what was the sense of being so particular? Surely the art of essay-writing consists in using the first word that comes and hurrying on."

" That's how I did," proudly says McLauchlan, the victorious competitor.

" I see," interposes another friend, " that McLauchlan speaks of there being a mask of people in the church. ' Mask' is a fine Scotch word."

" I thought of ' mask,'" says Tommy, " but that would have meant the kirk was crammed, and I just meant it to be middling full."

" 'Flow' would have done," suggested another.

" 'Flow' 's but a handful."

" 'Curran,' then, you jackanapes."

" 'Curran' 's no enough."

The friends throw up their hands in despair.

" I wanted something between 'curran' and 'mask,'" said Tommy, dogged, yet almost at the crying.

Then Ogilvy, the master of the victorious McLauchlan, but whose heart is secretly with Tommy, and who with difficulty has been hiding his admiration, spreads a net for him. " You said you wanted a word that meant middling full. Well, why did you not say 'middling full' or ' fell mask'? "

" Yes, why not? " demanded the others.

" I wanted *one* word," said Tommy.

" You jewel," muttered Ogilvy under his breath.

"It's so easy to find the right word," reproachfully adds another

"It's no', it's as difficult as to hit a squirrel." Again Ogilvy nods approval. But Cathro, Tommy's master, can restrain himself no longer. In a burst of fury he seizes Tommy by the neck and runs him out of the parish school of Thrums. As the others offer their congratulations to Ogilvy, master of the victorious McLauchlan, the school door opens from without, and the face of Tommy, tear-stained and excited, appears once more. " I ken the word now; it came to me a' at once; it is ' hantle.' "

"Oh, the sumph!" exclaimed McLauchlan; " as if it mattered what the word is now."

But Ogilvy gives his McLauchlan a push that nearly sends him sprawling, saying in an ecstasy to himself: " He *had* to think of it till he got it; and he got it."

When Cathro savagely says, " I have one satisfaction; I ran him out of my school," Ogilvy merely answers, " Who knows but what you may be proud to dust a chair for him when he comes back?"

How many of us know well this quest for the right word! How often we have struggled to find it when it was n't ' puckle' and it was n't ' manzy,' nor ' mask,' nor ' flow,' nor ' curran,' but ' hantle'! Sometimes we have found it, sometimes we have missed it; but the quest has ever been honourable, and has helped us to find and know the way to truth.

Cicero was well aware of the importance of what I am urging when he wrote those memorable words in his *de optimo genere oratorum*. Despite his thorough familiarity with Greek, he confesses that he found it a useful exercise to translate with care from Greek to Latin. In this way he prepared Latin versions of Demosthenes on the Crown and of Aeschines against

Cicero's Testimony.

Ctesiphon, not rendering word for word, but preserving the style and spirit of these two *orationes nobilissimae,* weighing their words, he adds, not counting them.

Compare also what Lowell says. Speaking before the Modern Language Association in 1889, after a life of wide

Lowell. observation and careful reflection upon the problems of education, he says: " In reading such books as chiefly deserve to be read in any foreign language, it is wise to translate consciously and in words as we read. There is no such help to a fuller mastery of our vernacular. It compels us to such a choosing, and testing, to so nice a discrimination of sound, propriety, position, and shade of meaning, that we now first learn the secret of the words we have been using or misusing all our lives, and are gradually made aware that to set forth even the plainest matter as it should be set forth is not only a very difficult thing, calling for thought and practice, but is an affair of conscience as well. Translation teaches, as nothing else can, not only that there is a best way, but that it is the only way. Those who have tried it know too well how easy it is to grasp the verbal meaning of a sentence or of a verse. That is the bird in the hand. The real meaning, the soul of it, that which makes it literature and not jargon, that is the bird in the bush, which tantalizes and stimu lates with the vanishing glimpses we catch of it as it flits from one to another lurking-place:

> Et fugit ad salices et se cupit ante videri.

Lowell may not have been a great teacher. His limitations in the class-room were probably very pronounced, but that, for all that, he possessed by nature and training a clear sense for what is vital and strengthening in education, I am thoroughly persuaded. At all events, the words I have quoted are the ones I have

always heard commended when mention has been made
of the address in which they are found.

This transcendent importance of translation as bearing upon an increased mastery of one's vernacular is so
generally recognised by educators that it seems worth
while to cite a few further similar expressions of opinion
as to its value. Thus we find Dettweiler declaring (Baumeister's *Handbuch der Erzie-* Dettweiler.
hungs- und Unterrichtslehre, iii. Lateinisch, p. 22): "We
must not forget that the real strength of Latin instruction lies in the recognition of the wide difference of
ideas, which is brought out in the choice of words and
phrases as one translates from Latin to German.
These ends we must reach . . . by *a constant comparison with the mother tongue*,[1] through the medium *of a
much more extensive employment of translation*[2] than
has heretofore prevailed." At a later point (pp. 54 ff.)
Dettweiler dwells more fully upon this topic. Aftei
enumerating a number of special principles to be observed in translation, he goes on to say: "The proper
treatment of these and many other points may exercise
an absolutely enormous influence upon the pupil's
German style. The Latin language in its means and
modes of expression is so remote from our own, that
the form of translation demands the exercise of a
stylistic power the application of which to the pupil
must in future constitute one of the noblest tasks of
the teachers in our *Gymnasien*. The experience of
other countries which is often cited with approval may
be utilized in Germany too. In France and Belgium

---

[1] The italics are Dettweiler's, *i. e.* they correspond to the spaced type
of the German.

[2] It is noteworthy that the revised courses of study for the Prussian
gymnasia promulgated in 1892 call for increased attention to translation
from Latin into German.

translations from Latin are regarded as an admirable
exercise in expression.   In England the superior style
of the gentry is ascribed to extensive practice in translating, and it is well known how Cicero [see above,
p. 17], that supreme stylist, formed his style by practising translation from the Greek.   'Translation from a
foreign language,' says one of our most experienced
school officials, ' is a lesson in German that cannot be
too highly prized, and is, alas!· too much neglected.
By a good translation, one conforming to the genius
of the German language, instruction in German is most
effectively promoted.' "   To a similar effect are the
remarks of Isaac B. Burgess and W. C. Collar as given
in the *Proceedings ɑf the National Educational Association*, 1896, pp. 563 ff.; also those of Laurie, *Lectures
on Language and Linguistic Method*, p. 108; Paton,
in Spencer's *Aims and Practice ɑf Teaching*, p. 61;
Shorey, " Discipline *vs.* Dissipation," in *The School Review*, 1897, p. 228: " Every hour spent by the student
in improving the accuracy or elegance of his version is,
apart from its practical service in mobilizing his English
vocabulary, an unconscious philosophic discipline in
the comparison of two sets of conceptual symbols and
the measuring against each other of two parallel intellectual outgrowths of the one sensational root of all
our knowledge.   Every time the student is corrected
for washing out in his translation some poetic image
found in the original, he receives a lesson in the relation
of the symbolizing imagination to thought.   As often
as he discusses with the teacher a word for which no
apt English equivalent can be found, he acquires a new
concept and a finer conception of nice distinctions.
Whenever an apparently grotesque or senseless expression is elucidated by reference to the primitive or alien
religious or ethical conception or institution that gives

it meaning, he receives a simple, safe, and concrete lesson in comparative religion, ethics, folk-lore, anthropology, or institutional history, as the case may be. And as often as he is forced to reconsider, in the light of the context, the mechanically memorized meaning of a word or phrase, he has impressed upon his mind the truth which the student of the more rigid working formulas of the physical sciences is so apt to miss, that words are not unalterable talismans, but chameleon-hued symbols taking shape and color from their associates. The effect of this kind of discipline is unconscious, insensible, and cumulative. It cannot, of course, cancel the inequalities of natural parts; it cannot take the place of practical acquaintance with life and accurate knowledge of a special trade or profession. But pursued systematically through the plastic years of youth, it differentiates the mind subjected to it by a flexibility, delicacy, and nicety of intellectual perception which no other merely scholastic and class-room training can give in like measure."

The English training derived from such careful translation as above described seems to me greatly superior to that gained by the usual methods of English composition. Original composition must necessarily deal only with the ideas already present in the pupil's mind. How elementary and crude these are in case of the pupils in our secondary schools, is a fact sufficiently familiar to us all. The reflective period has not usually begun at the age when the pupil enters upon the secondary education; he finds it difficult to write an English theme because he has nothing to write about. But set before him a passage of Latin, elevated in thought and well expressed, with the problem of putting this into the best English

Translation vs. Original Composition.

he can command; in the first place he is relieved of the necessity of hunting aimlessly about for ideas which do not exist in his brain; and in the second place he is raised above the plane of his ordinary thinking, and in this higher atmosphere grows familiar with concepts and ideas which might otherwise long remain foreign or at least vague to him. All things considered, I do not hesitate to say that I believe there is a considerable period in the secondary training when Latin translation, if rightly conducted, may wisely be made practically the exclusive instrument of special instruction in English composition. This view, too, I find, is shared by many. See the discussions in the *Proceedings of the National Educational Association*, 1896, p. 563 ff., especially p. 570. Probably no teacher who has ever systematically instituted this experiment of written translations has failed to regard the time it demanded as wisely expended.

I have said above that this training in English seemed to me to form a larger part of the advantages of Latin Other Effects study than all others together. Yet the other of Latin.   advantages are by no means insignificant. They are now to be considered.

Discussing with his usual sober thoughtfulness and lucidity of exposition the question: Wherein Popular Education has Failed,[1] President Eliot lays down the four essential educational processes which should be involved in any rational and effective system of instruction. These are:

1. The process of " observation; that is to say, the alert, intent, and accurate use of all the senses. Whoever wishes to ascertain a prèsent fact must do it through the exercise of this power of observation. . . .

---

[1] American Contributions to Civilization, p. 203 ff.

Facts, diligently sought for and firmly established, are the only foundations of sound reasoning."

2. " The next function, process, or operation which education should develop in the individual is the function of making a correct record of things observed. The record may be mental only, that is, stamped on the memory, or it may be reduced to writing or print. . . . This power of accurate description or recording is identical in all fields of inquiry."

3. " The next mental function which education should develop, if it is to increase reasoning power and general intelligence, is the faculty of drawing correct inferences from recorded observations. This faculty is almost identical with the faculty of grouping or coördinating kindred facts, comparing one group with another or with all the others, and then drawing an inference which is sure in proportion to the number of cases, instances, or experiences on which it is based. This power is developed by practice in induction."

4. " Fourthly, education should cultivate the power of expressing one's thoughts clearly, concisely, and cogently."

These, according to President Eliot, are the four essential processes of the educated mind: observing accurately; recording correctly; comparing, grouping, and inferring justly; and expressing the result of these operations with clearness and force.

Now it is precisely these four processes or operations which the study of Latin, when well taught, promotes in an eminent degree:

1 The study of Latin trains the observing faculty. To fathom the meaning of a Latin sentence requires a whole series of accurate observations. Thus Observation. the pupil sees the word *egissent* in a sentence; he observes that the word is a form of *ago ;* he takes

note of the voice, mood, tense, person, and number; he observes its position; he may make other observations. Or he is reading poetry and comes to the line, *Si qua fata sinant, jam tum tenditque fovetque.* The second word puzzles him at first; to the eye, it may be either a nominative plural neuter or an ablative singular feminine used adverbially. Observation (scansion of the line) teaches him that the latter conclusion is the true one.

2. Little of this observation is recorded in speech or writing in the preparation of a lesson, but *it is recorded mentally*, which according to President Eliot is entirely adequate. Moreover the process is constant. It is necessarily so. No lesson in a Latin author can be adequately prepared without sustained and repeated observing and recording from beginning to end.

Recording.

3. The study also necessitates the most thorough and rigid processes of reasoning. The pupil has observed that a certain word is in the dative case, or in the subjunctive mood, and has made also a mental record of the fact. He now proceeds to determine the relationship of the dative or subjunctive to other words in the sentence. This demands as severe an exercise of the reasoning powers as anything I know. The first combination the pupil tries may be found to be grammatically impossible; it offends against his consciousness of linguistic usage. Or it may be grammatically correct and yet be flatly absurd in point of meaning. Or it may make only a half satisfactory sense, somewhat inconsistent with the context. Every conscious endeavour, however, rightly to combine and accurately to interpret the words, phrases, sentences, and paragraphs of any passage of a Latin author is an exercise of the reason. It is not, to be sure, an exercise of the

Reasoning.

kind expressly mentioned by President Eliot in his allusions to the process of reasoning as one of the indispensable results of a rational education. He
mentions only inductive processes as entitled
to recognition in this sphere, and by implication excludes all recognition of deductive
reasoning. This seems to me extremely unfortunate
and unjust. Both processes are legitimate in education;
neither is to be disparaged. President Eliot's position
seems to be that only the inductive reasoning of the
observational sciences is reasoning properly so-called.
Yet of the popular fallacies and delusions which President Eliot enumerates (p. 224 f.), and which he justly
deplores, few, when evaded by intelligent and educated
men, are evaded by processes of inductive reasoning.
How many of the intelligent men who opposed the free-
silver heresy in this country in 1896 did so as the result
of inductive reasoning? Any such reasoning faintly
deserving the name would be simply impossible for the
average educated man. The process by which opinions
must be formed by most men on such matters is one
of deductive reasoning. Only the specialist can reason
inductively on such great questions, where honest settle-
ment by inductive processes demands almost infinite
time and pains, not to speak of special training. The
minds of the great majority of thoughtful men must
work otherwise. Faith in the honesty, intelligence, and
patriotism of others is probably the major premise in
the minds of most of us in determining our attitude on
large questions. The minor premise is the view of some
earnest, trained, and sagacious statesman or student of
affairs in whom we trust. Our conclusion, therefore,
represents the view of another person, logically made
our own by deductive process. Oftener perhaps our
own views on such matters are formed as a result of

[margin note:] Induction not the only Mode of Reasoning.

comparing the views of many others rather than by adopting the view of any individual. In such cases we adopt the preponderance of authority or the preponderance of evidence furnished by others and assumed by us to be fairly complete. But the process is still deductive. So in most of the serious things of life: our choice of a vocation, our preparation for its duties, our diet and recreation, the education of our children, our social, religious, and political affiliations, — all these must of necessity be determined by deductive processes of reason, so far as they are determined by reason at all. I cannot help thinking, therefore, that President Eliot attributes too important an educational function to processes of inductive reasoning, and allows such processes a much larger play than they can, under any conceivable conditions, ever have in the practical life of any individual. At all events, I think it proper to insist on a recognition of the part which deductive reasoning must always play in nine tenths of the lives of the most conscientious of us, and to urge this fact as of importance in estimating rightly the value of the deductive reasoning so inevitably associated with the study of Latin and other languages.

4. Lastly, the study of Latin involves in translation constant practice in expressing the results of one's observing, recording, and reasoning. Whether **Expression.** this be clear, concise, and cogent, as President Eliot would have it, is a matter entirely within the power of the teacher to determine. But I am confident that no teacher fit to be intrusted with giving Latin instruction, or in fact any instruction, will neglect this most important and crowning feature of Latin study.

Latin, then, would seem fairly to fulfil all the important functions demanded by President Eliot as essential in a rational system of teaching. Yet he himself is inclined to look askance at the present predominance of Latin and other language studies in the curricula of our secondary schools. Though not specifically declaring it, he implies his distrust in the efficacy of language study to achieve any of the results which must be admitted by all to be so eminently important.

To me all these results seem to flow of necessity from the study of Latin. Even with poor teaching, observing, recording, reasoning, and expressing are necessary daily processes of the pupil's intellectual life. This may explain why even poor Latin teaching often seems to have an educative influence. Where the teaching is of first-rate quality, the processes referred to are naturally given an accuracy, a power, and clearness of form, which cannot fail to prove of the highest educative power.

It is, of course, manifest that the foregoing arguments in favour of studying Latin, if valid, apply at least in some measure to other languages than Latin, Latin *vs.* and many persons doubtless will be inclined Modern to advocate the advantages of French or Ger- Languages. man, as superior to those of Latin. While not denying the usefulness of both those languages when taught with discrimination, yet, *if one language only can be studied*, I see two reasons for giving Latin a decided preference to either French or German. In the first place the concepts and ideas of the Latin language are much remoter from those of English than are those of the modern languages. All modern thought is essentially kindred. The same intellectual elements, so to speak, are common to all civilized nations, — particularly to nations so closely in touch as the English, French, and German. This is not true when we come to study either of the ancient languages. The ultimate elements of the thought, *i. e.* the language of the Greeks and Romans, are as different from our own as is their entire civilization. It is precisely this fundamental difference which makes either of the classical languages of such invaluable discipline. At every stage of study we are brought in contact with new phases of thought, new ideas; — the intellectual horizon is continually widening. The modern languages, on the other hand, suggest relatively much less that is new. Both the matter and the manner of expression are so directly in the line of our ordinary knowledge and speech, as to give much less occasion to processes of comparison or to that stimulating intellectual grapple which is essential to mental growth. This is particularly true of French, whose thought-forms are so closely kindred to our own. It is less true of German, though even that language suggests vastly fewer differences in ideas — and consequently vastly fewer opportunities for comparison — than does either Greek or Latin.

There is yet another reason which I should urge in favour of Latin as compared with either of the modern languages, and that is that Latin has supplied us with so large a share of our own vocabulary. Just what the exact percentage of such words in English is, I do not know. Nor is it material. The number, at any rate, is very large, and covers every department of thought. For this reason no educated person can safely undertake to dispense with a knowledge of the root words of the Latin language. I mean no such knowledge as comes from memorizing a list of the commoner roots and suffixes along with their meanings, but a knowledge at first hand, and sufficiently comprehensive and thorough to enable one to *feel* the full significance of the primary words of the Latin, a knowledge which reveals at once the full value of such English words as *connotation, speciousness, integrity, desultory, temperance, induction, deduction, abstract, ingenuous, absolute,* and scores of others whose precise apprehension marks the educated man. This point has been strongly though briefly emphasized by the Commissioner of Education, W. T. Harris, in " A Brief for Latin," *Educational Review*, April, 1899. See also Paton, in Spencer, *Aims and Practice of Teaching*, p. 41 f.

To the two foregoing theoretical reasons for preferring Latin to French or German as an instrument of secondary education, must be added a third reason, more cogent even than those already empha- Testimony of sized, namely, experience. I believe it well Experience. within the limits of accuracy to assert that no one who has had actual experience with the teaching of either of the modern languages to pupils of the same age and intellectual power will for a moment venture to compare the intellectual profit attained from French or German with that derived from Latin. In fact, so far as we have any testimony on this point, there is a striking unanimity of judgment in favour of Latin. Speaking at the first annual meeting of the Association of Colleges and Preparatory Schools in the Middle States and Maryland (*Proceedings*, 1893, p. 59), Principal Mackenzie, discussing the question, "Will any kind or amount of instruction in modern languages make them satisfactory substitutes for Greek or Latin as constituents of a liberal education?" said: " Twenty-three years ago, when I was a school-boy at one of our foremost academies, there was no scientific or English[1] course, — no course, that is, without Latin. Those who know the history of that school for the century closing in the seventies, know her brilliant achievements in developing mental power with Latin as the staff of the pupil's

---

[1] The scientific or English courses regularly omit Latin, and include either French or German, or both French and German.

mental life.   Meantime, in company with all our fitting schools, she, too, has established an English side without Latin.   I could give no umbrage nor be chargeable with indelicacy were I to repeat the statements made to me by her teachers as to the unfavourable change in the intellectual tone and character of the institution. There are in this Association an earnest, skilful, experienced body of teachers connected with our high-schools and other schools of secondary grade; I have yet to meet one such teacher who, administering courses of study both with and without one or two of the classical languages, does not, however reluctantly, affirm that satisfactory scholarship is found only on the so-called classical side, and that, therefore, no satisfactory substitute for Greek and Latin has yet been found." Subsequently President B. I. Wheeler, then Professor of Greek at Cornell, declared it his conviction that French and German cannot compare with the classics as effective instruments of secondary education, "simply because they don't."   These positive assertions based on experience went absolutely unchallenged in the protracted discussion of the question which followed. Compare also the testimony of an English educator, Mr. Paton, in Spencer, *Aims and Practice of Teaching*, p. 44: "Many argue that French and German would be just as efficient [as Latin], but their contention has never been practically demonstrated."   Similar testimony comes from Germany, France, and Belgium, to the effect that those boys who have received a classical training are on the whole superior to those who have received a training only in the modern languages (Fouillée, *Education from a National Standpoint*, p. 167).   Fouillée (*ibid.*, footnote) adds: "One of our most eminent critics [Ferdinand Brunetière], before his connection with the *Revue des Deux Mondes*, was on the staff of the École Normale Supérieure, and taught French literature to the pupils at the Collège Chaptal, and at the same time to the mathematical students at the Lycée Louis-le-Grand and the Collège Sainte-Barbe. At Chaptal almost every boy passed through his hands, as he took each class some time or other during the week, and in this way he knew the boys in six classes, of course of varying ages. Now, says M. Brunetière, ' I feel, after this experience gained under exceptional conditions, that for opening the mind and for general development, for a knowledge of our own tongue, and for literary skill, the boys who instead of a classical training have received a purely French education, with the addition of modern languages, are at least two and perhaps three years behind their fellows.' At Louis-le-Grand and Sainte-Barbe, M. Brunetière's pupils had done Latin and Greek grammar only, and had never had a thorough grounding in that, intending to devote themselves at an early period exclusively to mathematics. Here again the superiority of even a little classical training was equally marked. These observations," adds Fouillée, "agree with my own while I was engaged in teaching." Such testimony might be multiplied almost indefinitely.

From this verdict of experience we can hardly venture to appeal, until experience has new and different contributions with which to support the claims of the equality of the modern languages with Latin as educational instruments. The position of those who have advocated the equality of French or German on theoretical grounds is well represented by the late Professor Boyesen. In his remarks before the Association of Colleges and Preparatory Schools of the Middle States and Maryland (*Proceedings*, 1893, p. 38 ff.), he lays stress on the admirable quality of the French and

German literatures, comparing them favourably with the classical masterpieces. But the training of the secondary pupil who is studying a foreign language, as was shown above, is primarily *linguistic*, not *literary*. Literary study enters in to some extent, to be sure, but the *main* benefit of the study must come after all from the minute study of the elements of the thought, not from the contemplation of its larger literary aspects. And it is precisely on this linguistic side that French and German exhibit, as compared with Latin, such a striking lack of adaptation to the ends of a truly liberal training.

It is for the foregoing reasons that I feel justified in urging the superiority of Latin to either of the modern languages as an educational instrument in our secondary schools. Experience may ultimately prove French and German entitled to relatively greater consideration than we can at present concede to them, though the theoretical grounds against any such eventual result seem very strong.

As to Greek, for the pupil of the secondary school I am reluctantly forced to give it a place second to Latin. I do this chiefly because Greek has contributed so much less to our own English vocabulary than has Latin. These estimates of educational values, however, by no means imply that one or even more of the other languages mentioned may not wisely be added to Latin in the secondary school. I most certainly believe that this should be done wherever practicable, and would advocate the combination of two languages, as, for example, Latin and Greek, Latin and German, or Latin and French. Latin, however, I should insist upon *as the basal study for all pupils* of the secondary school who are capable of pursuing it. More than two languages (Latin for four years and Greek, German, or French for three years), I should not suggest for an individual pupil, though I am well aware that the colleges are enforcing demands in this direction. With all the advantages and allurements of language study, I feel that we can easily go too far, and may do damage by neglecting other sides of the pupil's intellect.

I have enlarged sufficiently upon what seem to me the primary ends of Latin study in the secondary school, namely, the power of accurate observation, the development of the reasoning faculties, and the superior facilities it affords for training in our own language, by which, as I explained, is meant not merely the apprehension of words, but the assimilation of ideas for which the words are merely symbols. Incidentally, too, we considered the fact that the study of Latin gives us the needed insight into the precise meaning of a vast number of English words derived from Latin, and that, by taking us out of ourselves, the study of Roman life and thought gives us a broader view of the significance of ideas and institutions, — what Laurie calls the "universal," as opposed to the merely "national" point of view (*Language and Linguistic Method*, p. 3 f.).

There are yet other humanizing influences of the study, which, though of less importance, yet deserve to be emphasized. Among these must be reckoned the *positive knowledge* of Roman history, **Historical Training.** thought, and institutions which comes from the study of Latin. No one can get so good a view of the personality of that great organizer Julius Cæsar, as the intelligent reader of Cæsar's own narrative; no one can so appreciate the constitution and workings of the Roman republic as the pupil who reads the pages of Sallust's *Jugurtha* and *Catiline* or Cicero's *Orations* and *Letters;* no one can so appreciate the one dominant principle of all Roman civilization, — the power of organization and administration combined with a sense of imperial destiny, — as he who comes face to face with that sentiment in the Latin authors. These are examples merely of the almost infinite suggestiveness of Latin study along historical and institutional lines; — not that the study of Latin should or can replace a formal study of Roman history and institutions, but it can and should serve to supplement such study.

I shall venture to emphasize also the value of the training of the æsthetic and moral sense which must **Æsthetic** come to every mind of ordinary endowment **Training.** by contact with the masterpieces of Latin writing usually read in our secondary schools. Here again I shall quote the words of Professor Shorey (" Discipline *vs.* Dissipation," *School Review*, 1897, p. 228 f.), " This scholastic study of language, through the careful interpretation of selected literary masterpieces, is a totally different thing both from mere gerund-grinding and the acquisition by conversational methods of the courier's polyglot facility. It is essentially a study of literature, — a fact overlooked by those who declaim against language while protesting their devotion to literature; and it is the only form in which literature can be taught to young students that offers serious guarantees of the indispensable accompanying discipline. It trains the intellect in close association with the sense for beauty and the sense for conduct as no other studies can. . . . The iridescent threads of cultivated and flexible æsthetic and ethical institutions must be shot through the intellectual warp of the mind at the loom. They cannot be laid on the finished fabric like an external coat of paint. The student who between the years of twelve and twenty has thrilled at the eloquence of Cicero or Demosthenes, has threaded the mazes of the Platonic dialectic, has laughed with Aristophanes, has pored over the picturesque page of Livy, or apprehended the sagacious analysis of Thucydides, has learned to enjoy the curious felicity of Horace and the supreme elegance and tender melancholy of Virgil, has trembled before the clash of destiny and human will in the drama of Æschylus and Sophocles, has been cradled in the ocean of Homeric song, or attuned his ear to the stately harmonies of Pindar, — the student, I say, who has received this or a like discipline in the great languages and literatures of the world, has insensibly acquired the elementary materials, the essential methods, and the finer intuitive perceptions of the things of the spirit, on which all more systematic study of the mental and moral sciences must depend."

We have dwelt sufficiently upon the various reasons for studying Latin in the secondary school. It remains to discuss briefly some of the objections which have been urged against the study at this stage of education.[1]

Objections Urged against Latin.

In 1861 Herbert Spencer published his work on *Education: Intellectual, Moral, and Physical*, consisting of a series of four essays which had previously appeared in various English Reviews. I shall not have the presumption to question the importance and value of these essays as permanent contributions to the discussion of educational problems. Yet with regard to the value of at least one classical language in any adequate scheme of secondary education, Spencer is singularly unjust. The title of the first essay is: " What knowledge is of most worth?" In discussing this question no at-

Herbert Spencer.

---

[1] It is impracticable here to discuss any utterances except those of a few representative thoughtful students of education.

tempt at a comparative estimate of the educational value of different studies is instituted. On page 23, Spencer observes: " If we inquire into the real motive for giving boys a classical education, we find it· to be simply conformity to public opinion. . . . As the Orinoco Indian puts on his paint before leaving his hut, not with a view to any direct benefit, but because he would be ashamed to be seen without it, so a boy's drilling in Latin and Greek is insisted on, not because of their intrinsic value, but that he may not be disgraced by being found ignorant of them."

This is the sum and substance of Spencer's examination of the worth of the pursuit of either Latin or Greek. The bulk of this first essay, the title of which assumes at least an honest attempt to institute a candid inquiry concerning the relative value of different subjects, is devoted to an exposition of the thesis that the study of science is of *some* worth to *some* people, — nothing more. Granting for the sake of argument that this thesis is adequately established, it by no means follows that other subjects are of less worth or that Latin is of no worth. Herbert Spencer has often, and with great acumen, justly convicted other thinkers of unwarranted assumptions and bad logic, but in the present instance he seems to cap the climax in his absolute begging of the question at issue. The value of Latin can never be proved or disproved by discussing the value of something else, nor can it be proved or disproved by passionate declarations of its worth or worthlessness. Spencer unfortunately has not attempted to go beyond these methods; and it is doubly unfortunate that this attitude has been assumed by a thinker who usually exhibits such exceptional seriousness, candour, and intellectual integrity, and the influence of whose utterances must inevitably be so great.

Much more commendable is the procedure of Alexander Bain in *Education as a Science* (London and New York, 1881). In chapter x., "Value of the Classics," Bain seriously undertakes **Bain.** to estimate the worth of Latin and Greek. Unfortunately he does not limit the question to any period of education, nor does he seem to recognise that the question of the study of Latin alone is a radically different question from the study of Latin and Greek. His discussion, however, is one that commands our attention. Bain first sets forth the alleged advantages of studying the classics, and then the drawbacks. His conclusion is that the latter decidedly outweigh the former. It is impossible here to take up his arguments in detail, but it is to be noted that, among the advantages of the study, Bain practically ignores the transcendent value of the increased intellectual power derived from the study of the classics, and the mastery acquired over the resources of one's mother tongue, *i. e.*, over the ideas which form the highest intellectual elements of our national life, — the very things which we set down above as constituting the prime reason for studying Latin. Of the other assumed advantages of the study of the classics, Bain finds no one of sufficient weight to be entitled to great respect. On the other hand he enumerates four positive objections to the study: **His Objections.** 1. The cost is great. 2. The mixture of conflicting studies distracts the learner. 3. The study is devoid of interest. 4. The classics inculcate the evil of pandering to authority.

As to the cost, it must be admitted that Latin does cost. It takes time and labour. If pursued as a daily study in our American schools for four years, it claims one-third of the entire secondary-school curriculum. The real question for us, however, and the question which Bain professes to be examining, is the question of *value*. To the discussion of that question the consideration of cost is irrelevant. When we have determined the value of Latin, the question of cost may properly influence the pupil's choice in individual cases, but it cannot affect the question of value any more than the length of one's purse determines the value of a fine watch.

That the study of Latin is devoid of interest (Bain's third objection), or that it inspires a blind pandering to authority (his fourth objection), is contrary to my own experience, and I believe to that of teachers in this country. I can only conclude that Bain is here advancing arguments which, if valid, are so only in Great Britain.

More importance attaches to Bain's second objection, which I intentionally reserve till the last. The mixture of conflicting purposes, he adds, distracts the learner, *i. e.* he would contend that it is distracting to the pupil of Latin to be gaining in intellectual grip and breadth of vision, to be mastering the resources of his mother tongue (*i. e.* the higher elements of the national life of which he is a member), to be gaining a profounder insight into the thought, life, and institutions of the Romans, to be advancing in the cultivation of the æsthetic and moral senses, — to be doing all these at one and the same time. I see no answer to make to this objection beyond declaring that experience does not seem to me to bear out its truth, any more than experience shows that the study of Latin is devoid of interest or that it inculcates a blind respect for authority. On the other hand, experience seems to me to show, and to show abundantly, that all the results whose contemporaneous realization Bain declares to be so distracting, do actually flow from the study of Latin. The reason they do flow is, in my judgment, due to the fact that *they are not consciously sought by either pupil or teacher.* Were such the case, I am quite prepared to believe that the joint quest would prove distracting and even futile. Fortunately, however, the valuable results of studying Latin are indirect results, while Bain's objection seems to have been formulated as a result of the erroneous conviction that the valuable ends of Latin study are always present to the pupil's consciousness. It is really their absence from his consciousness which is the salvation of the study.

Less radical in his attitude toward the value of Latin in secondary education is Friedrich Paulsen, who in 1885 published his important *Geschichte des gelehrten Unterrichts auf den deutschen Schu-* **Paulsen.** *len und Universitäten vom Ausgang des Mittelalters bis zur Gegenwart mit besonderer Rücksicht auf den klassischen Unterricht.* Paulsen's criticisms upon classical education as at present organized and conducted in German secondary schools (*Gymnasien* and *Realschulen*) are embodied in his concluding chapter. Before proceeding to their consideration, however, it will be necessary to get clearly before our minds the status of classical education in Germany. In the *Gymnasien* and *Realgymnasien* Latin is studied for nine years, — from about the tenth year to the nineteenth; while in the *Gymnasien* Greek also is studied for six years, — from about the thirteenth year to the nineteenth. A total of fifteen years of study is therefore regularly devoted to the classics in the *Gymnasien.* Another element that enters into the situation is that the amount of work in classics and other branches combined has long been something enormous for the student of the *Gymnasien.* For two generations the *Ueberbürdungsfrage* has been one uppermost in educational discussion. Accordingly when Paulsen undertakes to show the evils of existing conditions, and when he urges earnestly and cogently the dropping of Greek and the radical retrenchment of Latin, we must be exceedingly cautious what conclusions we draw from his observations for the study of Latin in the secondary schools of the United States. The time now spent on Latin in a German *Gymnasium* or *Realgymnasium* is more than equal to that spent by most graduates of our American colleges who have pursued Latin continuously from the lowest grade of the high school to the termination of their college course. A retrenchment of Latin in the German *Gymnasien*, therefore, may be entirely compatible with the maintenance of the existing attention given to Latin in this country, or even with its extension.

Paulsen nowhere goes so far as to advocate the abandonment of Latin as an instrument of German secondary education. His attitude on this point I believe has largely been misunderstood in this country, owing mainly to the prevalent incapacity of many minds to dissociate Latin and Greek. Paulsen's attitude as regards Greek is practically uncompromising. For the great body of students he is convinced it would better be abandoned, but as regards Latin, he nowhere goes beyond the demand for retrenchment. Thus on p. 762, while declaring positively that the present ideal of classical education in Germany must pass away, he unhesi-

Believes in Retaining Latin. tatingly asserts his belief that Latin must continue to be indispensable. As to the amount of time to be devoted to the study we get an expression of opinion on p. 774, where Paulsen thinks that the study may profitably be pursued through the lower and middle classes, — presumably to the end of *Obertertia*, or five years in all. On p. 782

he even goes so far as to admit that experience may show that for certain classes of students the traditional classical course will still be necessary. But in the main Paulsen's estimate of the value of the classics, Latin as well as Greek, is an exceedingly low one. Let us briefly consider his reasons.

First, he complains that classical training as pursued in Germany does not exert any marked influence upon the pupils' German style. In fact he goes so far as to assert that men who have enjoyed the classical training are conspicuously lacking in any sense for form, and the typical scholar is nothing less than a laughing-stock, — a handy conventional figure largely utilized in popular comedy to provoke merriment. This indictment is severe, and if well grounded certainly constitutes a weighty argument against the pursuit of Latin. But Paulsen's testimony is contradicted by his own countrymen, *e. g.* by Dettweiler, quoted above, p. 18 f. It is, I believe, contradicted also by the impressions received by most Americans in their contact with German gymnasial graduates frequenting the German universities. However, for us Americans the question is not one to be settled by the experience of Germany. The question for us is, whether Latin produces certain results upon our own pupils.

Alleged Defective Results of Latin Study.

Another of Paulsen's arguments is to the effect that, after all, vital results in education emanate from the personality of the teacher, not from the subject. Certainly there can be no underrating of the effect of personality in the teaching of any branch; but that fact has nothing whatever to do with the large question, whether there are not vast differences between the educational values of different subjects. Until experience faintly demonstrates the contrary, we must believe such differences exist; and so long as they do, the influence of personality in teaching can hardly be considered as bearing upon the question at issue. Even Paulsen himself, by the way, candidly admits that the ancient classics do afford an unusual opportunity for the *effective exercise* of personal influence, or at least that they would, were it not that inability to understand the lan guage in which they are written constitutes an impassable barrier between teacher and pupil. But it is difficult for an American who has witnessed the brilliant inter pretations of the classics in the upper forms of the *Gymnasien* to credit the general existence of any such barrier.

Paulsen passes on to urge that the pursuit of the classics does not tend to promote that sympathy, charity, **Moral** and brotherly love which might be expected **Influence.** from the *humanities*. But certainly Paulsen's own volume teaches us most clearly that the humanities (*studia humaniora*) were never so designated because they were supposed to make men humane, in the sense of sympathetic and charitable. Humanism was but the revolt from scholasticism: the one made *God* the ex- elusive object of speculation; the new tendency empha- sized *man*, his achievements, capacities, and aspirations. The implication, therefore, that the classics are specially under obligations to make men kindly and charitable is one hardly justified by the designation ' humanities,' nor has it ever been the professed ideal of these studies. But let us look at the facts adduced by Paulsen in support of his charge that the study of the classics promotes strife, hatred, pride, and all uncharitableness. He cites a letter of Jakob Grimm, in which complaint is made that of all branches of knowledge none is more arrogant, more contentious, and less indulgent toward the short- comings of others than philology. Goethe also writes in a similar strain to Knebel. But philology is not confined to the classics; it includes the modern languages as well, even German, which, as we shall later see, is specially recommended by Paulsen to take the place of Greek and Latin in the reformed program. Goethe's indictment also is not directed against the classics, but against liberal studies in general. But neither of these men was considering the effects of any of these studies upon pupils. They were obviously alluding to the exhibitions of jealousy and rivalry manifested between scholars of eminence. Such exhibitions must always be a more or less frequent result of keen intellectual competition. They are no more frequent in classical philology than in other departments. Nothing can exceed the virulence of some of the recent polemical literature evoked in Germany by the higher criticism of the Scriptures. Even philosophy (another subject which Paulsen cordially endorses as a substitute for the classics) is not without its amenities, and I vividly recall the polemic of a leading German investigator in this field, in which words were used that English literature has not tolerated since the days of Swift. Natural science, too, has not been exempt, — a study which Grimm and Goethe seemed to think more adapted to the development of a " sweet reasonableness." Such may have been the case in Germany at the beginning of the century. It may still be so. But certainly in the United States there are many exceptions to this rule, and one of my clearest boyhood recollections is of the vehement personal invectives hurled against each other by two eminent paleontologists.

Paulsen will attach no weight to the fact that men, even professional men, who have enjoyed the severe classical training of the *Gymnasien*, are prac- Social Phases. tically a unit in their advocacy of retaining this instruction in its present form. These men, he

asserts, are actuated not by any educational considerations, they are not impressed with any sense of the
value of the training they have received. What actu-
ates them is social pride, an aristocratic sense of the
recognised superiority which their education has con-
ferred. They wish to perpetuate the caste in all its
glory. How just this imputation of motives is, it is of
course impossible for us to determine, but one hesitates
to believe it well founded. At all events, in this country
no one will charge the existence of such sentiments as
a factor in the adjustment of educational problems.

Paulsen's last argument is based upon the observable
educational tendencies of the last four centuries. Ever
Tendency of since the Renaissance and the Reformation the
the Times. relative importance of the classics has been
diminishing. There was a time early in the sixteenth
century when these studies practically monopolized the
field of learning. Each succeeding century has seen
their relative importance diminish. Paulsen's reasoning
is that ultimately their place must vanish, and that that
era has in fact arrived. But any such argument based
upon the operation of a tendency is likely to be falla-
cious. No one can say with certainty how long a given
tendency may operate. The record of the American
trotting horse has been reduced in the last twenty-five
years from two minutes seventeen and one-quarter sec-
onds to a fraction over two minutes. But he would be
bold who should predict that this tendency will go on
without limit. Similarly, educational policies can hardly
be determined on the basis of observed tendencies.
They must be settled rather in the light of existing
conditions.

As substitutes for Greek and for so much of Latin as
it is proposed to banish, Paulsen suggests the introduction of philosophy and German. We hardly need to

discuss the value of the former of these studies. If introduced into the *Gymnasien*, it is obvious that philosophy could be intended only for the two higher **Proposed** classes of the *Gymnasium*, a department of **Substitutes.** education lying beyond what we designate as secondary, and corresponding rather to the lower years of our American colleges. But the proposition to introduce German as a substitute for the classics invites our careful attention, for if it is sound for Germany, it is also sound for us to replace the study of either or both the classical languages by the study of English. My reasons for questioning the soundness of the general principle involved are two:

1. Experience has never shown that any study of the vernacular is capable of yielding results in any way comparable with those secured from the study of **Inadequacy of** other languages. In fact experience has so **a Study of the** frequently illustrated the reverse as prac- **Vernacular.** tically to have demonstrated the impossibility of securing such results. 2. Reflection, too, reveals adequate grounds for believing that the study of the vernacular never can prove of any very high educative value. The case has been so well stated by Fouillée, *Education from a National Standpoint*, p. 108, that I quote his words: "From the point of view of individual development, the study of the mother tongue is only sufficient in the case of exceptionally gifted minds. Secondary education should be regulated according to the average, and not according to exceptional students. Now, on the average, to the culture essential to the humanities, the study of a tongue other than the mother tongue is the shortest and surest method. A Frenchman, for instance, has a quick mind and a versatile intellect; but the very facility with which he uses his intellect does not leave him enough time for reflection.

When a French boy is reading a French book, unless he enjoys unusual reflective faculties, his mind is carried away by the general sense, and the details and shades of expression escape him. As M. Rabier says, 'A French child reading a page of Pascal or Bossuet does not fully grasp it, *i. e.* only half grasps it.' Exercises and translations force the child to weigh every word, to ascertain its exact meaning, to find its equivalent; he must also consider the inter-relations of *the ideas and words* in order to fix the sense concealed in the text; finally, he must transpose the whole from one language to another, just as a musician transposes an air. The final result is that he has repeated for himself the labours of the thinker and writer; he has re-thought their thoughts, and has revived the living form which was organic to the writer's thought. He has had to reproduce a work of art. A cursory perusal of works in the mother tongue is rather like a stroll through a museum; translation from one language to another is like copying a picture; the one makes amateurs, the other artists. In this way the sense of depth and form are simultaneously acquired." My own experience confirms this view. For some years I was connected with one of our large universities, in which there was an " English " course. The preparation for admission to this course included neither classics nor modern languages, but was based primarily upon English itself. For years the students who presented themselves for admission with this English preparation were recognised as the most deficient in intellectual strength and training of any who came up to the University. Nothing, I believe, but a desire to give the experiment the fairest possible trial prevented the early abolition of that course.

In conclusion, Paulsen calls for the exercise of more common sense in the organization of education, particularly in the establishment of the curriculum. Common sense, he adds, suggests that languages are learned to be understood, and the inference is that, if understanding them is not obviously of transcendent value, then their study is profitless. All the fine phrases about the discipline and culture, he adds, supposed to result from language study are likely to make no appeal to sturdy common sense. If by sturdy common sense is meant the instinctive conclusion of the common man who has given no serious thought to the problems of education, Paulsen is probably right, but can we safely intrust the interests of our higher education to such hands?

Such are Paulsen's arguments against the study of Greek and Latin in the German secondary schools, and such are the substitutes he proposes. I have considered them partly because they repre- **Review of** sent the conclusions of an eminent thinker **Paulsen's Objections.** and earnest student of educational problems, partly because by many in this country Paulsen is popularly supposed to have demonstrated finally the absolute lack of any *raison d'être* for the study of either of the classical languages. Our examination of his arguments shows, I think, that they are very far from justifying the radical changes which he proposes in German secondary education. Much less do they warrant a lack of confidence in the pursuit of the classics as pursued in this country; while, as regards Latin, Paulsen expressly recognises the justification of retaining quite as much as is ordinarily pursued in American secondary schools.

In conclusion we may state the case for Latin briefly as follows:

Reason and experience show that Latin in secondary education is capable of producing intellectual results of great positive value, practically indispensable to the educated man. Experience has not yet shown that any other subject (excepting possibly Greek) is capable of producing equally good results. Theorists have often asserted the equal value of other subjects, or at least have asserted the capacity of other subjects to yield as good results. Some of these theories, *e. g.* that in favour of the study of modern languages, that in favour of the study of the vernacular, we subjected to criticism with a view to showing their defects. Still the empirical argument must ever be the stronger, and, say what one may, the stubborn fact remains of the unique educational influence exercised by Latin. By this it is not for a moment meant to disparage the legitimate functions of a single other study. Their special value is ungrudgingly conceded. But in the light of our present knowledge, it seems a plain educational duty to adhere to Latin as admirably meeting a distinct educational need which is not met by any of the other subjects with which we are so often urged to replace it.

At present, however, the danger seems to be not that too few will study Latin, but rather too many. Latin is a difficult subject, and the peculiar educative power it possesses is not capable of being exercised upon all minds, — only upon those of a certain natural endowment. In our intense democracy we are perhaps at times inclined to forget that no constitutional declarations of *civil* equality can ever make, or were ever intended to recognise, an *intellectual* equality between the individual members of the nation. Latin is good for those whose gifts enable them to profit by its study. It is not, however, capable of popular distribution like so much flour or sugar. Because Latin is a highly effective instrument for the training of certain minds, we must not think that the efficiency is contained in the subject *per se ;* there must exist in the pupil the mental endowment requisite to profit by Latin; else the time spent upon the study is worse than wasted. Observation convinces me that many parents and pupils labour from a serious misconception on this point, and that many are ambitious to study Latin whom nature has not endowed with the capacity to benefit by its pursuit.

The present enormous increase in the number of Latin pupils in our American secondary schools seems to justify calling attention to possible dangers in this direction.

CHAPTER II

THE BEGINNING WORK

IN the beginning work we are confronted with what is probably the greatest difficulty in the entire range **Difficulty of** of elementary Latin instruction. The pupil **the Problem.** who in his early study fails to become well-grounded in the elements of Latin — who fails to secure an accurate knowledge of forms and of the leading principles of syntax — is at once put at an immense disadvantage. The chances are that he becomes discouraged, and that his continuance in the work will prove increasingly uninteresting and increasingly profitless to himself, as well as increasingly burdensome to his teachers. The proper conduct of the beginning work also makes the severest demands upon the knowledge and skill of the teacher. Too often, beginners are intrusted to inexperienced instructors on the general theory, apparently, that the lower the class the easier it is to instruct it. But in every subject I believe that, if there must be differences, the ablest and wisest teacher should be put in charge of the beginning work. " Aller Anfang ist schwer," says Goethe. Certainly this is preeminently true of Latin. Only the well-trained teacher, whose knowledge of Latin is accurate and broad, is qualified wisely to direct the first steps of the beginner. For only such can and will inculcate that indispensable precision, and only such can judge what things are of vital importance and must be learned now, and what things are less essential and may be deferred to a later time.

Even for a well-trained and accurate Latinist, the difficulties that beset the teacher in charge of the beginning work are very great. Some of them are inherent in the subject; some of them are connected with the choice of method to be pursued. Their number and importance makes it desirable to consider them under different heads. I shall discuss successively I. The Beginner's Book. II. Pronunciation. III. The "Inductive" Method. IV. Reading at Sight. V. Unseen Translation. VI. Easy Reading.

I. The Beginner's Book.

No problem is greater than the wise choice of the first book to be put into the beginner's hands. The plan of the beginner's book used in this country has been rapidly and radically changing in the last twenty years. Twenty years ago the pupil usually began with the Latin Grammar and the Latin Reader. The Grammar served to give the facts of pronunciation, accent, declension, conjugation, *etc.*, while the Reader gave parallel exercises illustrative of the parts of the Grammar assigned from day to day. The development naturally followed the arrangement of the Grammar, *i. e.* the pupils were taught the five declensions in succession, then the adjective, pronouns, and the four conjugations. During the acquisition of the forms little attention was paid to syntax. Only a few indispensable principles of the most elementary kind were introduced at this stage, such as the rules for the predicate noun, appositive, subject, object, agreement of adjective with noun, *etc.* After the acquisition of the forms, and before the com-

The Beginner's Book of Twenty Years Ago

mencement of the regular reading of a continuous text, the beginner's attention was directed to the elementary syntactical principles of the language. Here again the Grammar was used as the basis of instruction, and the different constructions studied were accompanied by parallel illustrative sentences in the Reader. Like the study of the forms, the study of the syntax followed the order of the Grammar, *i. e.* all the constructions of one case were treated together, and all the case constructions preceded the constructions of mood and tense. This method of study yielded excellent results. Boys learned their forms with accuracy, they early became familiar with the Grammar, and so laid a solid

A Defect. foundation for future work. This plan of instruction, however, involved one feature which exposed it to attack from the theoretical side; it was urged that the isolated fragmentary words and phrases given in the Reader as parallel exercises to the Grammar were irrational. During the acquisition of the declension of nouns, adjectives, and pronouns, and largely during the study of the conjugations, the pupil was fed in the Reader on these isolated words and phrases. Complete sentences were almost unknown, — necessarily so until the verb was reached. Now, it was urged that it was an injustice to the pupil to be confined for weeks together to such unnatural exercises as *Dionysii tyranni; equum Balbi; vobis; templum quod- dam; audiveris; sunto; laudatos esse, etc.* The justice of this position is fairly debatable, but debate now is hardly necessary. To-day the use of the Grammar

The Typical Beginner's Book of To- day. and Reader as above described is a thing of the past. For two decades the beginner's book has been coming into more and more general use, until to-day its reign is prac- tically universal. These books are usually complete in themselves. They contain all the grammar supposed to be essential for the beginning pupil, along with copious illustrative sentences. Representing as they do, also, a reaction against the old Reader with its isolated words and detached phrases, they introduce complete sentences at the start. This is accomplished by treating certain parts of the verb in the very earliest lessons.

Had the makers of these books contented themselves with remedying what they characterized as the crying defect of the old Reader, the result would not have been so bad. But they have gone much further. Most of these manuals are absolutely without plan Unsystematic. in their distribution of material. Bits of the matic. noun, adjective, adverb, verb, and pronoun are found scattered here and there throughout the book, interspersed with various syntactical rules, now on the noun, now on the verb, now on one case, now on another. The most cursory glance at almost any one of the dozens of beginner's books published in recent years will amply confirm the accuracy of this statement.

The plan of these books has long seemed to me pedagogically unsound, and in practice I fear they have not enabled us to realize the best results in our elementary Latin teaching. To me it seems undeniable that pupils to-day are conspicuously inferior in the mastery of their inflections to the pupils of twenty years ago, as well as conspicuously inferior in their general familiarity with the Latin Grammar. This observation I find is quite general. The complaint comes from Harvard even, situated though it is in the centre of the finest preparatory schools of the country, — schools whose efficiency ought to increase, not diminish, with time. Both these results I trace in large measure directly to the type of beginner's books now in vogue; as regards the former, at least, I do not see how it can possibly be assigned to any other source.

Let us examine more closely the defects of these books. My criticisms will cover three heads:

Defects in Detail. 1. They separate things that logically belong together; also, in endeavouring to relieve the memory and to promote interest, they sacrifice accuracy of knowledge.

2. They separate things in the early stages of teaching which must later be associated.

3. In introducing the translation of English into Latin before the forms are thoroughly mastered, they involve a serious expenditure of time without any corresponding gain.

My first criticism was that things which logically belong together are in these books separated from one another. Thus the five declensions seem to me more like each other than like anything else; the same is true of the pronouns taken as a whole; it is also true of the four conjugations of regular verbs, and even of the irregular verbs taken as a whole. So also in the case of the syntax, the different constructions of the genitive, the dative, the accusative, or the ablative, the uses of the subjunctive, seem to me more like each other than like anything else. This intimate logical relationship is explicitly recognised, too, in all Latin grammars with which I am acquainted. Now both reason and experience have for years constantly tended to strengthen my conviction that facts which logically belong together are most easily acquired by being learned in conjunction with one another, and that it is a fundamental psychological mistake to dissociate such facts in teaching. Thus the pupil who is studying Roman private antiquities, for instance, can hardly expect to secure an easy

Dissociation of what belongs together.

mastery of his subject if in one lesson he learns a few facts about the Roman house, a few more about the toga, coupled with isolated allusions to the modes of marriage and the methods of disposal of the body after death. Similarly, the pupil who acquires in one lesson a bit of a verb, a paradigm of a declension, the inflection of a pronoun, along with a rule for the use of the infinitive, and then in the next, perhaps, the principles for the use of *cum*, the formation of adverbs, and the conjugation of *possum*, — such a pupil, I say, seems to me to be put at an enormous psychological disadvantage in his acquisition of the really essential facts whose thorough mastery is so indispensable.

A certain theory of interest is, I am well aware, sometimes urged in defence of the prevailing plan, but it is a serious question whether interest is really promoted by a plan which does violence to obvious psychological laws, and, even if interest were promoted, whether it would be wise to make so great a sacrifice for the end.

The Theory of Interest.

The combination of a study of syntax with the forms results apparently from the same motive, — that of increasing the interest of the subject by increasing its variety.

Alleged Overtraining of the Memory.

It is frequently urged, too, that the old method of vigorous, aggressive attack upon the paradigms (and upon them alone until mastered) involved a training of the memory at the expense of other faculties; hence the justification of combining the study of syntax with that of the declensions and conjugations. But even were the study of syntax taken up more systematically, I am convinced that it would be a mistake to pursue its study in conjunction with the study of the forms. It can hardly fail to distract the energy of the beginning Latin student to be studying contemporaneously two things so different as forms and syntax. Any such plan necessarily precludes, or at least enormously diminishes, any effective concentration. Without such concentration it must be more difficult to acquire a mastery of either forms or syntax. We hear much Importance of to-day of correlation in educational work, Concentration. but we need to exercise the greatest discrimination in the combinations we undertake to make; else under the name of correlation we are likely to find ourselves encouraging a serious dissipation of energy. Nor need we, I believe, cherish any fears of overtraining the memory by directing the pupil's efforts from the outset exclusively (or practically so [1]) to a systematic study of the forms until these are mastered. So far from there being any danger of overtraining the memory by this plan, I am convinced, by my experience with some twelve hundred freshmen whose work has all passed directly under my observation during the last ten years, that there is the greatest danger of training it too little. The age at which pupils ordinarily begin the study of Latin is one at which the memory is usually active and responsive. Later the keenness of its edge is dulled, and it seems unfortunate not to encourage its cultivation by putting upon it the legitimate burdens which at this period it is fitted to bear with ease. Nor is it a common experience that pupils qualified to pursue Latin with profit find this work either specially laborious or distasteful when pursued in the manner I am recommending. On the other hand, I

---

[1] There can be no objection to giving the pupil at the outset the paradigm of the present indicative active of a regular verb of the 1st conjugation, the present indicative of *sum*, along with a few fundamental syntactical principles (subject, object, predicate noun, appositive). This makes it possible to deal with complete sentences from the earliest lessons.

cannot reject the conviction that the labour is increased and the acquisition of the forms is made positively distasteful by assuming, even unconsciously, the attitude that a vigorous attack upon the forms and a most thorough memorizing of them is not desirable. As has been often observed, the pupil in the early weeks of his study of Latin is dominated by a veritable thirst for extensive acquisition, and it seems unfortunate not to gratify this spirit and utilize it, instead of wearying the pupil by unnatural restraint.

The exclusive exercise of the memory is certainly a pernicious practice, but we cannot afford to neglect the service of this intellectual process at any stage of education or in the pursuit of any subject. Least of all can we afford to neglect it in the study of a highly inflected language, the knowledge of whose paradigms is so absolutely indispensable to all future work. These paradigms must be memorized till they are as familiar to the pupil as the alphabet or the multiplication table. Only so can he be said to know them. The important question is whether it is best to pursue a halting timid policy or one of vigorous, sustained attack, recognising that nothing but the severe exercise of the memory will suffice for the purpose. Yet it is only in the very earliest stages of Latin study that any such extensive utilization of the memory can be necessary. The pupil comes soon enough to problems which demand the exercise of the reflective, the discriminating, and the imaginative faculties, and he will be all the better equipped to cope with these problems if he has first provided himself with a solid foundation in the forms. In fact, without such foundation he will be permanently at a fatal disadvantage.

The second defect of the beginner's book of the prevailing type is that *it separates in the initial stages of the*

work things which must later be associated. Thus the
pupil, let us say, learns the present, imperfect, and

Necessitates Later Readjustments. future indicative of *amo* in one lesson; in
another somewhat later he learns the perfect
indicative active, and long subsequently he
acquires piecemeal the remainder of the conjugation of
amo. So with the other conjugations, with the pronouns,
with the five declensions, particularly the third, which is
often dismembered and whose parts are treated at wide
intervals; so, too, with the various constructions of the
accusative, dative, genitive, ablative, *etc.* Sooner or
later the pupil comes to the Grammar, and here he
finds the facts with which he has previously become
familiar grouped in quite another way. In the review
of what he has already learned, and in forming a basis
around which to group systematically the new facts of
forms and syntax he may acquire, the pupil is forced
to make an entirely new distribution of his stock of
knowledge. All the subtle threads of association which
have hitherto been woven into the existing fabric of his
knowledge have to be rudely broken, and a new warp
and a new woof have to be created. I fear that the
amount of effort requisite for the consummation of this
redistribution and rearrangement is not fully appreciated. To my mind the requisite effort cannot fail to
be enormous.[1] I fear, in fact, that it is so great that
the redistribution and rearrangement frequently fail of
consummation by the pupil, and to this fact I believe
we must attribute in large measure[2] the deplorable
ignorance of Latin grammar which characterizes the

---

[1] On this point, *cf.* Dettweiler (in Baumeister, Handbuch der Erzie-
hungs- und Unterrichtslehre für die höheren Schulen, Vol. III. Part iii.,
Lateinisch, p. 36), who insists that the beginner's book and the Grammar *should agree in arrangement and in form of statement.*

[2] Another cause is mentioned later in chapter iv. p. 144.

pupils of our secondary schools to-day. Even where
the change of association and the necessary regrouping
are effected, it can be only at great expense of time and
energy. A true economy of acquisition should always
consider the ultimate form and arrangement in which
the student is to marshal and group the facts of his
knowledge. Unless we are to abandon the effective
study of the Latin Grammar, it seems to me indispensable to make the beginner's book conform in its arrangement and material to the order of the Grammar, so far
as the two books cover identical ground. In this way
the beginning book will be a distinct help to the later
study of the Grammar; in the other case, the difficulty
of the new adjustment is likely to prove a serious impediment to an effective mastery of the Grammar. The
old way of beginning Latin with Grammar and Reader
would, I believe, be sounder and easier than this.

The third fundamental defect in these books to which
I wished to call attention touches the introduction of
exercises in translating English into Latin
before the forms are mastered. So far as
any increased mastery of the *forms* is concerned, it seems a serious mistake to expect
to secure it by practice in translating from English into
Latin. Let us suppose, for example, that the essential
feature of the lesson for a given day is the inflection of a
noun of the first declension, or the indicative
mood of the active voice of *amo*. Is it likely
to be an effective employment of the student's time and
energy, for him to translate, say, a dozen or fifteen sentences from English into Latin, calling for the use of
different forms of *porta* and *amo?* The pupil in this way
gets but a limited amount of drill on the forms. Fifteen
sentences of the sort mentioned constitute a fairly long
exercise. My own experiments indicate that two and

one-half minutes is a very moderate average time allow-
ance for each sentence. This makes thirty-seven minutes
for such an exercise, a large proportion of the pupil's
Defective time. Moreover, the exercise is almost certain
Results. to be lacking in tonic effect. The pupil's natural tendency in writing the Latin for 'of the farmer,'
'of the girls,' 'to the inhabitants,' *etc.*, is to turn to
his printed paradigm and secure the desired form by
imitating; so in the verb, 'he will praise,' 'we have
praised,' 'you summoned,' 'they are calling,' *etc.*, are
not turned into Latin by an active effort of deriving the
required form from the pupil's present knowledge of
the paradigm, but almost inevitably the pupil follows the
line of least resistance and consults the printed paradigm.
This tendency on the pupil's part is so strong, I believe,
as to be practically irresistible, and, where yielded to,
must exert an influence which, so far from being tonic
and strengthening, is positively weakening to the pupil.
To me it seems possible to ensure the requisite inde
pendent exercise upon the forms only by oral methods
under the immediate direction of the teacher.

Let me illustrate what I have in mind. Let us suppose the lesson is on the first declension. Let the
A Practical teacher put to the entire class such questions
Suggestion. as the following, asking for a show of hands
as each pupil is prepared to answer: "What is the
Latin for 'of girls;' 'to the farmers;' 'farmers' as subject; as object; 'of the island'?" and so on, *i. e.* pursuing a series of questions in which the English is given
and the corresponding Latin form is demanded. Then
let the reverse process be instituted, and translation into
English be demanded where the Latin form is given.
The teacher asks: "What is the English for *puellae*,
for *insulis, incolarum, incolam, agricolae, agricolas ?*" *etc.*
Then a fresh turn may be taken and the form be given,

while the pupils are asked to give the number and case in which the form is found; and, lastly, the teacher may give the number and case, asking for the form which corresponds, *e. g.*, "What is the genitive plural of *insula;* the dative singular of *agricola;* the dative plural; the accusative plural of *incola?*", *etc.* Similarly with the verb; the teacher can give the meaning and ask for the corresponding form, or he may give the form and ask for the meaning; or he may state the mood, tense, person, and number in which a given form is found and ask the pupils to give the form; or, lastly, he may give the form and ask the pupils to locate its mood, tense, number, and person. By such an exercise the pupils are thrown entirely upon their own resources. They are forced to recall and to reconstruct; they cannot refer to a book; the process is stimulating and strengthening. They are indelibly imprinting upon their minds vivid pictures of the paradigms, filling in the relatively uncertain and shadowy outlines with definite and effective strokes. Another advantage of such an exercise is the amount of work that can be done in a relatively short time. The pupil who in thirty-seven minutes has written fifteen exercises has at best received only fifteen impressions illustrating the paradigm involved in the lesson for the day. There is the greatest danger, too, that these impressions have been feeble, — inevitably so if, instead of recalling the required form by a direct effort, the pupil has consulted the printed paradigm for it. On the other hand, by such an exercise as I describe it is easily possible in *two minutes* to secure these fifteen impressions, and to be sure that they have been secured by the only way possessing any educative value, — by a direct effort of the memory and reason. In ten minutes, therefore, five times as much can be done toward impressing upon the pupil's mind the paradigm of *porta* or of *amo* as in four times the same amount of time devoted to writing sentences involving the application of these forms, and the teacher can be certain too that the work has been honest. It is not difficult either to enlist the activity of an entire class in such an exercise. While only one pupil can answer any given question, yet I have never failed to feel convinced, where I have followed this plan, that the entire class were doing the work. Such work, furthermore, is intensive, whereas the writing of sentences — even of simple sentences — inevitably distracts the pupil's mind from the forms, and dissipates his energies upon a variety of things. One of these is the vocabulary. As the pupil progresses from lesson to lesson he is sure to forget some, at least, of the earlier Latin words, and when he needs them there is only one recourse, — to hunt them up in the Vocabulary at the end of the book. Another difficulty is the syntax, — slight, perhaps, but actual; yet another is the matter of word-order. All of these elements together conspire to prevent that indispensable concentration upon the forms without which they cannot be mastered. Instead of doing one thing, the pupil is doing several contemporaneously, and all probably indifferently. "*One thing at a time, and that done well,*" was a fine old motto of our fathers, which seems too much neglected in recent education. Still the writing of Latin undoubtedly has its place. When the pupil comes to the systematic study of syntax, such exercises are indispensable; but I hold it to be a self-evident proposition that for the purposes of effective drill in syntax the forms must be already thoroughly mastered, so that the pupil's entire energy may be devoted to the one central object of attention. Only then can we secure that definiteness of impression which is the foundation of real knowledge. The pianoforte pupil does not practise exercises the successive bars of which consist of arpeggios, trills, double thirds, octaves, and scales. These various elements of musical capacity are taken individually, and each is made the subject of intensive work. I cannot but feel that in all study and all teaching the same principle must apply wherever effective progress is to be made without deplorable waste of time and energy both on the pupil's and the teacher's part.

As to the vocabulary of the beginner's book, I believe it should be small. The principle above advocated of doing one thing at a time and doing that thing well, as opposed to undertaking to do several things at a time and inviting disaster, holds here also. If the beginner can learn his inflections and a few elements of syntax, even though his vocabulary be limited, he is equipped to begin some simple reading. A vocabulary can be acquired only slowly at best, and its acquisition will be retarded so long as the pupil still has an imperfect or incomplete knowledge of his paradigms, and is still under the necessity of devoting a large part of his energy to this feature of his Latin study. Even after the forms are mastered, it would still seem wiser, pending the acquisition of the fundamental principles of Latin syntax, to defer any special endeavour to extend the range of the pupil's vocabulary. When these indispensable preliminaries have been met the pupil may well enough make the acquisition of a vocabulary an important end of study, and may then, I believe, expect to make fairly rapid progress in his quest. But before that, I am convinced not only that his struggle will be futile, but that his general progress in other directions will be impeded by the multiplicity of his concerns, and the consequent distraction of effort and energy. Those educators, therefore, who

The Vocabulary should be Small.

advocate a vocabulary of 2,000 or 2,200 words in the beginner's book seem to me to be guided by unsound convictions. It is perfectly true, as these persons urge, that
the lack of vocabulary is the one great impediment to
more extensive and more rapid reading of Latin; but the
great question after all is how best to secure an extensive and accurate knowledge of the words one is likely
to meet in reading. Are we likely to succeed by dint of
a heroic effort at the outset when other and more serious
difficulties are encountering us at every turn? Is it not
better to restrict ourselves to other things in the beginning work, and leave the vocabulary for the later stages
of the study? Seven hundred words have been shown
by experience to be amply sufficient to lend variety and
interest to the work, and, by the abundant repetition of
the same words, to ensure that this small vocabulary
will be thoroughly mastered. But even this mastery
should hardly be made a conspicuous object. Probably
most pupils will inevitably become familiar with all or
nearly all the words of a vocabulary of that size by the
mere frequency with which the words recur. Any
effective vocabulary will certainly always be gained in
that way, *i. e.* by reading and frequently meeting the
same words used again and again in the same senses.
Nothing but wide reading can bring about this result,
and to read widely while pursuing the beginning work is
a contradiction in terms.

To sum up, then, on this subject of the beginner's
book, I feel convinced that most existing beginner's
Summary. books make a profound psychological mistake in combining the contemporaneous
study of forms and syntax from the outset; in dissociating not merely the different declensions and conjugations, but even the different parts of the same
declension and the same conjugation; in dissociating

related syntactical constructions; furthermore (as a result of these dissociations), in teaching the elements of the language to the pupil in an order that must be unlearned and mentally rearranged so soon as a systematic study of the Latin Grammar is begun; lastly, in laying stress upon the writing of Latin before the forms are mastered, — an exercise which can primarily be of value only in inculcating a better knowledge of syntax, and is of the very slightest aid, if not a positive detriment, in acquiring a knowledge of the forms themselves. When to all these defects is added, as in some books of the class referred to, a very large vocabulary, we have the climax of unwisdom applied to the teaching of elementary Latin. Reason seems to me to show us that in approaching a difficult subject the logical way is not to attempt to master all its difficulties at once, not to undertake from the outset to cope with every species of obstacle, howsoever heterogeneous these may be; but rather to choose for the object of first attack that side of the subject whose knowledge is indispensable to further advance, to master this, and then proceed to the next thing, building in orderly systematic fashion, doing one thing at a time and doing that honestly, conserving energy, clinging definitely to a purpose, and making that purpose obvious to the pupil instead of involving him in a blind maze, out of which nothing but a supreme act of faith can afford any hope of ever emerging. Personally I believe the pupil should first address himself to the forms, and devote himself to nothing else until they are completely mastered. I believe too that these should be studied practically in the order given in the Grammar,[1] illustrated of course by copious sentences for

---

[1] *Bonus* and other adjectives of the first and second declensions may well enough follow nouns of the first and second declensions. I can think of no other justifiable deviation.

translation.   Until the forms are mastered, syntax, I am convinced, should be kept in the background, beyond the introduction of the commonest syntactical principles, such as the case for subject, object, predicate noun, appositive, the agreement of the adjective with its substantive, and of the relative with its antecedent.   The writing of Latin, too, should be deferred at least till syntax is reached, and if it is deferred till after the first rough outline of elementary syntax is acquired, it will involve no harm.   The vocabulary should be brief; seven or eight hundred words, exclusive of proper names, are ample for the beginning work.   These, too, should be common words, and as concrete as possible; words, too, employed in their original senses, not in derived ones.

II. Pronunciation.

BIBLIOGRAPHY.

Bennett, Chas. E.   Appendix to Bennett's Latin Grammar, pp. 4–68. Boston. Allyn & Bacon. 1895.

Lindsay, W. M.   The Latin Language, Chapter ii. Oxford. Clarendon Press. 1894.

Lindsay, W. M.   Historical Latin Grammar. pp. 8–21. Oxford. Clarendon Press. 1895.

Seelmann, Emil.   Die Aussprache des Latin. Heilbronn. 1885.

Ellis, Robinson.   The Quantitative Pronunciation of Latin. London. 1874. A discussion of special problems.

Roby, H. J.   Latin Grammar. Vol. I., 4th ed. pp. xxx–xc. London. Macmillan & Co. 1881.

It is now something like twenty years since the so-called Roman or quantitative pronunciation of Latin was

The Roman Pronunciation. first generally introduced into the schools and colleges of this country.   Prior to that, most schools and colleges had used the English pronunciation; some few employed a pronunciation called the ' continental.'   This last, however, was not one pronunciation, but several; in the sounds of the vowels it adhered to their prevailing pronunciation in the languages of continental Europe, but the sounds of certain consonants, namely, *c, g, t, j, s*, were rendered with much variety. Both the English and continental pronunciations still survive in this country, though probably the two together are not represented by five per cent of the Latin pupils of the secondary schools; in the colleges the percentage must be lower still.

By the Roman pronunciation is, of course, meant the pronunciation employed by the ancient Romans themselves. This pronunciation naturally varied much at different periods;[1] hence it has been necessary to take the pronunciation of some well-defined epoch as a standard. The epoch conventionally adopted for this purpose is the golden age of Rome's literary greatness, — roughly the period from 50 B. C. to 50 A. D. Inasmuch as many intelligent and otherwise well-informed persons, including teachers of Latin, often cherish and express a skepticism as to the grounds on which scholars have presumed to reconstruct the pronunciation of a dead language like Latin, it may be well here briefly to indicate the nature of the evidence which supports this Roman pronunciation of Latin. The evidence may be brought under five heads.

Evidence for the Roman Method.

a. *The statements of Roman writers.* To a person unaware of the writings of the old Latin grammarians from the first to the eighth centuries of our era, the body of their works will be surprising. These works have been carefully collected by Keil, a German scholar, under the title *Grammatici*

Roman Grammarians.

---

[1] Thus *v*, to take but a single letter for the purposes of illustration, was pronounced as English *w* down to about 100 A. D.; later it became a bilabial spirant (a sound not occurring in English); and finally (5th century A. D.) it passed into the labio dental spirant, English *v*

Latini (Leipzig, 1855–1880), and fill eight large quarto volumes. These writers cover the entire field of grammar, and most of them devote more or less space to a systematic consideration of the sounds of the letters. As representative writers on this subject, may be cited Terentianus Maurus (flourished 185 A. D.); Marius Victorinus (fl. 350 A. D.); Martianus Capella (fourth or fifth century A. D.; not in Keil's collection); Priscian (fl. 500 A. D.). Even the classical writers have often incidentally contributed valuable bits of information; *e. g.* Varro, Cicero, Quintilian.

b. *Inscriptions* furnish a second important source of information. The total body of these is very great. The *Corpus Inscriptionum Latinarum*, in process of publication since 1863, consists already of fifteen large folio volumes, some of them in several parts, and is not yet completed. These inscriptions disclose many peculiarities of orthography which are exceedingly instructive for the pronunciation of Latin. Thus such spellings as *urps* and *pleps* by the side of *urbs* and *plebs* clearly indicate the assimilation of *b* to *p* before *s*. Similarly *termae, aetereas, etc.*, show clearly that at the time these inscriptions were cut *th* was still practically a *t*-sound, and forbid us to attach to it the value of English *th* as heard in either *this* or *thin*. Even the blunders of the masons who cut the inscriptions are not infrequently exceedingly instructive.

Inscriptions.

c. *Greek transliterations of Latin words* constitute a third source of knowledge. Not only Greek writers (especially the Greek historians of Roman affairs), but also Greek inscriptions, afford us abundant evidence of this kind. Thus the Greek Κικέρων (*Cicero*) furnishes support for the *k*-sound of Latin *c*; while Λιουία (*Livia*) and Ούαλεντία (*Valentia*) bear similarly upon the *w*-sound of Latin *v*. The

Greek Transliterations.

inscriptions are naturally much more trustworthy guides in this matter than our texts of the Greek authors, for we can never be sure that the MSS. have not undergone alterations in the process of transmission to modern times.

d. *The Romance languages* also (French, Spanish, Italian, *etc.*), within limits, may be utilized in determining the sounds of Latin. **Romance Languages.**

e. *The sound-changes of Latin itself, as analyzed by etymological investigation.* Modern scholars, particularly in the last forty years, have done much to promote the scientific study of Latin sounds **Philology.** and forms; their researches have thrown no little light upon the sounds of Latin.

As a result of all these sources of knowledge,[1] any one who will patiently review the evidence may easily assure himself that the Roman pronunciation rests upon a solid historical foundation, and is not a flimsy product of the imagination. As to certain points, the evidence is, of course, conflicting, and as a result the opinions of scholars diverge. Doubtless, too, there existed certain refinements of pronunciation which will always remain unknown to us. But it cannot be denied that we can to-day restore in its essential features the pronunciation of Latin substantially as the Romans spoke it.

Admission has just been made above of our inability to establish with certainty all the various refinements of pronunciation which must have existed in Latin. An exception must be made, however, in **Hidden Quantity.** regard to one point, — " hidden quantity." A hidden quantity is the quantity of a vowel before two consonants. Such a quantity is called hidden as distinguished from the quantity of a vowel before a *single*

---

[1] The detailed evidence will be found in the books above cited.

consonant, where the employment of the word in verse at once indicates whether the vowel is long or short.[1]

The determination of these hidden quantities is obviously of great importance if we would secure an accurate pronunciation of Latin. In a modern language the pronunciation of a long vowel for a short, or *vice versa*, will often effectually disguise a word.[2] At first sight the determination of these multitudinous hidden quantities seems a well-nigh insuperable difficulty. Scholarly research has, however, succeeded in definitely settling most of them.[3] The evidence is as follows:

a. *Express testimony of the ancient Roman writers.* Thus, for example, Cicero (*Orator*, 48. 159) lays down the general principle that all *vowels* are long before *nf* and *ns*. Nearly every Roman grammarian furnishes some little direct testimony of this kind.

b. *The versification of the early Roman dramatists,* particularly Plautus and Terence. These writers fre-

---

[1] Thus in the hexameter line beginning *conspexere silent*, the metre clearly shows that the *i* of *silent* is short; for if the vowel were here long, the syllable would be long. But the *e* of *silent* might be either long or short. All that the metre shows is that the *syllable* is long; it tells us nothing about the *vowel*, and we cannot (at least not by mere inspection of the verse) determine whether we should pronounce *ē* or *ĕ*. Hence we call the quantity of the *vowel* in such cases hidden. Pupil and teacher alike should always guard carefully against the prevalent confusion of quantity of *vowel* with quantity of *syllable*. Before a single consonant the quantity of the vowel and syllable are, of course, always identical, *i. e.* if the vowel is long, the syllable is also long, but before two consonants, while the *syllable* is long, the *vowel* itself may be either long or short, and must be *pronounced* long or short according to its actual quantity.

[2] Were one to speak of a *wĭck* as a *wēke*, or a *pool* as a *pŭll*, the metathesis would be the same as in Latin when one says *victor* for *vĭctor ;* or *ŭstus* for *ūstus.* I remember that in German my pronunciation of *Klöster* as *Klŏster ;* *Mōnd* as *Mŏnd ;* and *Wüste* as *Wŭste*, all completely nonplussed my listeners.

[3] A detailed discussion of the principles for hidden quantity, along with a full list of words whose hidden vowels are long, may be found in Bennett, *Appendix to Latin Grammar*, pp. 34–68.

quently employ as short many syllables which in classi
cal poetry would invariably be long by position. In
many of these cases it is manifest that the short *syllable*
quantity is owing to the fact that the *vowel* was short
and that the two following consonants somehow failed to
'make position.'

c. *Inscriptions.* Various modes of spelling and various
diacritical marks were in vogue to indicate long vowels.
Thus from 130–70 B. C. we find the vowels *a, e, u* written
double, when it was desired to indicate their long quantity, *e. g. paastores, pequlatuu, etc.* Long *i* was in early
times often written *ei, e.g. veixit.* Beginning with the
middle of the first century B. C. we find the *apex* (or
accent mark) set over the vowels *a, e, o, u,* while long *i*
was now designated by an I rising above the other
letters and called *i longa.* Later, *i* also took the *apex.*
Examples are: *tráxi, ólla, léctus, júncta,* QVInQVE,
príscus.

d. *Greek transliterations of Latin words.* This method
is most fruitfully applied in case of the vowels *e* and *o.*
The employment of Greek ε or η, ο or ω, makes the
quantity of the Latin vowel certain, wherever faith may
be reposed in the accuracy of the transcription. Thus
we write *Esquiliae* in view of Ἡσκυλῖνος, Strabo, v. 234;
Vĕrgilius after Οὐεργίλιος; *Vesŏntio* after Οὐεσοντίων,
Dio Cassius, lxviii. 24. The quantity of *i* also may often
be determined by Greek transliterations. Thus ει regularly points to Latin *ī, e. g.* Βειψάνιος = *Vīpsānius;*
Greek *i* points to Latin *ĭ, e. g.* Ιστρος = *Ĭster.*

e. *The vocalism of the Romance languages,* particularly the Spanish and Italian. These languages treated
e, i, o, u with great regularity according to the natural
length of the vowel in Latin. Latin *ē* and *ō* were close
vowels; *ĕ* and *ŏ* were open. The Romance languages
have preserved these original vowel qualities with great

tenacity. Hence Italian *crescere* with close *e* justifies our writing *crēscō* for Latin; while Italian *honesto* with open *e* points to Latin *honĕstus*. Similarly Italian *noscere* with close *o* justifies our writing *nōscō* for Latin, while Italian *dotto* with open *o* points to Latin *dŏctus*. In the same way Latin *ī* and *ū* remained *i* and *u* in Romance, while *ĭ* and *ŭ* became respectively close *e* and close *o*. Thus from Italian *dissi* we infer Latin *dīxī;* from Italian *dussi*, Latin *dūxī;* while *detto* with close *e* points to Latin *dĭctus*, and *-dotto* with close *o* to Latin *dŭctus*. This method of determining the hidden quantity of Latin vowels from the Romance has been applied most fruitfully in recent years.

As a result of the application of the five methods above described, there remain at present extremely few undetermined hidden vowel quantities in Latin words. Some slight divergence of opinion still exists among investigators as to the quantity of certain vowels; but this divergence is exceedingly slight, vastly less, in fact, than for any corresponding number of English words. Professors Greenough and Howard in the preface to their *Allen and Greenough's Shorter Latin Grammar*, p. iv, speak of this matter of hidden quantities as a subject still in its infancy. Such is far from being the case. Of the five methods above enumerated of arriving at a knowledge of hidden quantities, each one has already been utilized to practically the fullest extent of which it is capable. The works of the Roman gram marians and other Roman writers have been systematically searched, and their testimonies recorded and sifted; the versification of the Roman dramatists has been carefully studied with specific reference to this very point; the great body of Latin inscriptions has been conscientiously examined, and all instances of the use of the *apex* or *I longa* have been gathered and classified by

Christiansen (*De apicibus et I longis.* Husum, 1889); the form assumed by Latin words in Greek transliterations has been carefully studied for the body of Greek inscriptions by Eckinger (*Orthographie lateinischer Wörter in griechischen Inschriften.* Munich. Without date; about 1893); and, lastly, the testimony derivable from the Romance languages has been most minutely examined in a series of publications: Gröber, *Vulgärlateinische Substrata romanischer Wörter,* a series of articles in Wölfflin's *Archiv für lateinische Lexikographie,* vols. i.–vi.; Körting, *Lateinisch-Romanisches Wörterbuch,* Paderborn, 1891; d'Ovidio, in *Gröber's Grundiss der romanischen Philologie,* Strassburg, 1888, i. p. 497 ff. The authors of these last three works have not merely taken into consideration the leading literary Romance languages, but they have gleaned from the most obscure dialects whatever contribution these could offer.

All in all, it is not probable that we shall ever know the quantities of hidden Latin vowels appreciably better than we do to-day, for it is unlikely either that new sources of knowledge on this subject will be discovered, or that further study of the existing sources will yield results which will materially alter our present conclusions.

I have been speaking thus far of the Roman pronunciation as a subject of historical and linguistic interest. It remains to say a word as to its adaptation to the needs of our American education; and here I wish at the outset to declare frankly my conviction that the introduction of the Roman pronunciation was a fundamental blunder, and that its retention is likewise a serious mistake. My reasons follow:

    a. *The Roman pronunciation is extremely difficult.* This is sometimes denied, but only by superficial observers. Such persons call attention to the fact that,

Difficulty. under the Roman pronunciation, *c, g, t, s* are always uniform in pronunciation, whereas by the English method the sounds of these letters vary and depend upon rules. This, however, is a very slight consideration; for *c, g, t, s* under the English pronunciation vary in accordance with the normal mode of pronouncing the same letters in English words. Thus we instinctively pronounce *genus* as *jee-nus, propitius* as *propishus*, after familiar English analogy. What makes the Roman pronunciation of Latin really difficult is the quantity of the vowels. So far as these belong to inflectional endings, *e. g. -ī, -ōrum, -ōs, -ās, -ārum, -ibus, -ābam, -ēbam, -erō, -eram, etc.*, they can be learned as easily by one pronunciation as the other. But even when the pupil has acquired a knowledge of these, there remains the multitude of vowels in the interior of words, — in root syllables, in stems, and in suffixes. Here nothing but sheer force of memory can enable any one to become master of the vast number of vowels to be pronounced. Even the same root often varies, *e. g. fīdō*, but *fǐdes ; fǐdēlis*, but *fīdus*. Some few general principles can, of course, be given, but there remain literally thousands of vowels that must be learned outright and retained by memory alone; *e. g. stǔdium, gěrō, vǐtium, mǒdus, sexāgintā, sěněx, vǐdeō, lǎtus* ('side'), but *lātus*, ('broad'), *fěrus, etc., etc., etc.* To these must be added hidden vowel quantities by the hundreds; *e. g. frūstrā, cěssī, scrīpsī, tīnxī, mǐssus, ūstus, ǔssī, lūx, nǔx, dǔx, něx, lēx, ūsque, rōstrum, nǒster, sǐstō, sīstrum, māximus, lūctus, flǔctus, etc., etc., etc.*

Even the consonants create difficulty, particularly the doubled consonants; *e. g. pp, tt, cc, ll, mm, ss, etc.* In English we pronounce these singly. Thus we say *fery*, though we write *ferry ; kity*, where we write *kitty*. But in Latin we know that these doubled consonants were regularly pronounced double, just as they are in modern Italian. A distinct effort is necessary to achieve this pronunciation.

Another point of difficulty is the proper division of words into syllables. Recent researches have shown that our traditional rules for syllable division, though they rest upon the express testimony of the Latin grammarians, were purely mechanical directions, and did not indicate the actual pronunciation.[1] The actual division, moreover, must have been quite different from that which prevails in English under corresponding conditions.

Lastly, we have the difficulty of the Latin accent. It is beyond question that Latin was less heavily stressed than are the accented syllables in our English speech.

All these difficulties are really so great that anything like an accurate pronunciation of Latin under the Roman system is practically impossible except by the sacrifice of an amount of time out of all proportion to the importance of the end to be attained. As a matter of fact, few teachers and practically no pupils ever do acquire a pronunciation of any exactness. Out of some twelve hundred freshmen whom I have tested on this point in the last dozen years at two leading American universities I have never found one who could mark ten lines of Cæsar's *Gallic War* with substantial quantitative accuracy. Nor is this all. For eight years I have conducted summer courses for teachers at Cornell University. This work has been attended by some two hundred teachers and college professors, nearly all of them college graduates, and many of them persons who had had graduate work at our best universities. Yet few

---

[1] See the discussion in Bennett, *Appendix to Bennett's Latin Grammar*, p. 30 ff.

of these have ever shown any thorough grasp of the Roman pronunciation, and most of them have exhibited deplorable ignorance of the first principles of its accurate application. Even college professors of eminence often frankly admit their own ignorance of vowel quantity and proclaim their despair of ever acquiring a knowledge of it. It is not long since I listened to a professor of high position who gave at an educational meeting an illustration of his method of reading Latin poetry. The reading was prefaced with the candid declaration that the reader had never pretended to acquire an accurate knowledge of Latin vowel quantities and despaired of ever succeeding in doing so. The reading which followed proved the correctness of this statement. The opening line of Horace, *Odes*, I. 23, was read thus:

Vītăs ĭnūlĕō mē sĭmĭlĭs Chlŏĕ,

and was followed by similar violations of vocalic and syllabic quantity.

It is safe to say that only those who have devoted long and patient attention to the subject, and who practise frequent oral reading, can pronounce Latin with accuracy according to the Roman method. My observation teaches me that those who ever attain this accomplishment are so few in number as to constitute practically a negligible quantity.

The foregoing practical considerations, based upon the inherent difficulties of the Roman pronunciation, coupled with the practically universal failure to adhere to its principles, have long seemed to my mind valid grounds for its abandonment. Those who urge its retention on the ground of its ease certainly are inexcusably blind to the facts. Those who advocate it on the ground that it is a moral duty to pronounce Latin as the Romans did, may theoretically have a good case. But certainly it can no longer be held to be a moral duty to maintain a system of pronunciation which the experience of twenty years has shown to result in miserable failure, and the intrinsic difficulties of whose accurate application are so evident. We cannot hope, I believe, to secure appreciably better results than have thus far been achieved, certainly not without the ex- penditure of a vast amount of time and energy, which can ill be spared.

b. *It brings no compensating advantages.* This state- ment will doubtless provoke dissent, and some may wish to urge that the acquisition of the vocalic **Brings no** sounds of the Roman pronunciation of Latin **Compensating** is of assistance in the study of the modern **Advantages.** European languages. But this can hardly be deemed a serious argument. Some of the Latin vowels and diphthongs designate identical sounds in French and German, but quite as often they are different; *e.g.* French *ă, u, eu, ei, ai, oi;* German *ae, eu, ei.* Moreover, the apprehension of these constitutes an exceedingly slight difficulty.

Others urge the importance of the quantitative pro- nunciation of Latin for the reading of Latin poetry; and here, if anywhere, we might recognise a valid reason for the retention of the Roman pronunciation, if only our pupils acquired, or could reasonably be ex- pected to acquire, an accurate quantitative pronuncia- tion of the Latin language, and if they combined with this any just conception of the truly quantitative nature of Latin poetry.[1] But so long as the prevailing pro- nunciation is practically oblivious of the difference between long and short vowels, and so long as we

---

[1] See below, chapter vi., Latin Prosody.

follow the traditional practice of making Latin poetry
accentual, it is idle to support the retention of the
Roman pronunciation on the grounds that it contributes to a capacity to appreciate Latin poetry in its
true organic and artistic structure. A rigidly accurate
quantitative pronunciation will do this, provided we
eliminate the unjustifiable artificial stress ictus, but our
present proficiency in the Roman pronunciation, or any
proficiency we are ever likely to achieve, will hardly
enable any considerable fraction of our students ever
to appreciate Latin poetry as a quantitative rhythm.

c. *It does bring certain distinct disadvantages.* Chief
among these is the difficulty it adds to the beginning
Disadvantages. work in Latin. I am forced to believe that
the acquisition of the forms is very much
easier under the English pronunciation, where the entire
energy of the pupil can be devoted to the forms them
selves without the embarrassment which the difficulties
of a strange pronunciation inevitably impose.

Another serious disadvantage is the chaos it has
wrought in our current pronunciation of classical
proper names, Latin quotations, proverbs, technical
terms, legal phrases, titles of classical works, *etc.* It is
extremely difficult to reach any satisfactory basis for
pronouncing these. The Roman pronunciation seems
awkward and affected, and is to many unintelligible,
while to those who have been taught the Roman pronunciation any other is difficult. The result is a condition
of affairs that is keenly felt by many classes of society,
— by none perhaps more than by the teachers of Latin,
who, while protesting against the present anarchy, find
themselves at a loss to effect any radical improvement.

The foregoing are the considerations which have for
years weighed with me, and which have finally com-

pelled me to believe that the retention of our present unmethodical "method" of pronouncing Latin has proved itself a serious mistake. Fifteen years ago my zeal for the Roman pronunciation was unbounded. For years I have been a conscientious student of the historical and linguistic evidence bearing upon this subject. For years I cherished the hope that with time and better teaching a decided improvement in the results yielded by the Roman pronunciation would manifest itself. But I am now convinced that no such advance has been apparent, and that it will not, can not, ought not to be. So long as we retain the Roman pronunciation, while nominally making that our standard, we shall in reality be far from exemplifying that method in our practice. We shall be guilty of pretending to do one thing, while we really are doing something else. I hesitate to believe that such disingenuousness can permanently commend itself to thoughtful teachers. I have above mentioned the fact that certain educators advocate the employment of the Roman pronunciation on moral grounds, urging that it is our bounden duty to apply what we know to be true. It is equally on moral grounds (among others) that I would urge the immediate abandonment of the Roman pronunciation. We are not just to ourselves, we are not just to our students, so long as we encourage the present hypocritical practice. The English pronunciation is at least honest. It confessedly violates vowel quantity, though I doubt whether it actually does so any more than the Roman method as actually employed. But it is simple, easily applied, and relieves the beginner especially of one important element of difficulty and discouragement.

The educators of other countries have shown much greater wisdom in this matter of Latin pronunciation than have we. England and Germany have witnessed efforts to introduce the Roman pronunciation, but the sober conservative sense of·German and English educators has thus far resisted, and probably will continue successfully to resist, this unwise spirit of innovation. In America we are unfortunately too prone to view with favour any new idea, educational or other, and to embark precipitately in experiments which involve serious consequences. Undue pressure, I think, is often exerted upon the schools by college teachers. Many of these, in their enthusiasm for the scientific aspects of their own professional work, exhibit a tendency to demand that the teaching of their subject in the secondary schools shall be conducted with express reference to the ultimate needs of the higher scholarship. This attitude manifests itself in many matters of educational policy connected with Latin, and in my judgment involves great danger to the best interests of the schools. The prime question in the teaching of every subject in our schools should be the present educational needs of the pupils. Pedagogical procedure should be governed by these considerations. In other words, pupils do not exist for Latin, but Latin exists for the pupils. The needs, real or fancied, of the higher scholarship have no claim to consideration as compared with the rational satisfaction of the pupils' present interests.

III. The "Inductive" Method.

BIBLIOGRAPHY.

Cauer, Paul. Grammatica Militans, 1898. Chapter ii. "Induktion und Deduktion."

Wenzel, Alfred. Der Todeskampf des altsprachlichen Unterrichts. Berlin. Carl Duncker's Verlag. 1899. pp. 19–41.

A discussion of the "Inductive" Method may seem somewhat academic. At present certainly in this country such a discussion is no longer a practical one. Books constructed professedly on an inductive plan have met with severe criticism, and those specimens of them which have thus far been offered to the educational public have been, I think, quite generally recognised as involving serious pedagogical defects. Still, fairness compels the admission that the so-called "inductive" method has not yet had a fair trial upon the basis of its own merits. The radical defects of the "inductive" Latin books for beginners which I have known have seemed to me to lie not so much in the inherent weakness of the method professedly followed as in some other features. Harper and Burgess's *Inductive Latin Primer* will serve to illustrate what I mean. The defects of this book in my judgment are fairly represented by the type of beginner's books which were under discussion in an earlier part of this chapter, pp. 51–66. We note the same unsystematic arrangement, the same dissociation of things belonging together, the same mistaken endeavour to teach a little of everything at one time, which we considered above. These defects seem to me so serious as to have prevented the possibility of a fair judgment upon the merits of the feature which has given the title to the book, namely, its so-called "inductive" character.

In order to understand what this feature promises for Latin instruction, let us examine precisely what it involves. The essential feature of the method receives illustration in the opening lesson of the book referred to. Its essence seems to consist in giving an illustration of a principle, and encouraging the pupil to deduce the principle from the illustration. Thus it is pointed out that *Gallia* is accented on the first syllable, *dīvīsa, omnīs, partēs*, on the second, and from these facts the pupil is to study

What the "Inductive" Method is.

6

out the principles of accentuation. So with the other facts and principles of the language. Instead of the statement of a principle followed by an illustration of it, the pupil is to work out and determine the principle for himself by observation and reflection. The plan rep-

The Name a Misnomer.

resents, therefore, a definite educational theory. The name "inductive," however, seems a thorough misnomer. Any proper induction (in any sense of the word with which I am familiar) consists in bringing together *all* the facts or, at least, *all the possible types* of facts bearing upon some one problem, and then determining from these the principle which they prove. In the book before us, the pupil is given to understand that the facts *are* typical; hence he really institutes no truly inductive process;[1] he merely interprets the meaning of an example which some one else by processes truly inductive has discovered to be typical. This inaccuracy of nomenclature, however, does not bear vitally upon the merits of the method, except so far as it may mislead both teacher and pupil to believe they are pursuing a severer mental process than is really the case.

The purpose of the method, such as it is, may be presumed to be the stimulating of the pupil's observational and reflective powers. Whether it be wise to

Its Purpose of Questionable Wisdom.

utilize the beginning Latin work for this purpose seems open to serious question. Personally I have had no experience with this method of learning the elements of the language, — particularly the accidence; but the experience of those

---

[1] The process, in fact, is a truly deductive one. Formally, it amounts to this: 1. The example before us illustrates a universal principle. 2. The example before us illustrates the following truth (*e. g.* that the subject of the infinitive stands in the accusative case, or that adjectives of *fulness* are construed with the genitive). 3. Therefore it is a universal principle that the subject of the infinitive stands in the accusative, or that adjectives of fulness are construed with the genitive.

who have attempted to apply it has impressed me with the belief that it is neither effective nor economical. The later study of Latin is so rich in the opportunities it affords for the cultivation of the observational and reflective powers, that it seems safer to defer for the first three or four months of Latin study any special attention to these ends.   It certainly will be not only safe, but a positive duty, to do this, unless experience can show that this so-called "inductive" method of learning the sounds, accentuation, forms, and inflections of Latin is an easier and briefer way of mastering them. That experience ever will show this, I doubt.   Observation and reason have never proved very helpful assistants in memorizing any large body of facts, such as the forms of a highly inflected language.   Reason, I fear, hinders rather than helps in such a task.   Such a task seems to me rather a function of the retentive memory, a faculty whose importance we have lately shown such a mistaken tendency to ignore.   An exclusive cultivation of the memory at the expense of the other faculties is certainly most deplorable.   But memory has its important functions, and it is to be hoped that in avoiding the abuse of this faculty we may not be betrayed into ignoring and neglecting its legitimate utilization.

In his *Grammatica Militans*, Paul Cauer, one of the soberest and most thoughtful of German classical educators, thus expresses himself on the subject of the " Inductive " Method as its workings **Cauer's Criticisms.** have been observed by him in German schools (Chapter ii. : " Induktion und Deduktion," p. 25) : " In the exact sciences, all know how difficult — not to say impossible — it is to establish a complete inductive proof, and how difficult it is to avoid the errors which are necessarily involved in the limited material at one's disposal.

Yet in the school in studying grammar, after three,[1] four, or, if you will, ten examples have been adduced, the pupil is encouraged to conclude, ' Therefore it is always true that, *etc.*' Instead of this, the teacher should always remind the pupil that no proof has really been adduced, and that the principle to which attention has been called in one or two examples has been established by the labours of scholars who have carefully examined the literary monuments of the Greek and Latin languages. . . . Otherwise there is propagated by teaching, instead of the blessings of an inductive process, merely the tendency to precipitate generalization, — a tendency always too natural, — as illustrated in the case of the Englishman who returned from Heidelberg with the conviction that it always rained there, since he had twice so found it. . . . The passage from the particular to the general, from fact to law, is not the only method of acquiring new knowledge; the reverse process is equally justified. . . Which process is best, must be decided in each special case by the nature of the subject."

As regards "inductive" treatment of the forms, Cauer (P. 26) says: " In the first weeks of the study of a new language the pupil is inspired with a burning zeal for learning much; he has a veritable hunger for extensive acquisition. The teacher should gratify this disposition; he should utilize it, and not weary the pupils with a method which is in place only where one is reviewing matter already familiar for the purpose of discovering the laws to which it conforms. Later also in the syntax there are many instances in which it is both simpler and more instructive to derive the truth from the nature of the subject under discussion rather than from observation."

---

[1] Our American books have mostly contented themselves with *one*.

IV. Reading at Sight.

'Reading at sight' is used in two senses; in one sense it designates the reading of a passage from some classical author in the original Latin in such **What it** a way as to appreciate and feel its content **Means.** without translation mental or oral, but precisely as one would feel a similar passage in one's own vernacular. In the other sense 'reading at sight' designates the translation into English of a passage never before seen. In the discussion which follows I shall restrict the expression 'reading at sight' to the first of these two senses,[1] and in later discussing the second process shall employ the phrase 'translation at sight.'

With the appearance of Professor Hale's fascinating and stimulating paper, *The Art of Latin Reading* (Boston, 1887), the suggestion was first definitely **Professor** put before teachers and pupils that by the **Hale's** proper method of study it was possible at **Pamphlet.** a relatively early stage of one's Latin study to learn to apprehend even the more complex periods of Cicero's orations as rapidly as read by the eye or heard by the ear. To acquire this power, Professor Hale recommended habituating one's self from the very beginning of Latin study to extensive oral reading. As the Latin word-order constitutes one of the chief difficulties in the comprehension of a Latin sentence, the pupil was urged consciously to ask himself at each word of a new sentence, Just what bearing or bearings may this word have?, and holding his several conclusions in suspense was bidden to press on to the end, precisely as in the case of his own language. Faithful application of these

---

[1] It is, of course, obvious that the two processes are not necessarily mutually exclusive. I separate them for the purposes of discussion.

principles, it was promised, should enable the pupil, as he progressed in his Latin study, to understand Latin without the necessity of a translation. Professor Hale included in his paper well-chosen illustrations of the way the pupil's mind should act in attaining the promised goal, and new visions of the millennium thrilled the hearts of those who were so fortunate as to listen to the original exposition of his views at the Conference of Academic Principals held at Syracuse in December, 1886.

Since Professor Hale's pamphlet appeared (and incidentally before that time),[1] Professor Greenough has **Professor** given forcible expression to views practically **Greenough.** identical with those presented by Professor Hale. In the *Preface* to his edition of Eutropius (Boston, 1892) he thus concludes his remarks on this question: "The essence of all this is, that to learn to read a language the words must be taken as they come, with the ideas they are supposed to convey, *and must be forced to make a mental picture in that order*,[2] no matter whether the order is familiar or not."[3] More recently still the Commission of New England Colleges has urged[4] that a very large amount of attention be paid to reading at sight in the new scheme of instruction which they have lately recommended to the secondary schools of New England for adoption. The eminent standing of the advocates of the new theory naturally claims for their views the most serious consideration, and it is because I am not familiar with any

---

[1] For example, in the Introduction to his edition of Cicero's *Orations*. Boston, 1886.

[2] The italics are mine.

[3] *Cf.* also the similar tenor of Professor Flagg's remarks in the *Preface* to his edition of Nepos. Boston, 1895.

[4] See the Report of their action in the SCHOOL REVIEW for December, 1895.

previous discussion of the subject that I venture here to express some doubts as to the soundness and the practical possibilities of the theories so confidently championed.

A favourite appeal with those who lay stress upon the importance of reading at sight is to the fact that children in learning a language learn it not through the medium of objective study and transla- Subjective Acquisition of tion, but by direct interpretation of what they Foreign Languages. hear or read. "Why," they ask, "should not Latin and Greek be acquired in the same way?"

A proper answer to this question seems to involve the consideration of two others; first, What is the purpose of Latin study in the secondary school? and, Purpose of second, What is the nature of the intellectual Latin Study. training gained by acquiring a language in the subjective way that is regular with children?

To the first of these two questions I can still see no other answer than that which I undertook to formulate and defend in the first chapter of this volume. As there set forth, the only rational justification of the study of Latin in our secondary schools seems to me to be found in its unique effect in stimulating and elevating the pupil's intellectual processes, and most of all in the increased mastery over the resources of the mother tongue which it confers. As previously maintained, these results come naturally from careful daily translation under wise guidance.

In order properly to answer the second question, namely, that as to the value of the subjective acquisition of a foreign language, the attainment of a capacity for direct interpretation without the medium of translation, let us assume that an American boy of ten goes abroad and resides at Paris or Berlin. It is a familiar fact that such a boy rapidly acquires a certain command of French or German. To the person who has no oral command of those languages, the performance of such a youth after a year's foreign residence would be impressive to a degree. But what has the lad really acquired, and what is the significance of his acquisition from the purely educational point of view? The actual acquisition does not go beyond a capacity to express the limited range of his ordinary ideas. His vocabulary is small. As regards the educational worth of his new-found capacity, it has given him no mental stimulus, no new powers of discrimination or analysis. Least of all has it given him any increased mastery over his own native language. In fact, as he has become subjectively familiar with a new tongue, the chances are that he has proportionately lost command of his own. Educationally apparently the boy's new acquisition marks no positive intellectual gain, nor could it fairly be expected to do so; for the process of acquisition has been purely imitative, or practically so, and such a boy might go on indefinitely, learning a new language a year in the same way, without essentially strengthening his intellectual fibre or increasing his intellectual range. Educational processes after the very earliest years are no longer imitative. They are rather discriminative and constructive. They must involve comparison and judgment, and no employment of the pupil's attention which ignores this principle can be expected to yield fruit of value.

Those, now, who insist so strenuously on the importance of the direct subjective interpretation of Latin at the very outset of the study seem to me to advocate the acquisition of something which in the first place can be attained only by an imitative process, and which, if attained, is not likely to be of any greater educational utility than the capacity to understand colloquial French or German which an American lad might acquire by a moderate period of foreign residence. If, now, Latin is to be retained as a basal subject of instruction in our schools, is it desirable that the pupil be initiated at the outset into a subjective apprehension of the language? Would not the chief usefulness of Latin as an instrument of intellectual discipline vanish the moment the mind of the pupil passed from its objective to its subjective contemplation? So soon as such a transition was effected all need of translation would at once disappear, and with it those minute and searching mental processes, which now constitute the most important functions of the study, and which give it its superior title to a place in the curriculum of our schools.

Just so far then as reading at sight abridges attention to conscientious translation into idiomatic English, just so far must those who believe in the vitalizing and informing influence of such translation believe that reading at sight introduces into our secondary education an element which is undesirable, — simply because it interferes with what *is* desirable.

But it may be said by the advocates of reading at sight, " No one disputes the value of translation. All we maintain is that reading at sight furnishes a discipline just as good or better, and hence equally entitled to recognition." The validity of this last position seems so questionable that we shall do well to examine it more fully. The result which the exercise of Reading at Sight aims to achieve is the subjective apprehension of the language, a feeling for Latin as Latin. Obviously such a result can be obtained for Latin only in the same way as in case of other languages, namely, by imitative pro cesses. Professor Hale and others urge, in fact, that the beginning pupil put himself in the same attitude as the

Roman boy of nineteen centuries ago. But was such a process an educative one to the Roman boy? If it was not, is it likely to be to the boy of to-day? Or if it be claimed that to the Roman boy it was distinctively educative, why is not the acquisition of our own tongue in precisely the same way of distinctively educative value, and why does it not accomplish ideal results? It cannot be too clearly borne in mind, I believe, that it is not the knowing a language that is primarily of educational utility. If that were so, the polyglot couriers and kellners and portiers of the continental hotels ought to be the most highly cultivated persons of contemporary society. How many of them are able to speak with fluency and accuracy four or five different languages! These men have learned English, French, German, Italian in the very way that we are told is so desirable for Latin. They feel English as English, French as French, German as German, Italian as Italian. No details of word-order trouble them. No necessity for even a mental translation into terms of their own vernacular. All is subjective, as it should be. The appeal is as direct as was *Cave canem!* to a Roman boy. And yet what intellectual furtherance has ever come from such linguistic attainments? In fact, ought we to expect it to come? Must not such intellectual growth for pupils in the secondary school come from processes of reflection and comparison, rather than from those of imitation? Personally I am convinced that they must so come. And so I say again: To interpret Latin directly, to feel it as a Roman felt it, is a facility that can be acquired (if at all) only as the Roman acquired it, namely, by imitative processes; and these processes do seem to be lacking in any tonic educational value which warrants their recognition as instruments of the secondary education.

But there are those who advocate the subjective acqui-
· sition of Latin on other grounds, namely, æsthetic ones.
Is it worth while, they ask, for students to   Æsthetic
study Latin four years in the school, unless   Grounds are
they acquire a feeling for Latin and learn to   Urged.
enjoy it? Now I have a regard for what is beautiful, and
I certainly believe in cultivating the æsthetic sense, but I
cannot bring myself to believe that the purpose of Latin
study is primarily an æsthetic one, and that the chief
goal is the attainment of a nice feeling for the cadence
and rhythm of the Latin sentence, so that the culmination of a four years' course shall be a capacity to revel
in the flow of Cicero's periods or in the long roll of the
hexameter, or, failing this, to be condemned to look
back upon wasted hours and neglected opportunities.
If that be true, why is it truer of Latin than of geometry?
We hold up no such peculiar ideal for the latter study. To
reap value from geometry it is not thought necessary that
the pupil should feel a thrill of rapture over the contemplation of an isosceles triangle or an inscribed hexagon.
Why should we magnify the æsthetic aim of feeling
Latin any more than feeling geometry? There might
possibly be reason for so doing, did Latin offer opportunities for culture in no other way. But will any one
seriously maintain such a thesis?

There are still others who are incessant in their assertion that it is the reproach of Latin study that a youth
who has spent four years on Latin does not
acquire a sufficient mastery of the language   Present Re-
to enable him to read Latin with ease and   sults of Latin
speed, or to continue his study of Latin litera-   Study Defec-
ture with pleasure and enthusiasm. It certainly is be-   tive.
yond question that the great majority of young men
when they reach college do not turn with relish to Latin,
and it is even truer that in after years they do not evince

a disposition to beguile any considerable part of their leisure in the perusal of Latin literature. This condition of affairs I admit is beyond question. But what conclusions are we justified in drawing from it? Have we a right to assume that all young men when they enter college ought to turn with avidity to the study of Latin? Have we a right to assume further that after graduation the proper employment for one's leisure time is the continuation of one's study of the classics? And with this assumption as our major premise, have we a right to assume as our minor premise that students would turn eagerly to Latin in college, and that college graduates would assiduously pursue the study of Latin literature, if only the capacity for reading at sight were theirs? We should then get this syllogism:

1. All college students ought to study Latin with enthusiasm, and all college graduates ought to turn with zest to the study of Latin literature.

2. If the persons referred to could read Latin at sight they would do these things.

Therefore, all pupils should be taught to read at sight.

But with all my interest in Latin and all my conviction of its abounding importance, both for discipline and culture, yet I cannot assent to either of the two premises just mentioned.

As a preparation for college, both reason and experience seem to me to show that Latin is not only the best single instrument, but practically an indispensable instrument; but for the average man in college I say with all frankness I do not believe that extensive specialization in Latin is a *sine qua non.* The secondary education is essentially disciplinary. The college cannot afford, and does not pretend, to restrict its energies to that goal. It aims at imparting breadth of view, it aims at depth and soundness of knowledge in some few lines.

Above all, it recognises the relation of the educated man to the state and to society; it recognises the necessity of bringing the student into close and sympathetic touch with the problems of modern life and thought. Now, in the quest of this ideal the classics undoubtedly have their part, but with all their usefulness and all their pre-eminence they certainly do not contain the bulk of the " best that has been thought and said," and do not pretend to monopolize the field of culture. Professed teachers of the classics ought to be the first to realize this in theory, as I believe they actually do in practice, so far as they make any impression on the thought and action of to-day.

Let it not be thought for a moment that I believe a liberally educated college man can dispense with Latin or even safely with Greek in his college course, but can we any longer say in candour — if indeed we ever could — that these studies should form the chief and central object of attention of the college student, and that the test of his being on the right course is to be found in the spontaneous enthusiasm with which he addresses himself to their pursuit?

I have just been endeavouring to say that the college student may, in my judgment, be making wise use of his advantages for self-improvement even though he fail to manifest that absorbing devotion to classics to which I have referred.

I wish also to ask: Are there not other reasons, and valid reasons, why the average educated man in college and out should not be expected to evince a profound absorption in Latin literature? How much of Latin is primarily attractive to the average cultivated man? What are the Latin authors to communion with which such a man should be expected to apply his leisure? Shall he devote it to Plautus and Terence with their scant dramatic variety and wearisome repetition of brazen courtesan, tricky slave, simple father, and braggart soldier? Shall he devote it to Cato and Varro, with their old recipes of how to plant beans or the best way to manure a field? Shall he devote it to Lucretius even? Will the noble enthusiasm of that writer and his occasional magnificent bursts of poetry be compensation for the long and tedious discussion of puerile physical and metaphysical theories? Even when we come to Cicero, how many of that great writer's works can be counted on to make an appeal to the sympathy and intelligence of the average cultivated man of to day? He would be hardy who should say that the proportion is large. The best of Virgil and Horace, of Livy and Tacitus, has presumably been read in school and college, and to these he will often return; but will he find strength and inspiration in the other Augustan poets or in the later poetry of the imperial era, overloaded as it is with mythological detail and studied rhetorical embellishment? I am speaking of the average educated man. For such a man I do not hesitate to say that, when we consider the wealth of the world's literature outside of Latin, when we consider the masterpieces of the more recent centuries, many of the greatest of them in our own language too, — when we consider these, it seems to me that it is not to be expected that Latin literature should assert any such paramount claims.

To the special student of Latin the case is quite different. The professional teacher will and must spare no effort in familiarizing himself with all the literature, just as he spares none in studying the history and growth of the language, in tracing the development of institutions, social, religious, and political. He will and must endeavour to become saturated with ancient thought

and life. But men of this equipment cannot be relatively numerous, nor is it desirable for the interests of
modern society that they should be, any more than
that every man should be a profound physicist, a profound chemist, or profound biologist. Of the two premises, then, which we undertook to examine, neither one
would seem to rest upon a basis sufficiently solid to
warrant its acceptance. Even did our freshmen bring
to college an ability to read Latin at sight, I cannot see
how it would alter or ought to alter the attention given
to Latin in college or after graduation, simply because
adequate reasons appear why Latin should not constitute a more absorbing object of attention than it
actually does at present. When, therefore, Latin is
reproached because it fails to accomplish these ends,
it is pertinent to inquire whether the difficulty may not
be one inherent in Latin as a study, and not merely
the result of the traditional methods of Latin instruction in the schools, and also whether the ends which
it is claimed Latin as now taught fails to achieve are
themselves legitimate and indispensable ends of a liberal
education. Why, then, reproach Latin for failing to
consummate these ends? Why not rather commend
it for what it does accomplish, and endeavour by wise
and fostering care to make it realize even more richly
that which experience has so abundantly shown it capable of achieving?

In all this discussion thus far I have been conceding
what I really believe to be impossible, namely, the
acquisition in the secondary school of the Subjective
power to read Latin as Latin and to interpret Acquisition
of Latin Im-
a Latin text directly. My own conviction possible in
is that relatively little can be accomplished the School.
in this direction in the schools, even under favourable
conditions. Do we realize sufficiently the amount of

time that is indispensable in acquiring pronunciation, learning forms and vocabulary, analyzing words, tracing their history and development of meaning, studying syntax, and writing Latin?   Some time, too, is conceded to translation even by the most ardent adherents of direct interpretation.   When all this is done, how much time is likely to be left in any ordinary school program for the acquisition of a subjective feeling for Latin? Does it not take in the aggregate an enormous amount of time to acquire a subjective feeling for a modern language?   I do not mean a subjective feeling merely for a few current phrases sufficient to enable one to secure railway transportation and hotel accommodations in France or Germany.   We are speaking of a subjective acquisition of Latin which shall be adequate for the interpretation of literature.   Can any such subjective acquisition of French or German be attained without prolonged concentration upon the spoken language? Is it not a mistake, too, to imagine that the chief diffi culty in acquiring a sense for Latin as Latin is the word-order?   Undoubtedly the word-order does constitute one great obstacle to the pupil, but it is far from being the only one, or the greatest.   My own experience with elementary pupils has shown me that they are ignorant of the meanings of words, they fail to apprehend the force of inflections, they have hazy or inaccurate conceptions of syntactical possibilities, they are not adequately informed as to the subject matter with which the Latin text is concerned.   Under such circumstances, there are apt to be so many elements of uncertainty in a Latin sentence that the direct apprehension of its content is simply impossible to the average elementary pupil.   The capacity to understand Latin as Latin, and to interpret it directly, must, it seems to me, be a matter of growth, and with most pupils a matter of slow growth. I do not see how it can come until the pupil has grown very familiar with individual words for one thing, — so familiar that the word is no longer objective, but subjective, so that as soon as uttered its whole meaning flashes before him involuntarily. So, too, the pupil must come by long practice to feel the exact force of inflection, all the numerous variations of mood, tense, voice, case, *etc.* A keen appreciation for word-order must also have been developed as the result of repeated observations of its significance. All this takes time, and a great deal of time. Yet until it has been accomplished I fail to see how the pupil can be held to read at sight in the sense of directly interpreting a Latin author. Only then can one do this when the process has become thoroughly unconscious, and after an experience of many years with freshmen in four American universities, I have not as yet had the good fortune to meet with pupils who seemed to me to have reached this stage, anxious as I have been to discover them, and thankfully as I should hail them as my own deliverers from many a difficulty which has for years given me perplexity; for after thirty years of continuous study of Latin I am still bound to confess that I think it hard, very hard. I have read much, in fact most of the Latin literature. A few years ago I sat down to prepare a little edition of Cicero's *de Senectute.* For six months all my available leisure, which was then considerable, was devoted to the completion of this task. The *de Senectute* is what would be called easy Latin, hardly more difficult than one of Cicero's orations, and yet with the help of all the extensive literature on the subject and of several competent advisers, I am still bound to confess that there are many points of interpretation in that little essay which are by no means clear to me, and more where my own interpretation (though I am prepared to defend it) has been adjudged anywhere from improbable to absolutely impossible by other scholars. This in the case of a classic that is relatively easy, whose text is unusually sound, and for whose elucidation relatively so much has been done. I repeat, I believe Latin to be hard, and its accurate understanding and faithful interpretation no simple matter. We so often fail to realize the immense intellectual gulf that separates us from the past. It is not merely the structural difficulties of the Latin language that make Latin a hard study; it is even more the content of what is recorded in that language. Latin literature consists not of the doings, thoughts, and aspirations of nineteenth century Americans, but of a widely different people, different in all their social, intellectual, religious, and political endowments, attainments, and environment. When we read Latin, therefore, we must not merely master the technical difficulties of the

Some of the Difficulties of Latin. Roman speech, but we must surmount the obstacle of adapting ourselves to the totally new intellectual surroundings. Is not this the really difficult thing; and must not the key to it be furnished mainly by a slow and minute study of the literature itself? Until we have by gradual steps worked our way up to the new attitude, may we undertake to believe that we can interpret Latin directly? In other words, can we feel Latin (the speech of the Romans) as Latin, until we have first surrounded ourselves with the intellectual atmosphere of that ancient people? This is true of any modern language, even under favourable conditions. It takes in the aggregate a long time — longer than can ever be available in the schools, — to learn to think and feel in French or German, even when one hears those languages constantly spoken. How much more difficult must it be to do the same in the case of Latin, which we not only do not hear spoken, but practically not even pronounced to any extent worth mentioning, — a language, too, whose entire idiom is so much more at variance with ours than is either of the modern languages just mentioned. .

One other fact, too, remains to be considered. 'Latin' is an elastic term. 'French' and 'German,' on the other hand, are definite and precise concepts, Latin an Elastic Term. or relatively so. When we say 'French' or 'German' we mean the French or German of to-day, — of a single period. Latin may be the Latin of Plautus or the Latin of Suetonius, and between the two is an interval of nearly four centuries, containing writers of widely different style, vocabulary, syntax, word-order, sentence-structure, *etc*. The vastness of the difference between many of these various writers we often fail to appreciate, simply because it is so difficult for us to acquire an actual feeling for a language which we do not speak. But these differences exist, and they augment enormously the difficulties of acquiring a sense for Latin as Latin, especially in the beginner; for with a new author and a new period we practically come upon a new language. Latin is not one language, but practically several, according to its various periods and its various representatives.

All these difficulties and embarrassments must be frankly faced when it is seriously proposed to teach pupils in the secondary schools a sense for Latin as Latin, and to make the acquisition of that capacity the prime end of Latin study at that stage. It is very easy to recommend such a program, and even to tell how it should be carried out. Thus Mr. Hale tells us that the mind should hold in suspense. But the human mind is a peculiar organism. It is very obstinate for one thing. It has laws of operation which when they

become habitual it is well nigh impossible to alter. It is
one thing to be told we are to hold in suspense; it is
quite a different thing to hold something in suspense.
Similarly Professor Greenough urges us to force the
mind to make a mental picture, whether the given order
is familiar or not. I am free to confess that so far as
the secondary schools are concerned I believe both Mr.
Hale and Mr. Greenough to be at fault. I cannot think
that the true way to get a feeling for Latin is *by any conscious process,* — least of all by any conscious forcing
process as Mr. Greenough would have us believe.

Hamerton in his *Intellectual Life* has a dream of a
Latin island. " Let us suppose," says he, " that a hundred fathers could be found, all resolved to
submit to some inconvenience in order that
their sons might speak Latin as a living language. A
small island might be rented near the coast of Italy,
and in that island Latin alone might be permitted.
Just as the successive governments of France maintain the establishments of Sèvres and the Gobelins
to keep the manufactures of porcelain and tapestry up
to a recognised high standard of excellence, so this
Latin island might be maintained to give more vivacity
to scholarship. If there were but one little corner of
ground on the wide earth where pure Latin was con
stantly spoken, our knowledge of the classic writers
would become far more sympathetically intimate. After
thinking in the Latin island, we should think in Latin as
we read, and read without translating." Hamerton himself confesses that this is a Utopian dream, and so I am
confident it is, but not for the reasons that he advances.
To his mind the proposed plan is idle, because sooner or
later these isolated Latinists would be forced to return to
the corrupting influence of modern colleges and universities. But even on their island I must believe that the

Hamerton's
Proposal.

attempt to maintain a high standard of spoken Latin could terminate only in ignominious failure. Latin, as Hamerton understands it and as we all must understand it, was the language of a people who have long passed away. The Latin language, as we know it in its extant literature, records the mental attitude, intellectual attainments, sentiments, and aspirations of that people. For these it was an adequate expression. For the immensely altered conditions of our modern life, different in almost every conceivable detail from that of the Romans, it can be no adequate vehicle. Hamerton's young islanders, therefore, could not resuscitate the language of the Romans, because they would have none of the ideas that were essentially characteristic of the Roman people. The most they could do would be to create a new idiom, — Latin mayhap in outward form and structure, but in content as modern as our daily newspapers. Such an experiment could bring one no nearer the heart of ancient life nor do one whit to lessen the strangeness of the ancient civilization, the thing which really makes Latin difficult. To meet *this* difficulty we want not more method, but simply more knowledge.

I shall also venture to urge another point in this connection, and one which seems to me of fundamental importance. It is this: unless I am gravely *Relation of the* mistaken, the proposition to make direct in- *College to the* terpretation the central feature of Latin instruc- *School.* tion in the secondary school emanated originally from the college alone, and the pressure that has since been exerted to secure its recognition in programs of instruction has come from the same source. Now I make bold to raise the question whether college teachers can possibly understand the organization and problems of the secondary schools sufficiently well to warrant them in urging any such method of imparting instruction upon the schools.

Ought not any such detailed scheme of teaching, if it is to give promise of success, to originate primarily in the schools themselves? Ought it not to be the outcome of the observation and experience of the teachers who are in constant touch with secondary pupils, who know exactly their strength and weakness, their capacity and their limitations? Is there warrant for believing that any definite method of imparting knowledge, elaborated outside the schools by men of however exalted scholastic position, can be intelligently adopted and applied by the teachers? I do not believe there is. Any method really feasible and fruitful is sure to be discovered and applied by the secondary teacher long before it is formulated outside. I have therefore regretted not a little of late to note the increasing tendency on the part of the colleges to assume a responsibility for the interior economy of the schools, and not merely to prescribe the subject matter, but to urge definite ways of giving instruction. Any such attitude, I believe, does injustice to the schools. As one who has laboured in that department of education for some length of time, and knows something of the problems with which the secondary teacher is confronted, I earnestly deprecate the assumption that the secondary teachers are not the most competent agents to solve their own problems. Certainly if they do not possess the intelligence and patience to do so, I am at a loss to see how they can be thought capable of applying a solution devised by others.

The foregoing considerations were formally presented to a gathering of representative teachers a few years ago. In the discussion which followed, an eminent educator nominally took issue with my conclusions. As his remarks showed, however, his attitude on the main point under discussion was practically identical with my own. In fact he dealt the method I had myself been condemning some additional blows, calling attention among other things to the undue stress laid upon syntax to the practical exclusion of everything else. What this educator understood by 'reading at sight' was an exercise wherein the pupils under the teacher's guidance read a passage of Latin hitherto unseen. This is not reading at sight in the sense in which it is ardently championed by some, and in which I had endeavoured to discuss it. An exercise in which the pupils are taught by a competent guide the proper mode of attacking a new passage of Latin and getting its fullest and most accurate meaning, is one for which I have only commendation. Within limits it is most useful. But it should be obvious that it has not in the least been the subject of consideration in the foregoing pages.

V. Translation at Sight.

'Translation at sight' has already been defined above, p. 85. It means precisely what the words naturally suggest, namely, the translation of a passage of Latin which the pupil has never seen. I **Definition.** have already, at the close of the previous section, indicated what all will undoubtedly recognise as a legitimate employment of translation at sight for purposes of instruction. Where time offers — and it can usually be wisely taken — for such an exercise, it is likely to prove an efficient means of guidance and of imparting knowledge. It is nothing new, however, and has probably been recognised as an effective instrument from time immemorial. More serious is the question how far 'translation at sight' should be made the **As the Basis** basis of college admission tests. Were this **of College,** **Admission** question one which affected the colleges **Tests.** alone, or the student after leaving the secondary school, it would be an impertinence to discuss it here; but as it has vital bearings upon the teaching of Latin in the schools, the relevancy of considering these bearings must be apparent.

Some persons advocate making such translation (combined with the writing of Latin) the sole test of the candidate's knowledge, to the exclusion of any examination upon prescribed work. Against an examination upon prescribed authors, it is urged that such a test is *quantitative*, whereas an examination on a passage set for translation at sight is qualitative. Such a comparison, however, seems to me exceedingly unfair. To characterize an examination upon prescribed work as *essentially* quantitative implies that its primary object is to discover *how much* has been read, combined with the policy of accepting or rejecting the candidate according as the amount is found to be great or small. No one seriously supposes any such thing for a moment. As a matter of fact, an examination upon prescribed work is, and always has been, primarily a qualitative test. The essential difference between such an examination and an examination by translation at sight is not that one is qualitative and the other quantitative, but that, both being qualitative, the range of selection is somewhat greater in the one case than in the other. My own objections against an exclusive sight test are based quite as much on the practical effects of the system, as upon any theoretical grounds. Practically I believe the tendency of such a test is to tempt many teachers to employ the time of their classes on the rapid reading of large amounts with consequent failure on the part of their pupils to acquire that precise knowledge of the grammar and that fine feeling for the language which are so indispensable to true scholarship. This I believe, because I have thought I discovered the effects of this practice in the deterioration in the quality of classical preparatory training which is now so generally deplored. In the secondary study of Latin, I am convinced that our greatest danger at present is that of slovenly, superficial work. In the eager quest of the magic power to translate at sight, it is all too easy to lose sight of the most indispensable conditions of ever attaining proficiency in the language, — namely, a painfully thorough grammatical discipline. At no period in a four years' course should such discipline be relaxed. It is with learning to read a classical language, as it is with learning to play a musical instrument. The technique of the art cannot be neglected, and he who is the most perfect master of technique will be surest of making a player in the end, — at least he will never make a player without it. So in reading Latin the process is not one of divination, but of sober inference from positive knowledge of the meanings of words, the force of inflections, word-order, and the subtleties of syntax; and no one who is not master of these can any more translate at sight, than he can read music at sight without having previously mastered the technique of the particular instrument on which he wishes to perform.

Another practical objection to the plan of an exclusive sight test is the great difficulty in setting passages which are just and fair. I base this conclusion partly on a comparison of passages actually given at different institutions, and partly on my experience as a secondary teacher and a college professor. It is no exaggeration to say that passages are often set which, in view of their inherent difficulty and the absence of the context, are altogether beyond the power of any ordinary pupil; in fact it is no secret that the secondary teacher is sometimes seriously puzzled to interpret the passage set for his own pupils.

If a sight test is to be made the basis — wholly or partially — of a college entrance examination, I should recommend as the best possible preparation for such a test the most careful and thorough preparation of the traditional prescribed authors, Cæsar (or Nepos), Cicero, and Virgil.

The pupil who has faithfully and accurately studied his four books of the Gallic War, his seven speeches of Cicero, and his six or eight books of the *Æneid*, need have no fear of any passage set him for translation at sight that ought to be put before a candidate for admission to college. It is because so many teachers fail to see this, and because the colleges so often set extremely difficult passages, that new "methods" are becoming prevalent and vitiating the quality of preparatory Latin teaching.

With a definite amount of time at our disposal only two possibilities present themselves to me: Either the traditional prescribed authors and honest work, or an increase of the amount read and a consequent lowering of quality. I leave it to the candid judgment of all teachers, which course is likely to prove the better either for the student who is to end his Latin study in the secondary school or for the prospective collegian.

VI. What Latin Reading should follow the Elementary Work?

When the elements of Latin have been once mastered the question arises, What is to be done next? It was long common to begin at once the reading of Cæsar; and probably that custom is still somewhat prevalent. Yet the difficulties of Cæsar or even of the alternative Nepos are undeniable, and have led teachers more and more to prefer the use of some simple Latin to serve as a transition from the simple sentences used in connection with the elementary work to the first regular continuous prose author. I am myself de- Reading cidedly of the opinion that some such simple Proposed. Latin should precede either Caesar or Nepos. Several things offer themselves for this purpose:

a. *Viri Romae.*

b. Roman History (*e. g.* Jacobs's extracts).

c. Eutropius.

d. Some simplification of a part of Cæsar.

Let us consider these in turn.

Viri Romae is of more value than its barbarous Latin title might suggest. It was prepared a century and a half ago by an enthusiastic French teacher, Viri Romae. Lhomond,— a man whose whole life was dedicated to the service of secondary education. As the title of the work suggests, it is a history arranged biographically. It contains some thirty lives of Roman worthies from Romulus to Augustus. In composition the work is a cento, *i. e.* the different sentences of which each life is made up are drawn from various Latin writers. Often they are abbreviated or otherwise simplified for the purpose of producing a narrative which shall avoid the difficulties that characterize almost all continuous prose. Lhomond evidently had the teacher's instinct; he knew the advantages of the biographical treatment, with its keen appeal to the youthful mind; he was quick, too, to see and utilize those historical and biographical features which were striking and essential, and to bring these out in strong relief. His little work is therefore extremely interesting to the average pupil of the class for which it is intended. For years it has been widely used abroad, and recently it has met with much favour in this country.

Jacobs's extracts from Roman (and Greek) history have also done excellent service both abroad and in this country. They were originally prepared by Jacobs, an eminent German educator of the early part of this century, for his *Latin Reader*. The arrange-

Jacobs's Extracts. ment is historical, as opposed to biographical, but the material is put together on much the same plan as that in Lhomond's book. It is, however, drawn from fewer sources (chiefly from Justin and Eutropius), and the changes from the original have been fewer than in *Viri Romae*. Though brief, and sketchy, it is not devoid of interest, and impresses upon the pupil who reads it a number of the essential happenings which constitute the basis of Roman history. Few freshmen, I must confess, bring to college as much knowledge of Roman history as is contained in these brief selections of Jacobs, meagre as they are. A possible advantage possessed by this work as compared with *Viri Romae* is the great simplicity of the Latin, particularly in the earlier portion of the selections.

Eutropius[1] has never been much used in this country or elsewhere, so far as I know, and the reception accorded to recently published editions of the

Eutropius. work fails to encourage the belief that it will ever be popular. The work lacks life and, above all, it lacks perspective; it is an exceedingly dry annalistic account of events important and unimportant. It can hardly be expected to inspire interest, especially in young pupils.

The last type of simple reading to be considered consists of some simplification of a part of Cæsar. An ad-

Cæsar Simplified. vantage of such matter is that the pupil becomes familar with Cæsar's vocabulary, his subject matter, and his general style, without encountering the severer obstacles of his continuous narrative.

---

[1] See Redway, J. W., The *Breviarium* of Eutropius, in The Educational Review, vol. xii. (Dec. 1896), p. 509 ff.

Still it is difficult, I think, to secure any simplification of Cæsar without a decided diminution of such interest (perhaps not very great at best) as is possessed by the original.

With the exception of the last, all the foregoing works suffer from one defect. The Latin is much of it far from classical. Eutropius belongs to the fourth century of our era; Justin to the second. Similarly many of the other sources embodied in *Viri Romae*, and in Jacobs's *Extracts from Roman History* are late, and exhibit striking variations from the norm of classical usage. This is a serious fault. The pupil learns from his elementary book or his grammar that *quamquam* is construed with the indicative, but is at once introduced to Latin in which he finds this particle used with the subjunctive; he learns that *ut* or *postquam* referring to a single past act takes the perfect indicative; he finds them used with the pluperfect; he learns that in indirect discourse verbs of ' promising,' for example, are followed by the future infinitive with subject accusative, but he meets expressions like *promisit dare*, obviously employed in the sense ' he promised that he would give.' These are but illustrations of the very numerous violations of the most ordinary canons of standard usage as laid down in all our grammars. If *Viri Romae*, Jacobs's *Extracts*, or Eutropius are to be used in our schools, they certainly ought to be adapted, as can easily be done, to recognised classical standards. Otherwise the task of inculcating any accurate grammatical knowledge must be immensely increased.

The foregoing enumeration of books containing simple reading makes no pretence at completeness. There are numerous other books. Many suffer from the same objectionable features of unclassical Latin; others introduce modern or mediæval subject matter in a Latin dress. This last procedure seems a serious mistake. To the extent that we withdraw the student of Latin from the thoughts and ideas of ancient Rome, we are missing one important element of culture which ought to come from the study of Latin, namely, better understanding of the present through an understanding of the past. This end is certainly not reached by stories from the *Arabian Nights* or English history put in Latin form by modern scholars.

CHAPTER III

WHAT AUTHORS ARE TO BE READ IN THE SECONDARY SCHOOL AND IN WHAT SEQUENCE?

REFERENCES.

Wagler, F. A., Cäsar als Schulbuch, in ZEITSCHRIFT FÜR DAS GYMNASIALWESEN, 1857, pp. 481–503. This article has been excellently translated by F. H. Howard in THE SCHOOL REVIEW, 1897, pp. 561–587.

Report of the Committee of Ten of the National Educational Association. Latin. 1893.

Report of the Committee of Twelve of the American Philological Association on Courses in Latin and Greek for Secondary Schools. 1899.

I. What Author should be read first?

THERE has been much discussion in recent years as to what regular prose author should be read first. For years Cæsar's *Gallic War* had been chosen for this purpose, and this practice had become so universal as to be regarded almost as a permanent and necessary feature of our educational economy. In the Report of the Committee of Ten of the National Educational Association, published in 1893, the suggestion was formally made that Nepos be substituted for Cæsar as the first prose author to be read in our secondary schools. Nepos *vs.* Cæsar. This suggestion of the Committee of Ten was but the adoption of a recommendation of the Latin Con ference appointed by the Committee in December, 1892. The Conference devoted two days of careful discussion to the consideration of several problems of secondary instruction in Latin, and was practically unanimous in its recommendation that Nepos be made optional with Cæsar. As the question of choice is of some importance, it seems worth while to discuss the relative merits of these two authors with reference to their adaptation to the needs of secondary instruction. I cannot do better perhaps than to enumerate the considerations which weighed with me (and I think with others) as a member of the Latin Conference which reported to the Committee of Ten, and then to add the reasons which have tended subsequently to modify the position then taken. While not explicitly expressing disapproval of Cæsar as the first author read, yet the recommendation of the Conference was intended to indicate a certain distrust of the fitness of Cæsar to retain the place it had held so long. In recommending Nepos, though only as a permissible alternative, the Conference meant to suggest the superior fitness of that author for the special stage of Latin involved.

Objections to Cæsar. Against Cæsar (and by Cæsar is meant his *Gallic War*) it is urged:

a. *Cæsar is undeniably difficult.* Indirect Discourse abounds, particularly in the first book, which from natural inertia will always be the book generally first read, despite the frequent recommendations of educators to begin with the second, third, or fourth book. But even apart from the indirect discourse and apart from the first book, Cæsar cannot be called easy reading, especially for the beginner.

Difficulty.

b. *Cæsar is not interesting.* The writer does not impress us as gifted with imagination, historic or other. He is exceedingly dry. There is little to excite the enthusiasm. The narrative, moreover, is monotonous. We have practically an unbroken chronicle of marches and victories, in which the triumph of trained Romans over undisciplined and poorly

Lack of Interest.

equipped Gauls and Germans is nothing surprising. Patches of interest appear here and there, to be sure, as where Cæsar gives us descriptions of the customs of the Gauls, Britons, or Germans. These are brief, however, — hardly more than oases in the surrounding desert of military details; — some of them, moreover, are found in portions of Cæsar not usually read.

c. *The bearing of Cæsar's narrative is not obvious.* The pupil cannot see the point, — the drift of it all. It is apparent, of course, that Cæsar is con- Obscure quering a lot of turbulent Gauls and Germans. Bearings. But what it all signifies, must necessarily be very obscure to the average pupil; at least it does not appear in the narrative itself. With the exception of the few chapters already referred to on the customs of the Gauls, Germans, and Britons, all of Cæsar's commentaries on the Gallic War might easily be summed up in a few brief lines, to the effect that for seven years he waged unceasing war against the Gallic and German tribes, and finally subdued them all. This is practically the substance of the historical knowledge acquired by the student in reading Cæsar. Without doubt Cæsar's Gallic campaigns were profoundly significant. They had a motive, — perhaps a double motive. On the one hand Cæsar was strengthening himself by his military success for future schemes of ambition. By winning prestige and power in Gaul, he aimed to be able to return to Rome at the critical juncture and make himself master of the situation, as he actually did. On the other hand he may have been exercising that far-sighted statesmanship, with which Mommsen credits him, in preparing for the organization of the West as a part of the Roman Empire. But though all this is true, yet it does not appear in Cæsar's *Commentaries.* The *Commentaries* themselves, in all their weary detail of battle, siege, and march, never suggest their own connection with contemporary or future history. To all intents and purposes they stand outside of the events of their own day. They do not contain facts the knowledge of which is of value to the average pupil or the average educated person of mature years. Some have compared the similar choice of Xenophon's *Anabasis* as the first Greek usually read. But it must be admitted in favour of the *Anabasis* that, while it has for the pupil no visible connection with Greek history and no visible bearings upon it, it is at least neither difficult for the beginner nor dull. Cæsar, on the other hand, is regarded by many as unique in its combination of difficulty, its dulness, and its dearth of valuable information. If anything of Cæsar's were to be read, it is often urged that it

The Civil ought rather to be his Commentaries on the
War. *Civil War* than those on the *Gallic War*.
The account of the Civil War at least contains valuable information of an important epoch in Roman history. We see the very death-struggle of the old order of things, — the Republic passing away to make room for the Empire. We see Cæsar leave his Gallic province and become an active maker of Roman history at its most critical era. We follow him from the beginning of his strife with the Senate and Pompey through all the stirring events of the next three years (49–46), at Pharsalus, in the East, in Egypt, in Numidia, until he finally comes back to Rome to lay the foundations of the imperial organization. There is no doubt here as to the bearings of the narrative. The most ordinary pupil cannot fail to apprehend its import. Nor is it dull. It may, however, possibly suffer from one defect: it is difficult, — too difficult perhaps for the average pupil who is approaching his first Latin author.

In defence of Cæsar the chief point to be urged is

the purity of his diction and the accuracy of his style. That he is a correct writer, no one can deny. He thought, as he acted, with a directness and *In Defence* precision which were admirable, and he ex- *of Cæsar.* pressed himself in writing with equal directness and precision. At the same time nothing could be more grotesque to the minds of most than to attribute a literary character or quality to Cæsar. He simply gives us a plain and colourless statement of facts, which makes hardly any nearer approach to literary charm than does a clear statement of a proposition in geometry. Such a statement may be clear and precise and direct, — yet its literary quality would be grudgingly conceded.

We pass to the considerations which are *Nepos.* urged in favour of Cornelius Nepos.

a. *Nepos's Latinity is good.* This is disputed by some, and I have even heard it charged that Nepos did not know how to write Latin. That he *His Latinity.* was an elegant writer, possessed of command-ing stylistic powers, no one will maintain, but that he was a correct writer and represents in the main with great fidelity the standard classical usage of the best period cannot be gainsaid. To verify the impressions of my own reading, I have recently re-examined Bern-hard Lupus's book of some two hundred pages, *Der Sprachgebrauch des Cornelius Nepos*, Berlin, 1876. This work is a detailed syntactical study of Nepos, and supports abundantly the assertion made above regard-ing the correctness of Nepos's style. Nepos, to be sure, omits the auxiliary *esse* with the future active and perfect passive infinitives, but this is the prevailing usage with many excellent writers. He also uses *dubito* with the infinitive, where Cicero and Cæsar preferred to use a *quin*-clause; but while Cicero himself never uses the infinitive with *dubito* in this sense, several of his correspondents employ it, the accomplished Asinius Pollio, Trebonius, and Cicero's own son Marcus. *Dum,* 'while,' in standard prose usually is construed with the historical present. Nepos once uses it with the perfect; but Cicero also does this. The perfect subjunctive (for imperfect) in result clauses is exceedingly frequent in Nepos, — so frequent as to be a striking feature of his style. Yet the usage is thoroughly good. Cæsar and Cicero use it, though rarely. The only two striking exceptions to standard usage that I have noted in Nepos are *fungor* with the accusative and *quamvis* with the indicative. Yet Cicero also is credited with *one* instance of the latter construction, and Sallust once uses *vescor* with the accusative. On the whole Nepos writes like his contemporaries, barring the fact that he does not exhibit their stylistic gifts. He shows none of the symptoms of the so-called "decline." So far as his diction is concerned, he is an eminently fit author to put into the hands of young pupils.

b. *Nepos's lives are interesting.* Though they are the lives of Greeks, they are the lives of famous Greeks, men who stand out as great exemplars in human history, whose achievements and whose characters have always evoked admiration. Were they the lives of Romans, they would undoubtedly be better adapted to pupils of Latin, yet Nepos's point of view and his mode of treatment are so thoroughly Roman that one catches much of the Roman spirit in reading and studying them.

Interest

c. *They are composed in short instalments.* This is exclusively a psychological advantage, perhaps, but it is not without importance. Where the pupil sees the end, he receives a stimulus to counteract the fatigue of study. When the end of what he is reading lies but two or three pages ahead, he is eager

Form.

to press on and gain the goal. When he reaches this, he enjoys the satisfaction of having accomplished one whole thing and of having it behind him. Very different are his feelings when he begins one of the long books of Cæsar, where he must read for weeks before he can really get the setting to enable him fully to understand what he reads, and where the remoteness of the end of the book tends to produce a certain discouragement and despair of ever reaching it.

d. *The method of treatment by biography is attractive.* The hero-worshipping instinct of the young pupil takes delight in the recital of the deeds of noble men, a point already touched upon above in connection with *Viri Romæ.*

Biographical Treatment.

The foregoing, I believe, were the main considerations which prompted the recommendation of the Latin Conference in 1892 which was later embodied in the Report of the Committee of Ten in 1893. Subsequent experience has shown that most teachers cling tenaciously to Cæsar. Some doubtless do so from sheer inertia, but I am convinced that there are many who are thoughtful and deliberate in their choice. I have been surprised to find how many pupils find Cæsar interesting, not merely more interesting than Nepos, but possessed of a positive human interest *per se.* Where samples of both Cæsar and Nepos have been read by a class, I have been told the pupils often prefer Cæsar. Possibly the greater energy of action displayed in Cæsar's *Commentaries* may explain this attitude on the part of those pupils who manifest it. Boys in particular take an interest in accounts of *achievement.* Nepos is not altogether lacking in this feature, but many of his lives are prevailingly devoted to an analysis of character; while with Cæsar we have practically a continuous account

Reasons why Cæsar is still Preferred.

Not Dull to All.

of skilful triumph over difficulties. Upon most mature minds not of the Miles Standish type, this narrative soon palls; but it seems to be a fact that to the minds of many young pupils it has a positive attractiveness.

One other reason in favour of Cæsar of a somewhat subtler nature may not be without its weight, and may have acted subconsciously perhaps in determ-

Cæsar's Greater Concreteness in Vocabulary. ining the adherence of many teachers to the traditional *Gallic War*. I refer to the vocabulary of Cæsar. A very careful comparison of the vocabularies of Cæsar and Nepos undertaken in connection with the preparation of my *Foundations of Latin* revealed to me the much greater *concreteness* of Cæsar's diction. This is largely a natural and necessary adjunct of Cæsar's subject matter. He deals mainly with facts; Nepos indulges much more in character analysis, and, while this is never deep or subtle, it necessitates the employment of words in transferred, figurative, abstract senses. This fundamental difference is of vital importance for the beginner. He should, if possible, first become acquainted with concrete ideas and with the literal meanings of words, particularly in the case of words that also possess figurative senses. These words and these meanings make the most direct appeal, and leave the most vivid impress on the mind. An apprehension of the literal meaning affords, too, the best guide to all figurative, transferred meanings which have later developed from it. These consider-

Progress more Noticeable. ations may perhaps explain the fact often noted by teachers that pupils who have read one book of Cæsar find the next book much easier, and the subsequent books easier still, while with Nepos this increased facility is not noticed, the tenth life being no easier than the first and the twentieth scarcely easier than the tenth. Yet even apart from the vocabulary, it must be manifest that the range of ideas is considerably greater in Nepos than in Cæsar; this constitutes a permanent difficulty in Nepos, so that, though this author is somewhat easier at the outset, it may after all be doubted whether on the whole he is more so than Cæsar.

On the whole, I for one feel to-day that the considerations which are so often urged in favour of reading Nepos instead of Cæsar are by no means weighty enough to warrant our giving the preference to the former author. The choice between the two may properly vary with the temper and taste of teachers and the disposition of their pupils. Yet reflection tends to make me think that for most pupils Cæsar is the better book for the purpose we have been considering.

II. Should Cicero Precede or Follow Virgil?

There is a difference of opinion as to whether Cicero should precede or follow Virgil, and practice varies accordingly. The question is one of enough importance to receive consideration here; two reasons suggest themselves for postponing Virgil.

a. *On the ground of the language.* The pupil who has finished Cæsar or Nepos has not yet a sufficient mastery of the language. He probably knows the forms, if he is ever going to, but he is not Linguistic Reasons. yet posted as he should be on the syntax of the language, on its vocabulary, on the order of words, and many other points of idiomatic usage. If he enter upon the study of Virgil in this state of mind or of knowledge, the chances are that what little knowledge of the language he possesses will be pretty thoroughly unsettled by reading poetry. The use of cases, the employment of words, and the arrangement of the sentence are all so different from prose usage, that unless the pupil has already acquired settled convictions on the subject great damage will be done.   On the other hand, if he takes his Cicero immediately after Nepos or Cæsar, he becomes so familiar with normal prose usage by the time he finishes that author, that not only does the poetical diction of Virgil work no injury — it rather helps, by virtue of the contrast it furnishes to the idiom of prose.

b. *On the ground of the literature.*   Virgil is a poet, whose product is one of the choicest that Roman litera-

Literary Reasons. ture contains.   Let the pupil wait until he is best qualified to do justice to the fine quality of the *Æneid*.   A year makes a great difference, and will often decide whether the pupil shall read Virgil with sympathy and profit, or the reverse.

Attention must also be given to another sequence recently suggested in the reading of Cicero and Virgil.

Another Arrangement. I refer to the course tentatively outlined in the *Preliminary Report of the Committee of Twelve on Courses in Latin and Greek for Secondary Schools*, issued in 1897.   This committee consisted of members of the American Philological Association, and was appointed at the request of the National Educational Association in July, 1896.   The suggestion is made in this report that in the third year of an ordinary four years' Latin course Cicero's four speeches against Catiline be read, followed by Books i. and ii. of Virgil's *Æneid* in the same year, and that in the fourth year Books iii.–vi. of the *Æneid* be first read, to be followed by two more orations of Cicero.   It is difficult, however, to believe that this suggestion represents the mature judgment of any considerable number of educators. To break the continuity of one's reading of Cicero's orations by Virgil's *Æneid*, and to break the continuity of the *Æneid* by the long vacation, seems an unjustifiable waste of energy without any compensating advantages.

III. Should Virgil's Eclogues be read in the Secondary Schools?

The Latin Conference which met at Ann Arbor in December, 1892, and which reported to the Committee of Ten of the National Educational Association, advised against reading Virgil's *Eclogues* in the secondary schools. This recommendation of the Conference was adopted by the Committee.

The considerations urged against reading the *Eclogues* are probably familiar. Stress is often laid upon their difficulties. That they are difficult in parts, is undeniable. They abound in mythological allusions, while several of them involve allegorical conceptions whose precise interpretation is still debated by the critics. Another argument often urged against the *Eclogues* is, that where they are not allegorical they are mainly imitations of the *Idyls* of Theocritus; that the names and allusions are chiefly Greek, and are taken from the pastoral life of the Sicily of the third century B. C. Hence it has been urged that the study of the *Eclogues* is properly adapted only to advanced college students of comparative literature, — students who know Theocritus and who can trace the Virgilian poems back to the Sicilian originals.

Considerations Urged against the Eclogues.

But the experience of teachers and pupils denies validity to the foregoing arguments. Pupils who have read the *Eclogues* in the schools have, with practical unanimity, declared that they enjoyed these poems more than anything else in the entire Latin course of the secondary school. Despite their allegorical and mythological features, and despite

Their Literary Charm.

the fact that they are palpable imitations of Greek
originals, they nevertheless do make a strong appeal
to the youthful mind which cannot be ignored. There
is danger, perhaps, of condemning too precipitately
every literary work which bears traces of imitating
some previous work. All of Virgil bears the same
impress of his Greek originals as do the *Eclogues*.
The prime question in all these works and all similar
works is not merely whether they exhibit traces of
borrowing, but whether they exhibit anything else. In
Virgil   the case of all of Virgil's works we may say
Recreated.   that, despite the obvious evidences of indebtedness to his predecessors, he is no irresponsible
plagiarist or slavish imitator. He is a true poet, with
the genius and endowment of a poet. In form, in
phrase, in metaphor and simile, he has drawn with
freedom, in accordance with the spirit of his own age
and of all antiquity, upon Homer, Hesiod, and Theocritus. But in spite of this he has transformed all he
took with the spirit of his own genius; he has recreated. It is this which makes the *Æneid*, the
Georgics, the *Eclogues* all great poems, and which
makes each in its totality as different as can possibly
be from the *Iliad*, the *Odyssey*, the *Works and Days*,
or the *Idyls* of Theocritus. Precisely the same thing
is true of Shakspere and of Milton.

I believe, therefore, that the *Eclogues* have a clear
title to a place in the curriculum of our secondary
schools, and that where time is available, it would be
wise to read them. They exhibit to us a phase of ancient literature not so well exemplified by anything else
I know. They breathe the breath of spring, the per-
Tennyson's   fume of flowers; they suggest the charm of
Tribute.   nature — trees, brooks, hills, lakes, sun, air,
stars — in her manifold phases. They touch upon

the abounding joys of country-life. Tennyson's three stanzas well exhibit the spell which these unique poems exercised upon himself:

> " Poet of the happy Tityrus
>   piping underneath his beechen bowers;
> Poet of the poet-satyr
>   whom the laughing shepherd bound with flowers;
>
> " Chanter of the Pollio, glorying
>   in the blissful years again to be,
> Summers of the snakeless meadow,
>   unlaborious earth and oarless sea;
>
> " Thou that seëst Universal
>   Nature moved by Universal Mind,
> Thou majestic in thy sadness
>   at the doubtful doom of human kind."

This, to be sure, is the tribute of a poet, but I am convinced that the attitude of pupils will be generally analogous, and that it will justify the study of these poems wherever time allows. All their subtleties will not be apparent to the young student; some of them have not even yet been settled by the critics, and may never be, but there is enough that is obvious, that is stimulating, that is elevating, to make them legitimate and worthy objects of study for the pupils of our schools.

IV. Sallust.

In point of content and style, Sallust is well deserving of representation in the curriculum of the secondary school. Both the *Jugurtha* and the *Catiline* are valuable and interesting specimens of historical prose which will well repay careful study. The *Catiline* in particular is instructive as correcting the one-sided conception of the famous conspiracy derived from reading only Cicero's Catilinarian speeches; Sallust's narrative also largely supplements Cicero's account and makes the historic picture much fuller and completer.

The great difficulty, however, with the average school is to find time for reading this work. The Latin curriculum of the secondary school is already full, and our school programs are now so congested that in most cases to add more work is to increase a tension already too great and to run great risk of lowering the quality of the instruction given.

V. Ovid.

There is no denying the charm of Ovid's *Metamorphoses*. Their style, too, is simple, while they afford no little instruction in classical mythology. What has long existed in the pupil's mind in more or less vagueness, now takes on definite shape, as he reads Ovid's picturesque details of the Deluge, of Phaethon, of Daphne, *etc.* Yet the same difficulty confronts us here as in the case of Sallust, and desirable as both these authors are in an ideal secondary curriculum, it is greatly to be feared, despite the recent recommendations of the Committee of Twelve,[1] that no large number of schools will find it practicable under existing conditions to introduce either of these authors into the Latin program.

VI. Five-year and Six-year Latin Courses.

The foregoing discussion has been based upon the assumption that the course of Latin study in the secondary school is a four-year course of five periods a week. Many schools, however, already have five-year and six-

---

[1] Report, p. 28 f.

year courses, and the number of such longer courses appears to be constantly on the increase. In view of these conditions, the Committee of Twelve of the American Philological Association, in its recent report to the National Educational Association, makes the following observations: [1]

" The demand seemed imperative that it should undertake to formulate courses extending beyond the four-year limit. It accordingly presents a five-year course, drawn in double form. The first form is the standard four-year course, with the work of the first year extended over two years in order to give twice the amount of time for grammar lessons, the writing of simple exercises, and easy reading. This form is intended to meet the needs of students who commence Latin a year earlier than in the ordinary four-year course. All educational experience shows that the best results may be secured from the study of Latin when the subject is commenced somewhat earlier than is usual in this country, and at least two years are given to the elementary work before the pupil begins the reading of Nepos or Cæsar. The second form is designed for schools which have more mature and stronger pupils. The work of the first four years of this course coincides with that of the four-year standard course; the additional year is devoted mainly to reading. The recommendation is made that Virgil's *Æneid* be completed in order that pupils who have the time for a five-year course may enjoy the satisfaction of reading to the end the greatest Latin epic, and viewing it as an artistic whole. An additional amount of Cicero is also recommended: the two essays *On Old Age* and *On Friendship*, which are short and

Recommendation of the Committee of Twelve.

A Five-Year Course.

---

[1] See their *Report*, p. 35.

complete in themselves, together with some of the briefer and more interesting *Letters.* Thus the pupil's acquaintance with Cicero's many-sided literary and intellectual accomplishments will be extended, while the selections suggested will furnish the best possible model of style for the writing of Latin in the latter part of the course.

" A six-year course may be established at once by introducing Latin into the last two years of the grammar
Six-Year   schools; such was the method adopted in the
Course.   city of Chicago. Or a six-year course may
be developed out of the five-year course, through the use of either of the forms which have been suggested. In either case it is obviously desirable to aim at a fair degree of uniformity in such courses, and thus avoid for them the inconveniences from which our present four-year courses suffer. In the six-year course, at any rate, two years can be given to that careful and thorough preparation for reading which not only forms the best foundation for all later work in Latin, but also con stitutes, for this period of the student's education, the most effective instrument of training in exact habits of thought and of expression. If two years are given to this sort of work, most of the difficulties felt by the young pupil in entering upon the study of Cæsar will have been anticipated and overcome. Thus arranged, the first five years of the six-year course and the five-year course in the first form presented will be identical in respect of the subjects taken up and the order of arrangement. The work of the sixth year will then correspond closely with that of the last year of the five-year course as given in the second form; that is, it will be devoted to the finishing of the *Æneid,* to the reading of Cicero's essays *On Old Age* and *On Friendship,* and of selected *Letters,* and to weekly exercises in prose com-

position based on Cicero. Here also the principal object should be, not to extend widely the range of authors taken up, but so to adjust the work of the course to the needs of the pupil's intellectual life as most effectively to promote his development at this period.

"In a number of cities it has been thought advantageous to give two years of Latin in the grammar school rather than one. The reason is that, since the length of the high-school course, by common consent, remains fixed at four years, the study of Latin for only a single year before entrance into the high school is not only less fruitful in itself, but is also less satisfactorily adjusted to the other studies of the grammar-school course. The arrangement is also found to be advantageous from the point of view of the adjustment of the grammar-school and high-school courses to each other. In a city in which two years are given to Latin in the grammar school, the high school also will undoubtedly continue to give a four-year course. Pupils, then, who come up from the grammar schools with two years of Latin will in the high school find it possible to enter upon work which corresponds with that of the second, third, and fourth years of the four-year course, and will need to be taught separately from other high-school students only in the sixth year of their Latin study; in other words, immediately upon entering the high school they may be united with the second-year students in the four-year course. In large high schools separate sections need to be formed in any case for each Latin class, and probably it will be found advantageous to teach the students of the six-year course by themselves. In like manner, the adjustment of a six-year or five-year course to an already existing four-year course will be found easy in the case of academies and private schools.

"A plan by which the work of the four-year Latin course may be correlated with that of the six-year course is indicated in the following diagram:

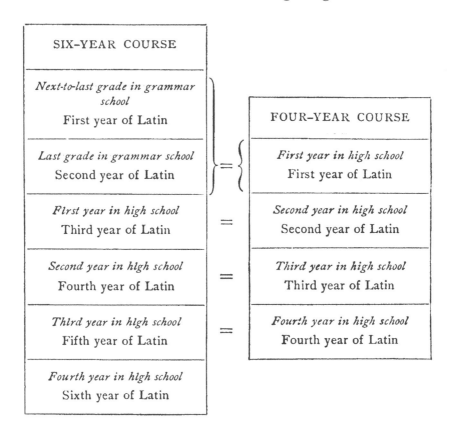

"Led by the considerations which have been briefly presented, the Committee, after careful deliberation, has framed the three programs subjoined: one for a four-year course, one for a five-year course (in two forms), and one for a six-year course. We commend these programs to the consideration of the schools, hoping that they may be found convenient as standard or model courses.

FIVE-YEAR LATIN COURSE.

FIRST FORM.

(Five periods weekly throughout the five years.)

FIRST AND SECOND YEARS.

The same as the first year of the four-year course.

THIRD YEAR.

The same as the second year of the four-year course.

FOURTH AND FIFTH YEARS.

The same as the third and fourth years of the four-year course.

FIVE-YEAR LATIN COURSE.

SECOND FORM.

(Five periods weekly throughout the five years.)

FIRST YEAR.

The same as the first year of the four-year course.

SECOND YEAR.

The same as the second year of the four-year course.

THIRD AND FOURTH YEARS.

The same as the third and fourth years of the four-year course.

FIFTH YEAR.

Virgil's *Æneid :* completed.

Cicero : *De Senectute* and *De Amicitia ;* selected Letters.

The equivalent of at least one period a week in prose composition based on Cicero.

The reading of Latin aloud. The memorizing of selected passages.

9

SIX–YEAR LATIN COURSE.

(Five periods weekly throughout the six years.)

FIRST AND SECOND YEARS.

The same as the first year of the four-year course.

THIRD YEAR.

The same as the second year of the four-year course.

FOURTH AND FIFTH YEARS.

The same as the third and fourth years of the four-year course.

SIXTH YEAR.

Virgil's *Æneid:* completed.

Cicero : *De Senectute* and *De Amicitia ;* selected Letters.

The equivalent of at least one period a week in prose composition based on Cicero.

The reading of Latin aloud. The memorizing of selected passages."

It is earnestly hoped that these recommendations may receive careful consideration from Latin teachers wherever it may be feasible to put them into effective operation.

CHAPTER IV

REFERENCE.

Miller, F. J. The Preparatory Course in Latin. SCHOOL REVIEW. 1897. p. 588 ff.

I. General Points on which Emphasis should be laid.

ASSUMING that the purposes of Latin study in the secondary school are those already indicated in Chapter I., namely, training in English, the strengthening of the mental powers, the better comprehension of the history of Roman thought and institutions, the quickening of the higher literary sense, we shall easily draw certain conclusions as to the fundamental principles of Latin teaching. I have no special scheme to advocate, but wish simply to call attention to one or two important particulars, in which it seems to me there is often neglect of duty on the part of teachers — frequently to the great and, under the circumstances, deserved discredit of Latin as an educational influence.

a. *Translation.* To begin with, if Latin is to be a means of training in English, the form of the English translation becomes a matter of the first im- The Form of portance It is not enough for the pupil Translation. to grasp the idea, and then to render it in a mongrel idiom half Latin and half English. From the very outset of Latin study the standard should be set high, and no translation accepted which will not stand the sever-

est test as to the orthodoxy of its English. It should
not merely be idiomatic; it should possess the merits
and even the graces of style. Wherever a rendering is
unnatural and smacks of the original, a halt should be
called, and improvement demanded. I believe I am
not extreme when I insist that no translation should
ever be accepted which would not, when written out, be
accepted as fit to print. It the pupil is not capable of
this, it must be either because he does not understand
the passage to be rendered, or else because he cannot
express in English a thought which his mind clearly
apprehends. Either of these difficulties, if it exist,
admits of remedy by judicious instruction. Such instruction may be slow, — both at the outset and often
afterwards, — for it involves frequent discussion as to
the choice of words and sentence-structure; but precisely herein lies the advantage of the study. I am well
aware of the pressure for time, and can appreciate the
temptation of the teacher to accept any rendering of a
passage, however un-English, provided it indicates that
the pupil apprehends the thought. But I insist that
there is no falser economy than a surrender under such
circumstances. Compromises of this sort not only do
not save time in the long run, but they ignore the very
principle and purpose of Latin study, and ought to
make that study stand in even less respect among the
general public than it actually does to-day. Yet I am
convinced that the habit of ignoring the form of translation, provided the pupil gets the sense, is practically
epidemic. More than this, the custom is even defended.
I know of teachers who soberly maintain their preference for a perfectly literal translation on the ground
that such a rendering facilitates the teaching of Latin
syntax. This attitude, I think, gives us the key to the
prevailing methods of translation from Latin into Eng-

lish. Grammatical knowledge is often made the end of Latin study instead of a means. Grammar is undoubtedly indispensable to the reading of Latin authors; but is it not a fact that many teachers stop at this point of the subject, and rest content, if their pupils can dispose successfully of the ablatives and genitives, the subjunctives and infinitives? Is not " construction " made the culmination of the study, and the text used as though it were but a convenient lay-figure upon which to drape in imposing folds the robe of grammar and syntax? I am convinced that there are many teachers whose attitude and practice are not misrepresented by this comparison. My own view is that in reading an author the amount of grammatical catechizing should be reduced to a minimum; let only so much be demanded as is absolutely necessary to the proper understanding of the text. Let all the effort be directed to the most discriminating interpretation of the passage in hand as language and literature. Let the study be an ethical and spiritual one; let the pupil feel when he approaches it that he is to receive each day some fresh revelation of the nature of mind and its workings.

b. *Subject matter.* As regards the subject matter of authors read, I believe our secondary schools quite generally make one very serious omission. **Subject** They fail to emphasize the importance of **Matter.** grasping the narrative or argument of a writer in its continuity. The tendency is to read simply from day to day. Too little effort — often none at all — is made to bring successive lessons into relation, to show the bearings and connection of the different parts of a narrative or speech. How few pupils after reading a book of Cæsar or an oration of Cicero have in their minds any clear and consistent picture of the course of thought, the line of argument, its strength and defects, or apprehend the real drift of the piece as a whole! Is not the piece commonly made a succession of "takes," the order of which might be varied *ad libitum,* so far as concerns interference with any systematic endeavour to show their organic connection? And is not the impression left upon the minds of pupils often one of utter vagueness as to what it is all about? I believe the alleged defect to be very general; and if it is, it surely ought to be remedied at once. I know of no surer way to kill all literary sense and encourage mechanical formalism, than the exclusive employment of the analytic method of study, without ever a thought of synthesis, — always taking apart, never putting together. Such a process is *destructive* in more senses than one. Let us not abandon analysis in our study of Latin, but let us combine with it a larger use of synthetic **Importance** methods. After a pupil has translated a **of Synthetic** book of Cæsar or an oration of Cicero, let **Work.** him, under the teacher's guidance, go carefully over the whole; let him build up thought on thought, until he comes to see and feel the piece as a unit. I believe that reform in this particular is widely needed in the schools where Latin is taught. The ancient languages are held to be instruments of culture; and so they are when rightly used. But culture implies the apprehension of things in their relations. It is not merely a familiarity with "the best that has been thought and said." If it were,' the *Dictionary of Familiar Quotations* would be the place to find it. Let us bear this in mind as we teach the Latin classics; let us remember that they are not merely language, but — what is much more — literature.

c. *Grammar.* Attention has been called above to the danger of laying undue stress upon the importance of syntax in connection with translation, even to the extent of neglecting the form of the English rendering and the proper understanding of what is read. Grammatical work, however, has its place, **Grammar.** and a very important place, in the study of Latin in the school. Even in connection with the daily translation it must command some attention, while besides this it should also be studied separately, I believe, by way of regular lessons to be assigned for formal recitation.

Considered from the purely intellectual point of view, grammar is by no means the arid, profitless study that many conceive it to be. Far from it. On **Logical Discipline in Study of Grammar.** the syntactical side in particular it brings us face to face with the severe problems of logic, and forces upon us the minute and conscientious consideration of complex thought relationships. Take the conditional sentence, for example. It is the function of grammar to offer some classification of the mass of material falling under this head. Usually the basis of classification is found in the logical implication of the protasis of such sentences. Thus in one type nothing whatever is implied as to the truth or falsity of what is assumed in the protasis ('If death ends all, let us eat, drink, and be merry'). In another type, the protasis suggests that the substance of its content may eventually be realized (' Should he come, I should refuse him admittance '); while yet a third type as distinctly implies that the supposed case is contrary to fact ('Were I a rich man, I should gladly help you'). The differentiation of these three types of protases is something requiring a definite logical effort, and the pupil who has learned accurately to distinguish the three has made important attainments in the way of grasping logical relationships. Particularly instructive in this line is a study of the Latin equivalents of those

treacherous modal auxiliaries 'may,' 'should,' 'would.'
Logical analysis shows that we have not merely one
'may,' and one 'should,' *etc.*, but several, — all clearly
distinct from each other in present logical value; so
that the pupil who is translating from English to Latin
is forced to make a mental equation of his 'may,'
'should,' or 'would' before he can undertake to
render the thought in Latin. 'The class may please
turn to page 52' is one 'may'; 'Men may come and
men may go, but I go on forever,' is another 'may';
'To-morrow it may rain' is another; while 'From this
evidence we may easily conclude'; 'You *may* think
to succeed in this audacity'; 'May I take this book?'
all represent yet other varieties of this elusive auxiliary,
whose capacity is by no means exhausted by the above
examples. As all of the above 'may's' represent distinct logical ideas, so each one will demand a different
form of rendering in Latin, as will be readily recognised
by teachers. Equally varied are the ideas represented
by our English 'should' and 'would;' and equally
varied, too, the mechanism of reproducing in Latin
the logical values which they represent. In short, conscientious grammatical study brings out, as nothing else
can, the fact that grammar is not a mechanical occupation dealing with dead formulas, but that its substance
is human thought in its infinite and stimulating variety.

Exceedingly valuable too is the insight afforded by
grammar into the psychology of language, — its life and
growth. Illustrations in abundance may be
drawn from sounds, inflexions, word-forma- Gives In-
tion, and syntax; but the latter field alone sight into
must serve our present purpose. The pupil Psychology
of Language.
is puzzled at first to find the Latin ablative used with
comparatives in the sense of 'than,' but he easily sees
the psychology of the idiom when he learns that this

use goes back to the true ablative or 'from'-case. 'Marcus is taller than Quintus,' was, therefore, to the Latin mind, 'Marcus is taller (reckoning) from Quintus (as a standard)'; similarly the ablative of agent with *a* is seen to go back to a 'from' use of the case. The sentence *a Cæsare accusatus est,* originally at least, and perhaps always, must to the Roman mind have meant 'he was accused from Cæsar,' *i. e.* the action proceeded from Cæsar as the agent. An especially instructive illustration of the operation of the Roman folk-consciousness is seen in the construction used with verbs of fearing. *Timeo ne veniat* means 'I fear he will come'; *timeo ut veniat,* 'I fear he will not come,' — to the pupil's mind an apparent inversion of all reason. But the explanation of this apparent anomaly is easily furnished in the fact that the Latin forms of expression have developed from subjunctives of wish: *ne veniat* and *ut veniat.* These expressions originally meant respectively 'may he not come,' 'may he only (*ut*) come' *Timeo* was at first added half-parenthetically to express a fear that the wish might not be realized. Thus *timeo, ne veniat,* from meaning 'may he not come; I am afraid (he will),' soon came to be felt as virtually equivalent to 'I am afraid that he will come'; so *timeo ut veniat,* 'I am afraid he will not come.' What we thus translate, however, is not what is explicitly stated in the Latin, but what is implied in that which is stated. The foregoing are but familiar examples of what is meant by the insight into the psychology of language afforded by the study of grammar. Grammar takes the pupil back to the origin of constructions, and impels him to trace the evolution of the conventional forms of speech.

We see other psychological forces at play also. Analogy is a powerful factor in syntax, as it is in

sounds and inflexions. Verbs of 'filling' normally take
an ablative (developed from the ablative of means),
Analogy.   yet owing to the analogy of the genitive
with *plenus*, and adjectives of 'fulness,' we
find compounds of *-pleo* occasionally construed with
the genitive at all periods of the language. In *oro,
uxorem ducas* ('I beg you to get married'), the subjunctive, by origin, was a jussive, — 'Get married, I
beg you to.' But by analogy the subjunctive soon
came to figure in expressions where this logical explanation could not apply, as seen in expressions like *non
oro uxorem ducas* ('I don't ask you to marry'), where
the explanation 'Marry a wife; I don't beg you to,'
would be manifestly absurd. Grammar, too, shows how
arbitrary language is. To denote price, definite or
indefinite, the ablative was originally employed; to
denote value, definite or indefinite, the genitive was
employed. As a result of the near relationship of
these two conceptions of value and price, the two constructions naturally began to invade each other's territory. Four genitives, *tanti, quanti, pluris, minoris*, from
the earliest times on were mandatory with verbs of
'buying' and 'selling'; yet the construction of the genitive with expressions of 'buying' and 'selling' went
no further; with all other expressions of indefinite price,
e. g. magno, maximo, parvo, minimo, etc. the ablative·
was as mandatory as was the genitive in *tanti, quanti,
etc.* There can hardly be profit in speculating upon the
causes for this distinction; it simply illustrates the
fundamental arbitrariness of language in its historical
development. Language was not primarily a creation
of the logician, but an emanation from, and an evolution of, the folk-consciousness. The same forces which
brought it into existence determined in the main its
entire future career, and forever precluded the existence

of an ideally perfect and consistent scheme of expression. What we see in syntax, therefore, is largely the waywardness and inaccuracies of the popular mind. Literary masters exercised a certain influence in giving currency and character to those forms of speech which they deemed superior in accuracy, simplicity, or effectiveness; but they could not create the forms themselves or alter their moulds when once the forms were cast.

Syntax, too, shows us often the battle of two rival constructions in a struggle for supremacy. No better illustration of this general principle can be found than is exhibited by the history of the constructions with *similis*. Speech-Rivalry. In our earliest Latinity (Plautus), *similis* is construed with the genitive alone. Later, probably under the influence of *par* and similar words, *similis* begins to be construed with the dative. The genitive, however, still continues in vogue and is practically mandatory when the governed word is a pronoun or the designation of a person. In point of meaning, absolutely no distinction between the two cases can be discovered; we see simply a struggle for supremacy between two rival forms of equivalent value. As time goes on, it is evident that the invader (the dative) is gaining ground rapidly. In the post-Augustan writers the territory of the genitive becomes narrower and narrower; for a time the genitive of pronouns is usual, but with other words, whether designations of persons or of things, the dative occupies the field. Ultimately even the pronouns succumb to the levelling tendency, till by the time of Apuleius the dative is practically left in undisputed supremacy.

I have thus far been considering the functions of grammar study, particularly syntactical study, — as a training in logic and as illuminating general linguistic psychology. Grammar has yet one other function which demands

recognition, — æsthetic training.[1]   Such training is an inevitable result of a contemplation of excellences of style
Æsthetic   in the choicer masterpieces of Latin read in
Phases.   the schools.   Being subtler than the other
kinds of training, to which attention has above been
called, it is less certain of effective communication by any
of the customary methods of instruction.   We can explain facts and relationships, genesis and development,
to our pupils with tolerable assurance that they will
apprehend a lucid exposition of the truth.   But when
it comes to matters of taste and feeling, the case is
different.   We may indicate our own emotions and
our own appreciation, but there is no certainty of a
response on the pupil's part, as there is in the case of
a matter presented exclusively to his understanding.
Still the difficulties of communication on the teacher's
part and the limits of appreciation on the pupil's part
do not obliterate the existence of the function here
claimed for grammatical study; they simply prove that
there is less certainty of making this function effective.
But it is grammar that guides us through word-order
to a right appreciation of the relative prominence of
words, phrases, and clauses; it is grammatical study
that shows us the force of such rhetorical devices as
synchysis and chiasmus; and that tells us the difference
between the rapid summary of an asyndetic series as
compared with the cumulative effect of a polysyndeton.
It is nothing but objective grammatical study that can
tell us the subtle differences between the multitude of
synonymic constructions, revealing their shades of meaning, their inward character, their elevation or their com-
monplaceness, their literary dignity or their every-day
colloquial nature.

---

[1] See particularly Gildersleeve, *Essays and Studies*, p. 127 f., 'Grammar
and Æsthetics.'

d. *How scientific should a school grammar be?* In a strictly scientific grammar of Latin or any language, the facts must be classified on the basis of historical origin and historical relationships. A school grammar, however, is not exclusively scientific, — at least not in its arrangement of material. It must consult largely pedagogical expediency. While faithful to the facts, it must so state these and so arrange them as to facilitate their ready comprehension and permanent retention by the pupil. Yet within limits the scientific ideal may be consulted and followed to advantage even in a school manual. In our own country, Recent the tendency during the last twenty years Tendencies. has been to narrow so far as possible the chasm between the purely pedagogical and severely scientific mode of treatment. Wherever the scientific exposition or the scientific grouping of facts can be readily adapted to the understanding of pupils, there can hardly be any question as to the propriety of conforming to the scientific treatment. Writers of school grammars have not been slow to see this, as is shown by the improvements made in recent years in the direction of scientific accuracy. Thus it is not so very long ago that *i*-stems were indiscriminately classed with consonant-stems of the third declension. Yet historically these *i*-stems were as distinct from the consonant-stems as were nouns of the fourth declension (*u*-stems). Originally they had terminations (in the accusative and ablative singular, and in the genitive and accusative plural) which were not shared at all by the consonant stems. Our recent grammars recognise this fact explicitly; many of them also recognise a mixed class, consisting of those consonant-stems which have partially adapted themselves to the declension of the *i*-stems. Similarly the verb, *do, dare,* despite the short *a* of its infinitive and its short root vowel in several inflected forms, was classed as a verb of the first conjugation. Historically, however, *do, dare*, is an irregular verb, — just as irregular, and irregular in the same way, as *sum, fero, volo, eo ;* *i. e.* it was unthematic, the personal endings being appended directly to the root without the use of any connecting vowel. This fact is now quite generally recognised in our grammars. In the same way the Latin syntax of a quarter of a century ago has experienced many radical improvements. The ablative with *utor, fruor, fungor, potior*, and *vescor* used to be designated as an ablative in special construction. This was arbitrary and unsatisfactory. To-day the pupil learns that the ablative with these verbs is simply an ablative of means. The naturalness of this is perfectly apparent even to the elementary pupil so soon as he is reminded that all these verbs were originally reflexive middles, *utor* meaning 'I profit myself'; *fruor*, 'I enjoy myself'; *fungor*, 'I busy myself'; *potior*, 'I make myself master'; *vescor*, 'I feed myself.' Similarly in the syntax of the verb, the tendency is strong at the present day to introduce into our school grammars the true scientific explanation of substantive clauses developed from jussives and optatives. I refer to such expressions as *postulo abeas ; postulo ut abeas ; sino dicat ; licet abeas ; oportet dicas ; velim veniat ; cupio ne veniat, etc.* That the dependent subjunctive in clauses of this type is not a substantive clause of purpose, as it was formerly explained, is made sufficiently clear both by the meaning and history of these clauses. The subjunctive is simply a jussive or optative that was once used paratactically and later came to be felt as the object or subject of the main verb. This origin is so simple and natural that it is capable of easy demonstration to the secondary pupil. It is easy to show him that in *postulo fiat* or *postulo ut fiat*, the original sense was 'let it be done; I demand it'; so *cupio ne veniat*, 'may he not come; that's my wish.'

In general it seems a safe principle that, wherever the results of scientific advance in our knowledge of Latin grammar are of such nature as to be apprehended by the pupils of the secondary school, these results may claim a place in our school grammars. Such incorporation would seem not merely the right and privilege of the writer of a school grammar; I believe I am not going too far when I assert that it is also his duty. In some cases a certain arbitrariness even is justifiable. The construction of the ablative with *opus est* is almost certainly of instrumental origin. Yet this point cannot possibly be made clear to the elementary pupil. To my mind, however, in a case like this and in some similar cases, it is better to treat the construction in the light of our best knowledge rather than deliberately to inculcate what is untrue. Care must, of course, be taken to distinguish between what is scientifically established and what is mere tentative hypothesis. Care must be taken, too, to avoid the introduction of unnecessary and difficult explanations of origins. Thus the subjunctive of result and the subjunctive of characteristic are almost certainly developments of the potential (the 'should'-'would') subjunctive. Yet it is questionable whether it is wise to treat these uses of the subjunctive as subordinate potentials, as is done in a recently published Latin grammar. For the ordinary pupil will detect no trace of the 'should'-'would' idea in a sentence like *Persæ ita territi sunt ut ad naves perfugerint*, or in *nemo 'fuit qui non vulneraretur*. While subjunctives like this were almost certainly extensions and developments of the 'should'-'would' use, traces of the original value of

A Safe Principle.

these clauses have vanished so completely that probably they can no longer be detected in one per cent of the clauses of result and clauses of characteristic actually met by the pupil. In cases of this kind it seems far better, therefore, to offer to the pupil no explanation of origins, but to content one's self with simply stating the facts of usage.

e. *The grammar a book to be studied and learned.*
A deplorable tendency has manifested itself in recent

Recent Neg-
lect of the
Grammar.

years to make the grammar primarily a book of reference instead of a book to be thoroughly learned. The results of this attitude are inevitable. From nearly every quarter come complaints that students are steadily growing away from the grammar; that they no longer know it as they once did, in the days when the confident boast was made that, if every copy of Andrews and Stoddard's *Latin Grammar* were blotted out of existence, the boys of

One Reason
for this.

the Boston Latin School would restore it in a fortnight. One reason for the changed attitude has been the excessive bulk of most of our Latin grammars. Twenty years ago they were books of modest size covering scarcely more than three hundred pages of open typography. Since that time they have quite generally swollen in bulk with successive editions. Of these books the smallest now contains four hundred and fifty pages, while of the others one approaches five hundred pages, and a third nearly six hundred pages. The open page, too, of the older books has in their later editions become crowded; where small pica, long primer, and bourgeois formerly met the eye, one now finds extensive paragraphs of minion or even agate.

In all these changes the pupil of the secondary school has distinctly suffered. The immense mass of material offered by these bulky grammars has made it extremely difficult even for many teachers to determine what is essential and unessential. Hence, the extensive resort to the use of the grammar as a book of reference and its extensive abandonment as a subject of thorough formal study. This aloofness from the gram- Significance of mar has led quite naturally to the copious Wholesale In-troduction of introduction of grammatical references in the References in notes of our secondary school texts. In the Our Texts. days when pupils used to become masters of the Latin grammar the introduction of such wholesale references would have seemed little less than an impertinence. To-day when the grammar is no longer regarded as something for independent mastery, these references are naturally welcomed by the pupil and teacher alike. But experience shows that they do not teach grammar. A recent Virgil contains in the notes to six books of the *Æneid* no fewer than one thousand grammatical refer-ences, — many of them to such familiar constructions as the ablative of means, the subjunctive of purpose, *etc.*, showing that even in his fourth year the pupil still seems to need assistance in the simplest syntactical problems. It is entirely natural that he should still need such assistance, for the very abundance of gram-matical references always supplied in the notes of the text studied inevitably begets the habit of depending upon such references for grammatical help and as irre-sistibly destroys the independent acquisition of what every Latin pupil of the secondary school ought to know with the greatest certainty and accuracy.

The bulky grammars of the last decade or more have been valuable manuals for the advanced college student, but they have, I believe, signally proved their lack of adaptation to the needs of secondary pupils. If such pupils need to master some grammar, it is indispensable that they be provided with a grammar that can be learned. What is needed is a manual that states the essential facts of the language with scientific accuracy and in clear form. In this matter we Americans may well be guided by the experience of the Germans. German experience in recent years has tended to restrict the bulk of school grammars both of Latin and of Greek, and has demanded the incorporation of the main principles of the language in compact manuals of less than three hundred pages. Books of this compass now hold the field in Germany, and have for the last fifteen years proved more and more conclusively their ability to meet the severe demands of the German gymnasial course, — a course representing quite as much in scope and content, and more in thoroughness, than that pursued by the average American graduate who has studied Latin in school and college. To be adequate for the requirements of the average student, a Latin grammar does not need to include *all* the facts of the Latin language. Isolated or peculiar idioms of form or syntax met in the course of reading are properly explained in the accompanying notes; it is quite unnecessary and quite unwise, especially in a grammar intended primarily for beginners, to give an account of every special deviation from normal usage. To give space to these is to incur serious risk of distorting the true perspective of actual usage. What the pupil needs to know is the main facts of the language. If he acquires these as his primary equipment, he will the better appreciate the relative importance and frequency of exceptional usages by noting such points in connection with his reading.

Necessity for a Compendious Work.

Dettweiler's Postulates for a Latin Grammar. In discussing the features which should to-day characterize a Latin Grammar intended for use in secondary education in Germany, Dettweiler [1] emphasizes, among other points, the following:

1. The Latin Grammar must limit itself to a statement of those facts and laws of usage which are common to all Latin writers. All individual peculiarities should be left for the philologians.

It has been justly observed that Latin syntax conveys the impression of something definite, fixed, and energetic; that it is dominated by a spirit of strict subordination, and that these features of the language are an accurate mirror of the essential spirit of the Romans themselves with their respect for authority and for law. Yet this impression of the language certainly fails of being gained by the pupil if he is confronted with a host of exceptions and linguistic peculiarities which hold only for individual writers. The grammar should give systematically the fundamental laws of the language, therefore; the exceptions should be noted as they occur in the individual authors.

2. There should be *but one grammar, not a shorter and a longer.*[2] If the grammar is to be used, it must be a book in which the pupil can become thoroughly at home. The acquired local memory for things as they stand on the printed page is something that comes only with time, and is a not inconsiderable factor in promoting an intelligent retention of what has been learned. The grammar, too, should, in its arrangement and its diction, agree with that of the beginner's book.

3. The Latin grammar should not be ultra-puristic in its basis; *i. e.* it should not assume a single author as the sole representative of correct or model Latin, and base the laws of the language upon his diction. For a

---

[1] In Baumeister's Handbuch der Erziehungs- und Unterrichtslehre für höhere Schulen, vol. iii. Part iii. Lateinisch, p. 32 ff.

[2] The italics correspond to Dettweiler's spaced type.

long time Cicero's usage was taken as the basis of standard Latin. What was found in him — and nothing else
— might be imitated. The tendency was even carried
further, and certain special features of Cicero's diction
were canonized as specially qualified to serve as representatives of pure Latin. This is not only irrational; it is
ludicrous. It betokens a desire to be more Roman than
the Romans themselves. ˙ We may fairly take the attitude that anything found in representative writers of the
best period is correct Latin, even though it do not once
occur in Cicero. The fact that a form of expression
is not represented in that author is by no means con-
clusive evidence that he would have repudiated it.
Even assuming that he would, it is unreasonable for us
to exalt any single writer, however gifted in his style,
to the position of authority which in the past has so frequently been ascribed to Cicero.

4. It is desirable that the Latin Grammar in a supplementary chapter embrace the chief features of Latin
style, *i. e.* the essential points of stylistic difference between Latin and the vernacular of the pupil.

Most Latin grammars which have appeared in Germany in recent years recognise the validity of the foregoing propositions. Particularly as regards the first and
second of the four points enumerated, there prevails the
most hearty unanimity, as may be seen by a glance at
the appended lists [1] of the leading Latin grammars now
in vogue in Germany.

LIST A.

Books Shortened in Recent Years.

Ellendt-Seyffert.   34th ed., Berlin, 1890, 303 pp.; 37th ed. 1893,
265 pp.; 53d ed. 1909, 265 pp.

Lattmann-Müller.   6th ed., Göttingen, 1890, 324 pp.; 7th ed. 1892,
256 pp.

---

[1] Brought down to 1909.

Schmidt, Karl, 5th ed., Vienna, 1880, 296 pp.; 6th ed., improved and abbreviated, 1883 270 pp.; 7th ed., again improved and abbreviated, 1894, 236 pp.; 10th ed., 1904, 236 pp.

LIST B.

Books slightly Lengthened in Recent Years.

Harre, Kleine Lateinische Grammatik, Berlin, 2d ed., 1901, 228 pp.; 3d ed., 1908, 252 pp.

Scheindler, Leipzig and Vienna. 1st ed., 1889, 212 pp.; 2d ed., 1892, 239 pp.; 7th ed., 1908, 240 pp.

Landgraf, Bamberg, 3d ed., 1893, 263 pp.; 9th ed., 1908, 300 pp.

Stegmann, Leipzig, 5th ed., 1890, 250 pp.; 10th ed., 1908, 289 pp.

Schmalz-Wagner, Bielefeld, 1st ed., 1891, 233 pp.; 5th ed., 1901, 315 pp.

LIST C.

Books whose Bulk has remained practically unaltered in Successive Editions, or which have recently appeared in a First Edition.

Holzweissig, Hannover, 5th ed., 1894, 224 pp.; 25th ed., 1909, 222 pp.

Goldbacher, Vienna, 2d ed., 1886, 284 pp.; 9th ed., 1907, 286 pp.

Friedersdorff, Berlin, 1st ed., 1893, 201 pp.; 2d ed., 1897, 204 pp.

Harre, Berlin, 3d ed., 1893, 358 pp.; 4th ed., 1899–1900, 366 pp.

These lists are exceedingly instructive. Of twelve leading Latin grammars now published in Germany but two exceed three hundred pages. Three popular grammars in extensive use have been reduced from books of over three hundred pages to an average of about two hundred and sixty pages each. Of books lengthened in recent years but one exceeds three hundred pages; while the same is true also of the new grammars of recent years.

Significance of these Lists.

Recent movements in this country tend to show that the working grammar of American secondary schools is to be a book constructed upon the plan so extensively and so successfully followed abroad, namely, that of a clear and concise statement of the essential facts with careful elimination of superfluous erudition. Within the last five years no fewer than six grammars of moderate compass have appeared in the United States, while as many more are reported to be now in preparation. This timely recognition of the interests of the secondary pupil is a gratifying augury for the future of Latin study in our schools.

II. Special Points to be Emphasized in Connection with the different Latin Authors read in the Secondary School.[1]

a. *Cæsar.*[2] 1. Study the military system of the Romans, and make it the subject of systematic presentation to the class. Have the pupils understand how the legion was organized and officered. Study military evolutions, methods of siege, equipments, arms, engines, — in fine, everything that is embraced in this department of antiquities. All our editions of Cæsar now have admirable summaries of the chief facts belonging under this head, so that well-digested information is easily accessible to the student.[3] A familiarity with these military details cannot fail to lend greater interest to the reading of Cæsar's narrative;

Cæsar.
Military System.

---

[1] The attempt is here made merely to suggest a few salient points whose recognition in teaching seems of importance for a proper understanding of the author read. Many other points will inevitably suggest themselves to the teacher.

[2] See in general the exhaustive work of T. Rice Holmes, *Cæsar's Conquest of Gaul.* The Macmillan Co. 1899.

[3] A somewhat fuller presentation is found in H. P. Judson, *Cæsar's Army*, Boston. Ginn & Co. 1887.

it possesses, too, an undoubted culture value which will well repay the time devoted to its attainment.

2. At some stage in the study of the commentaries set forth the motives that actuated Cæsar in his Gallic campaigns. Have the pupil understand that all this seven years' fighting was not without Cæsar's Motives. a purpose, that very likely it was begun and continued in the exercise of great political sagacity by a master-mind, — a mind that apprehended the superiority of the Roman civilization and foresaw the inevitable clash between the expanding dominion of Rome and the politically defective institutions of her neighbours. Show further what were the specific defects of the Gallic civilization of Cæsar's day. Explain the forces at work among the Celts, — all eccentric; the growth of the city arrested at a primitive stage, as in Greece; no tendency toward centralization or national unity. All this may easily be put so that the pupil will easily understand how necessary it was that Rome should intervene with her institutions in order to secure political stability among the Gauls and to lay solid foundations for the future civilization of western Europe. On this subject the pupil will find some admirable suggestions by Mommsen in his *Roman History*, Book v. chapter vii ' The Subjugation of the West.'

3. Lastly, the attempt may be made to give some little sketch of the institutions (civil and religious) of the chief nations mentioned by Cæsar, namely, the Gauls, the Germans, and the Britons. Much Institutions. of the material on these topics will naturally be furnished by Cæsar himself, but it will need supplementing with matter from other sources.

b. *Cicero*. Cicero is important not only for his good Latin and his usually good style, but particularly for the light that his orations throw upon contemporary

history. The speeches against Catiline are of the
first importance, revealing, as they do, the
political and social unrest of the day, — an
omen of the complete collapse of the republican
organization.

Cicero.

All the orations, too, afford the best opportunity for
the study of the actual workings of the machinery of
the Roman state. Every pupil ought to
understand, at least in its main outlines, the
Roman constitution, the functions of the
magistrates, — consuls, prætors, ædiles, cen-
sors, tribunes, quæstors, *etc.,* — the organization and
jurisdiction of the Senate, the functions of the various
popular assemblies, especially the *Comitia Centuriata,*
the *Comitia Tributa,* the *Concilium Plebis,* the methods
of provincial administration, and the other fundamental
features of the old Roman public life. Here again the
introductions to our recent editions of Cicero's speeches
afford excellent guidance. Gow's *Companion to School
Classics* also contains some condensed information on
this point.

*Roman
Political
Organiza-
tion.*

Cicero's character, too, stands out in clear relief in his
orations. It is important that the teacher endeavour
to guide the pupil to an understanding and
appreciation of Cicero as a man, — always of
good intentions, and of high moral purpose, yet vain,
of narrow political vision, and often lacking strength of
character in emergencies. If possible, the pupil should
be stimulated to read parts, at least, of some of the
more recent lives of the great orator, *e. g.* Trollope's
Life of Cicero or Strachan-Davidson's *Cicero and the
Fall of the Roman Republic.*

*Cicero's
Personality.*

Even despite Cicero's undeniable merits as a stylist,
yet he is far from faultless. It will be a mistake to
endeavour to conceal this fact from the pupil. Cicero

is often culpably redundant. Worse than that, this very exuberance of diction is not infrequently the cloak for defective-logic or lack of argument. Again, Cicero is often guilty of gross exaggeration of the truth. In short, even in his political speeches, it is often the attorney that stands before us rather than the statesman or the candid student of affairs. All this is perfectly natural when we consider the heated partisanship and desperate struggles of the day; yet it is nevertheless a factor which cannot be ignored in any fair judgment of Cicero's speeches when considered by the standard of absolute truth, sincerity, and artistic form.

Cicero's Stylistic Defects.

c. *Virgil's Æneid.* The *Æneid* is one of the world's great poems. Yet the pupil needs guidance and assistance in order properly to appreciate this fact. He is naturally inclined to judge the *Æneid* by purely modern standards. Considered in this light the poem undoubtedly possesses glaring defects. To our modern sense, Æneas is anything but a romantic character. His desertion of the fated Dido brings him instant condemnation on the part of all of us. But the pupil should be made to judge this act in the antique light. As a servant of the gods, and the instrument for executing their decrees, Æneas's only course was to obey their commands. His abandonment of the Punic queen was not the result of the waning of a brief fancy; it was dictated from on high, and demanded the resolution and courage of a hero for its execution. The epithet *pius*, too, conveys to the English and American mind an unfortunate connotation. The English *pious* does not to us suggest the hero. It suggests instead a combination of dogmatic theology and respect for the forms of some established cult. This suggestion is so strong that, where

Virgil. Greatness of the Æneid.

The Character of Æneas.

pious is used (and it generally is) as a rendering for the Latin *pius*, in *pius Æneas*, the pupil attaches the qualities of weakness rather than of strength to the central figure of this great epic. *Pius Æneas* almost defies translation in our own language. Virgil wishes to depict his hero as faithful to his whole duty toward his parent, his wife, his child, his fellow-men, and above all toward the gods. This was *pietas*, — one of the cardinal Roman virtues, as it is one of the cardinal virtues of all times. Virgil wishes to exhibit Æneas to us as devoted, as tender, as loyal, faithful, just, sympathetic, reverent, and obedient; — all of this and doubtless more is contained in the one epithet *pius*, for which our own language possesses no adequate single equivalent. Nor is Æneas deficient in the sturdier virtues so prized by the ancients. He is patient in trouble; he is courageous in disaster; he is valiant in the fight. As a representative of martial prowess he is, of course, less conspicuous than the Homeric heroes. But while most of these excel only in hewing and smiting, Æneas exhibits a robustness of moral virtue almost totally lacking in the great figures of the *Iliad*, and not yet prominent even in the *Odyssey*.

The character of Æneas, then, must be interpreted by antique, not by modern, standards. To understand Æneas we must go back to the conception of society, of the state, and of man's place in the world, which prevailed twenty centuries ago. Viewed in this light Æneas will be seen to be the embodiment of the moral qualities that constituted the very essence of the Roman character.

Another feature of the *Æneid* which sometimes causes adverse criticism is the great extent of Virgil's **The Charge of Imitation.** indebtedness to Homer and to earlier Latin poets. This borrowing is evident on every page. In phrase, in epithet, in figure, in simile, Virgil has freely appropriated whatever served his purpose. But in so doing he was only following the prevailing custom of his day, and this free appropriation of the structural elements of which the *Æneid* is composed should not blind us to the majesty of the original ideas which Virgil has incorporated in the poem. After all, it is only in unessential externals that the *Æneid* is an imitative poem. Just as the character of Unique Roman Æneas himself is instinct with the cardinal Features. Roman virtues, so the *Æneid* as a whole breathes an intensely national spirit, in that it gives such decisive expression to the idea of Rome's mission in the world; her consciousness of imperial destiny; her function as mistress of the nations and the civilizer of mankind. This idea is finely wrought into the whole fabric of the poem, reaching its climax in vi. 847 ff.:

> " Excudent alii spirantia mollius aera,
> Credo equidem, vivos ducent de marmore vultus,
> Orabunt causas melius, caelique meatus
> Describent radio, et surgentia sidera dicent:
> Tu regere imperio populos, Romane, memento —
> Hae tibi erunt artes — pacisque imponere morem,
> Parcere subjectis et debellare superbos."

Linked with this intensely national spirit is the poet's sincere admiration for the Emperor Augustus. Profoundly impressed with the horrors of Rome's recent past, conscious of the necessity of a Augustus. new political order, and imbued with a deep faith that in Augustus lay the only hope for the moral and political regeneration of the state, Virgil lent his whole energy to the glorification of the Julian house, surrounding its past with the most splendid halo that his imagination could suggest, in the evident endeavour to increase its present prestige and perpetuate its beneficent influence.

It is well that the pupil should appreciate the fore-going points in reading the *Æneid*. For only so can he appreciate the true proportions of the character of Æneas and the genuine originality and majesty of the poem as a whole. For some further excellent sugges-tions concerning the study of the *Æneid*, see Elizabeth H. Haight, " An Experience with the *Æneid*." SCHOOL REVIEW, Vol. XVI (1906), p. 578 ff. At p. 585 f. a very full bibliography of the literature on Virgil is given.

d. *Use of translations.* In connection with the daily work of the pupil it is often possible for the teacher to make effective use of translations. This work may take two forms·

1. The teacher may read aloud to the class a transla-tion of the work thus far covered by the pupils. This procedure helps greatly to intensify the pupil's synthetic conception of what he has already studied. He now sees as an organic whole the campaign, the speech, or the epic episode which he has previously studied slowly and laboriously in Cæsar, Cicero, or Virgil.

2. Again, the teacher may read to the class other por-tions of Cæsar and Virgil than those read in the course, or other speeches of Cicero. Only relatively few pupils read in school all of the *Gallic War* or all of the *Æneid*, while none ever read more than ten or a dozen of Cicero's speeches. By means of translations, oppor-tunity is thus offered for widely extending the pupil's apprehension of Latin on the " content " side of the study. The concluding portions of the *Gallic War* constitute beyond question the most absorbing part of Cæsar's entire narrative. The last six books of the *Æneid* also, while perhaps inferior in interest to the earlier books, are well worth careful reading. It is a satisfaction, too, to have read all of these two works, even though partly in translation. Of Cicero's orations

there are many that give the pupil a better conception of the political conditions of the day than can well be secured by any other means. Thus the Verrine orations give us a picture of the extent to which the maladministration of the provinces might be carried by an unscrupulous governor. The *pro Milone* exhibits the excesses of partisan turbulence in the last days of the republic, while the whole series of the *Philippics* shows us Cicero in the fullest dignity and loftiness of character manifested during his entire career.

Thoroughly satisfactory translations of all the foregoing works, it must be admitted, are not at present easily accessible. For Virgil we have numerous good versions both in prose and verse. For Cæsar we have the vigorous and scholarly rendering of T. R. Holmes (London, Macmillan & Co. (Ltd.); New York, The Macmillan Co.). But for Cicero the Bohn translation is the only available one known to me. Still this last, with all its defects, may be made to do good service, while the demand for something better is sure in time to be amply met.

CHAPTER V

LATIN COMPOSITION

THERE is probably no subject in the entire range of secondary Latin teaching upon which there exists such a radical difference of opinion as upon the best way of **The Two Dif-** teaching Latin composition. This divergence **ferent Ways** of view is clearly represented in two kinds of **of Teaching it.** manuals prepared for use in the secondary schools. These books may be conveniently designated as the old-fashioned and the new. The plan of the old-**The Tradi-** fashioned book, which still commands great **tional Method.** confidence and respect (as I shall hope to show it deserves), is to take up the various grammatical categories in turn. The treatment is severely systematic, following closely the order and classification of the same material as presented in the Grammar. Thus the various case- and mood-constructions are taken up in turn. The lesson begins with references to the Grammar covering the subject under discussion. These references are followed by sentences to be memorized, illustrating the syntactical principles involved. A vocabulary of new words (also to be memorized) is added, and the lesson culminates in a series of English sentences to be turned into Latin; these sentences, of course, involve the repeated application of the syntactical principles which the lesson is designed to illustrate and enforce. This is the old-fashioned plan of teaching Latin composition.

The new-fashioned plan was first championed and made available in this country in the books of Mr. Collar and Mr. Daniell. Almost simultane- The Newer ously in the year 1889, each of these educators Plan. issued a *Latin Composition* of a novel sort. The plan is this:

The pupil is given a piece of continuous discourse to turn into Latin. This piece of continuous discourse is based upon a passage of original Latin which the pupil has already read, and to which he is now specifically referred. The book is furnished with no English-Latin vocabularies, either special or general. It has no model sentences to be committed to memory. The English given for translation into Latin is naturally a rather close imitation of the original. A fair sample of what is usually set may be seen by comparing a translation of Cæsar, *De Bello Gallico*, iv. 19, with an exercise of the sort mentioned which is based upon it.[1] The translation of the Cæsar passage runs as follows: " Cæsar having lingered a few days in their territory, having burned all their villages and dwellings, and cut down all their grain, marched into the country of the Ubii; having promised these his help in case they should be hard pressed by the Suebi, he heard the following news: The Suebi upon learning through scouts that a bridge was being built, held a council according to their custom, and sent messengers in all directions urging the people to move away, and place their wives, children, and all their possessions in the woods."

The English modelled upon this, and set for translation, is as follows:

"Cæsar tarried a few days in the territory of the Sugambri until he could cut down their grain; then went

---

[1] Taken at random from Moulton, *Preparatory Latin Composition*, p. 75.

to the country of the Ubii, whom he promised to free from the oppression of the Suebi. Meanwhile the latter had sent messengers in all directions announcing that a bridge was being built over the Rhine by Cæsar, and urging the women and children to flee to the woods."

Before making any comments upon this exercise, let us get well before us, if we can, the purpose of Latin composition. Why is it to be studied in the schools? What does it accomplish? The field may be partially cleared by stating, first, what it does *not* accomplish, at least in the school, namely, an ability to write continuous Latin with fluency and ease. Whatever be the purpose of the study, it cannot be that. For I am convinced no one ever does learn to write Latin of this kind in the school by any method of study yet devised, despite the occasional prescription of an ability to write simple Latin prose in the entrance requirements of our colleges. In fact, even in the college itself the ability to compose continuous Latin prose is a capacity acquired by but few, — chiefly those who specialize somewhat carefully in the classical field.

The Purpose of Studying Latin Composition.

What it does not Accomplish.

What, then, is the purpose and function of Latin composition in the secondary school? So far as reason and experience enable me to judge, the study of Latin composition is primarily intended to increase the accuracy, breadth, and certainty of the pupil's grammatical knowledge, — more particularly his knowledge of syntax. He first learns the Subjunctive of Purpose, let us say, or the Gerundive construction, by learning to recognise these idioms when he meets them in his reading. But this is only partial knowledge. A completer knowledge of the Subjunctive of Purpose or the Gerundive construction is acquired when the pupil

To Increase Knowledge of Grammar.

How it Achieves this.

learns to employ these in actual phrases of his own making. He then sees these constructions from a new side, and a practical side. The act of constructing sentences which contain these, fixes his mind more intently upon the construction than ever before. His knowledge of it is fuller and surer. Hence it is primarily as contributory to a better knowledge of the gram mar, that the study of Latin composition is of value. Incidentally it does give initial instruction in composing Latin, should the pupil ever get far enough along in his study of Latin to venture to undertake actual serious composition in that language. But the school can give nothing but the elementary technique of composition, if we use this word in the sense of composing continuous Latin. Just as in the case of drawing in the schools, the object of the study is not to make artists of the pupils: the elementary technique of the art is given them; but the justification of the study must be found in the quickened observational power, and in the training of the hand which drawing brings.

Such, now, being the purpose of the study of Latin Composition, namely, the acquirement of a deeper and surer and more subjective mastery of Latin grammar, the question presents itself, Which of the two plans sketched at the outset of our discussion is likely to prove the better, the old-fashioned plan or the new-fashioned? My conviction is emphatically in favour of the old-fashioned plan. The old-fashioned plan is systematic. The problem is to teach the various grammatical categories, to enforce them and bring them home to the pupil, so that he will feel them with a new intensity. The old-fashioned plan seems to me admirably adapted to bringing this about, because, I say, it is systematic. It takes the different constructions, one at a time, and treats them

The Traditional Method more Systematic.

11

by a large number of illustrative sentences. Thus, under the Clause of Characteristic, or under the Ablative Absolute, so many illustrative sentences are given that a definite and deep impression is conveyed, and one may count on the pupil's getting a firm hold of the idioms under discussion. In the new-fashioned plan, on the other hand, there is no such massing. The Ablative Absolute or Clause of Characteristic may be involved in a single sentence of a given exercise, and then not met again for weeks. Now a vital psychological principle seems to me to be involved here. All my experience with pupils has taught me to believe in the virtue of the **Advantages of Massing Illustrations of a Principle.** amplest possible illustration of everything difficult, and of massing this illustration at a given time, instead of scattering it sporadically over a longer period of time, and further of massing it on one thing at a time, and not distributing diluted illustrations on a multitude of different things. Thus, to be concrete: The Clause of Characteristic is difficult. It needs much illustration. Let us say, illustration by means of twelve English sentences to be turned into Latin. My experience leads me to believe that these twelve illustrative sentences would better be massed at one time, than distributed over a dozen separate lessons, as done by the new-fashioned plan, and that until that massing is consummated, and the Clause of Characteristic, or whatever else it may be, is amply illustrated and the intended impression made upon the pupil's mind,— until this is done, other idioms and constructions would better stand aside. It is for precisely this reason that I distrust the new-fashioned way of pursuing the study of Latin composition. To me it seems psychologically defective. It does not mass; it scatters.

Moreover, the old-fashioned plan employs yet other

resources for massing which the new method lacks. The systematic grammar lesson, and the illustrative examples which precede the exercise, help materially to intensify and deepen the impression intended to be conveyed by the lesson as a whole.

The new-fashioned plan also seems to me open to criticism on the ground of the extremely slight degree of effort which it demands of the pupil in **The Newer** those parts of the exercise really within the **Plan De-** **mands Less** pupil's power, while on the other hand nearly **Independent** every exercise bristles with difficulties whose **Effort.** adequate solution is far beyond the capacity of nearly all pupils and of very many teachers. The existence of these difficulties is implicitly recognised in **Yet in Parts** the publication of keys for teachers to accom- **it is too** pany books of the new-fashioned kind. But **Difficult.** if teachers find books of this sort so difficult as to feel compelled to resort to keys, what is to be said of the adaptation of such exercises to the ordinary pupil?

Reverting now to the exercise based on Cæsar, *De Bello Gallico*, iv. 19, let us examine somewhat minutely the nature of the discipline which a pupil in **A Concrete** the secondary school is likely to derive from **Illustration.** the attempt to put it into Latin. The passage is an extremely fair sample of the exercises in all books of this type. It was chosen by a random opening of the book.

The passage for translation into Latin begins: " Cæsar tarried a few days in the territory of the Sugambri." Turning to the Latin on which this passage is based, the pupil will easily see that he is to write: *Cæsar paucos dies in Sugambrorum finibus moratus est,* or, following the hint of the foot-note, *moratus* alone. The exercise continues: " until he could cut down their grain." This clause in its English is unfortunately inexact. Taken as they stand, the words mean that Cæsar waited until he should have the ability to cut down the grain, *i. e.* procure tools and command the necessary leisure for the operation. But it seems much more likely that the author means that Cæsar tarried for the purpose of cutting down the grain. If we adopt this latter view of the meaning of the clause, the Latin will be *dum eorum frumenta succideret ;* if we take the words literally, the Latin will be *dum eorum frumenta succidere posset.* But it is not easy to see how the pupil is to command the proper form of expression in either case, unless he has received some formal drill on employing *dum*-clauses of this kind, — the very feature which books of this type avoid on principle. Thus, while in the first clause of the sentence before us, practically no effort was required of the pupil in providing the Latin rendering, in the second clause he is likely to meet with difficulties beyond his capacity. Let us pass to the next sentence of the English: "then went to the country of the Ubii, whom he promised to free from the oppression of the Suevi." A glance at the original Latin shows the pupil at once that " went into the country of the Ubii " is *se in fines Ubiorum recepit.* The concluding relative clause, however, involves a difficulty, in the use of the proper mood, tense, and subject accusative, which only a minute and sustained study of the principles of indirect discourse will enable the pupil to meet with confidence and certainty. The Latin equivalent for the relative clause is: *quos se obsidione Sueborum liberaturum esse pollicitus est.* But to my mind there seems slight probability that many pupils can be counted on to know this unless they have had the special training in this idiom which books of the type under consideration expressly evade giving.

The next paragraph of the English begins: " Mean-

while the latter had sent messengers in all directions."
If the pupil's memory is good he will probably begin by
writing *Hi interea* and continue by changing the *nuntios
in omnes partes dimisisse* of the text into *nuntios in
omnes partes dimiserunt.* But if he momentarily forgets
his Latin equivalent for " meanwhile," as he may easily
do, or the Latin equivalent for " the latter," as the average pupil is likely to do, his only recourse is to omit
this part of the Latin sentence, for books of this type
give no English-Latin vocabulary to supply aid at such
junctures. The pupil, therefore, is likely to find himself
in the awkward predicament of neither knowing nor
being able to learn what he wants to know and is will-
ing to devote pains to discovering. Such a lacuna in
the present instance is not particularly serious, but at
times it may easily prove so; for often the form of other
parts of the sentence may depend upon these missing
elements.

The English goes on: "announcing that a bridge
was being built over the Rhine by Cæsar." A cross-
reference informs the pupil that no word for " announcing " is necessary in the Latin; " that a bridge was
being built," however, is furnished directly by the origi
inal: *pontem fieri.* But how many pupils will without
assistance correctly render " over the Rhine"? The
Latin idiom is regularly *in Rheno, in Danuvio, etc.*

The passage ends: "and urging the women and
children to flee to the woods," which, by referring to
the Cæsar passage, the pupil will without difficulty
(unless he has forgotten *√fugio* or confounded it with
√fugo) render: *uti liberi et uxores in silvas fugerent.*

Doubtless in this same book could be found other
exercises where the resemblance between the original
Latin to which the pupil is referred and the English
given for translation into Latin is even closer than in

the exercise above examined. Certainly in some books of this type the resemblance amounts practically to identity. Thus, from another book, I take at random the following, in which I have indicated clause by clause the original Latin (Cæsar, *B. G.* iv. 21) on which the exercise is based, and which by a few extremely slight changes on the pupil's part is transformed into the required Latin: " Caius Volusenus was sent forward with a galley (*Gaium Volusenum cum navi longa praemittit*), and was commanded to investigate all things and to return as soon as possible (*Huic mandat, ut, exploratis omnibus rebus, ad se quam primum revertatur*). He returned in five days, and announced that he had not dared to disembark and intrust himself to barbarians (*quinto die revertitur . . . renuntiat . . . navi egredi ac se barbaris committere non auderet*). Meanwhile, because ambassadors had come from many parts of Britain (*Interim   a compluribus insulae civitatibus ad eum legati veniunt*) and had promised to submit to the authority of the Roman people (*qui polliceantur . . . imperio populi Romani obtemperare*), Commius, King of the Atrebates, was sent to the island with them (*cum eis una Commium . . . regem, . . . mittit*) to urge the Britons to continue in that purpose (*hortatus, ut in ea sententia permanerent*)."

Yet in the passage which was first considered, the resemblance is so close that any pupil of average ability ought to be able without great effort to do all that practically any pupil may with confidence be expected to do. If we eliminate a few special difficulties likely to baffle most pupils, and for whose solution no adequate resources are accessible, the few changes necessary to adapt the phrases and sentences of the original Cæsar passage to a Latin equivalent of the English exercise are exceedingly easy to make. But an exercise so simple as this, it seems to me, cannot be tonic and strengthening, simply because it demands practically no effort on the pupil's part. Such exercises do not call for reflection, for judgment, or for memory; they simply involve that weakest of all intellectual processes, — mechanical imitation.

The absence of vocabularies in books of the new type also seems to me a serious defect. Most words needed in any exercise are, to be sure, sup- Vocabu-plied in the Latin passage on which the Eng- laries. lish exercise is based; but not all. Where the pupil is unable to discover the needed word in the original Latin and cannot recall it by memory, he must either resort to the pernicious expedient of hazarding a guess or else remain in ignorance. The special vocabularies, too, of the old-fashioned books seem to me a wise feature. These special lesson-vocabularies are given to be learned. Personally I believe it not merely legitimate but important for the pupil in his composition work to commit regularly to memory a certain number of the more common words of the Latin language. A reluctance to do this seems to me to be dictated by the same unwise attitude toward the exercise of the memory to which I have above referred (p. 55).

Thus far I have been criticising what seems to me the defects of the new-fashioned way of teaching Latin composition. It remains to examine the rea- Reasons sons which are advanced in its favour. These Urged in are best set forth by Mr. Collar in the Preface the Newer to his *Practical Latin Composition*, Boston, Plan. 1887. Mr. Collar owes the suggestion of his method to certain passages in Ascham's *Scholemaster*, in which Ascham's own method is set forth. The Ascham. method is this: The pupil is to take a passage of some Latin author, and master it in detail with the teacher's help and guidance. Then he is to make a careful English translation of the same. After at least an hour's pause, he is to re-translate into Latin this English version. Ascham incorrectly speaks of this method of study as suggested by Cicero, *De Oratore*, i. But Cicero goes no further in that work than to speak with approval of the practice of careful written translation from a foreign language into one's vernacular. The question of writing in a foreign language is not even remotely suggested. For his own method, Ascham says that he knows by good experience that with ease and pleasure and in a short time it " workes a true choice and placing of words, a right ordering of sentences, an easle understanding of the tonge, a readiness to speak, a facilitie to write, a true judgment, both of his owne and other men's doinges, what tonge so ever he doth use."

I shall make no criticisms upon Ascham's method; I shall not even pause to urge that the extravagant claims made for it by its author may properly excite in us a good degree of distrust. But Mr. Collar's method involves neither of Ascham's fundamental processes; it does not include a careful translation by the

Mr. Collar's Method not Ascham's. pupil into English to start with; it does not include the effort of re-translating this English, after an interval, into Latin. It is an entirely different method, in which the pupil, with the text before him, engages in a feeble imitation of the Latin phrases which he finds in the original passage.

As regards Mr. Collar's own method, not all will be able to assent to his fundamental proposition, which is

Mr. Collar's First Assumption. this: Latin writing must go hand in hand with *Latin reading*. Nor does Mr. Collar himself advance any reasons for this position. He assumes it as though a self-evident proposition. The traditional view is that Latin composition should go hand in hand with *Latin Grammar.* In other words, Mr. Collar thinks that Latin composition is primarily helpful as illuminating the *content* of what is read ; others regard it as of value in improving and increasing the pupil's mastery of the *linguistic form* of what is read, — the technique of the language. This last statement reduces the question at issue to its very lowest terms, I believe. Beyond it we can hardly go. Is Latin composition primarily of value as a direct aid to reading in the sense which Mr. Collar maintains, and is it, as he asserts, an abandonment of common sense to give a boy sentences to write about Balbus when he is reading about Themistocles and Miltiades? As above stated, Mr. Collar advances no reasons for his attitude, and as none occur to me, I shall not attempt a refutation of his thesis. I think, however, that it needs to be supported by cogent arguments if it is to meet with acceptance as a valid truth. Mr. Collar, however, does advance certain objections to the old way. For one thing he asserts that it " is ' a very perfite waie ' of muddling the learner, because it breaks all the threads of association. He [the pupil] is still supposed to be studying Latin, but the subject matter of his study and his mental processes have no relation to those from which he has been diverted. Certain principles are enunciated, certain rules are laid down, certain words are given, and the problem is to form sentences of these words in accordance with the rules." But how all this muddles the learner, I fail to see in theory, just as I have never been able to observe it in experience. Mr. Collar declares " it effectually breaks all the threads of association." This is but a re-statement in other terms of his fundamental position, namely, that Latin composition ought always to go hand in hand with reading (in the sense that it ought to deal with the same subject matter). As above noted, this position needs support before we can accept it as sound. Till then we may question the propriety and necessity of the existence of any such intimate association between the subject matter of the author read and the subject matter of the exercises in Latin composition; and, unless this association is shown to be something necessary and organic, we may with perfect justice deny that there is any breaking of threads of association; there may be failure to bring certain threads *into* association; but if they do not naturally and necessarily belong together, then there has been no act of severing.

From the point of view of those who believe that Latin composition is of value primarily as the handmaiden of Latin grammar, there certainly is in the old method of teaching Latin composition no breaking of any threads of connection that ought to remain associated. On the other hand, the very associations are preserved which ought to be preserved. The study of Latin composition deepens and strengthens the pupil's knowledge of syntax and forms. If a minute, accurate, broad, and certain knowledge of Latin grammar is of the first importance for the Latin pupil of the secondary school, then anything that promotes the attainment of this must be regarded as rational and legitimate. If Latin composition promotes this end, its natural and organic associations would seem to be with grammar rather than directly with the content of the authors read in the schools.

Mr. Collar's position seems to me singularly analogous to the hypothetical attitude of a teacher of music who **An Analogy** should urge that scales, arpeggios, octaves, **from Music.** trills, thirds, sixths, *etc.*, should be studied only in connection with regular musical compositions, and should protest against breaking the threads of musical association by practising the foregoing elements of musical technique in isolation. The technique of a language is of no less importance than the technique of the fine arts. To me it seems analogous in many ways. Minute knowledge of the structure, particularly the syntactical and stylistic structure, of a language is as indispensable an instrument for the proper interpretation of its literary monuments, as is a thorough musical technique for the rendering of a sonata. Neither of these, however, can be attained without laborious and sustained attention to the elements which constitute them. Mr. Collar calls the process by which this technical familiarity is acquired in the traditional way of studying Latin composition " mechanical"; and the product he calls " artificial." Both these allegations are to a certain extent just, but they are, I believe, far from possessing the significance which he would attach to them. The traditional method of teaching Latin composition is mechanical in The Traditional just the same way that all Latin grammar is ditional Method not mechanical. It involves repeated illustration Unduly Mechanical. of principles to the end that they may become very familiar, — so familiar as to be always subconsciously present to the pupil's mind. Only in this way can the whole energy of the pupil be devoted to the most effective interpretation of what is read, just as in rendering a musical composition the technique of the instrument must be so thoroughly mastered by the performer that all his energy may be devoted to the musical interpretation. But to me this mechanical drill seems indispensable, and I have deplored with increasing anxiety its partial disappearance in our schools in recent years.

So the product of the traditional method of teaching Latin composition is also, as Mr. Collar urges, to a certain extent artificial. But the same is true of many of the fundamental elements of every liberal education. For

Certain Limitations of All Teaching. the average student I can conceive nothing more artificial than the study of geometry, trigonometry, analytics, and differential calculus. In the sense that these mathematical branches deal not with what is vital and of permanent intellectual worth to the student, they are artificial. Yet I assume that their value is conceded by most students of education. Despite their artificiality they possess proved educative efficiency. So I think it is with the traditional mode of teaching Latin composition. It is in a sense artificial, but is an indispensable disciplinary element of the Latin course.

I am entirely at one, therefore, with Mr. Collar in his contention that Latin composition is not an end in

Conclusion. itself; I am at one with him also in thinking that its ulterior purpose is to aid the pupil in reading and understanding Latin authors. I cannot agree with him, however, that the traditional method fails to do this, and my dissent is based primarily upon extended experience. Undoubtedly the results of the traditional method are not as large as the teacher would desire; but we must not forget the limitations of teaching. Few of us ever get more than distant glimpses of our ideals. If we only succeed in remaining faithful to them in our hearts, we have cause for satisfaction. But I have not, as a college teacher, annually meeting a hundred or more new freshmen, been able to discern that those trained under the new method have begun to acquire the ability to write even simple detached sentences which I have often seen realized under the traditional method.

Mr. Collar's method also lays great stress upon the principle of continuity, *i. e.* of having the pupil write continuous passages instead of detached sentences. The experience of years with college freshmen has convinced me (I might almost say, has proved to me) that this attempt to teach pupils to write continuous discourse before they can write detached sentences is a prodigious mistake. Possibility of Learning to Write Continuous Discourse.

It is like teaching pupils to play a sonata before they can play a musical phrase. The attempt is too ambitious, and is, I believe, doomed to failure. Such pupils not only do not learn (in the schools) to write continuous discourse; they do not even learn to write detached sentences; and their failure, I think, should not excite surprise. It is true, as often urged, that no one ever learns to write Latin by writing detached sentences. But, on the other hand, no one ever learns to write Latin who has *not* learned to write detached sentences. The pupil who has learned to write simple isolated sentences involving the fundamental logical relations expressed in Latin, has secured a solid basis — and an indispensable basis — for more ambitious composition in the Latin language. The Easy must Precede the Difficult.

Possessing the art of expressing in phrase and sentence the various elements of Latin thought, he may then proceed to join these phrases and sentences in continuous paragraphs, studying the best methods of bringing successive sentences and successive paragraphs into organic relation. But this is a function of college teaching. I should rejoice to see the day when graduates of our secondary schools brought to college such a capacity to write simple detached sentences as would make it possible to avoid the necessity of spending part of the freshman year in acquiring this very power.

In the last few years an undoubted reaction in favour of the traditional method has manifested itself. This

reaction is attested not so much by the welcome accorded to new books prepared on the traditional plan,
A Reaction as by the circumstance that books of the new-
Noticeable. fashioned sort are in their revised editions
so remodelled as to include systematic drill in syntax.
This is conspicuously true of Moulton and Collar's
Preparatory Latin Composition, which, though in its
first edition (1897) constructed on the strict lines of
Mr. Collar's earlier work above considered, has recently
(1899) been enlarged by the addition of " Part ii. Systematic Drill in Syntax. 75 pp." Practically the same
is true of Daniell's *Latin Composition* in its revised edition. Whether these tendencies point to an ultimate
return to the traditional method of teaching Latin composition, the future alone can determine.

CHAPTER VI

THE difficulties of reading Latin poetry are sufficiently familiar. Extremely few pupils, and not many teachers, ever learn to read Latin verse with that keen consciousness of its artistic form which ought to attend the reading of poetry. The main causes of the trouble are two:

a. A failure to apprehend the truly quantitative character of Latin poetry;

b. An inaccurate pronunciation of the Latin.

Two Fundamental Difficulties.

Let us consider just what is meant when we say that Latin poetry is quantitative. We shall best understand the significance of this term if we pause a moment to consider the nature of English poetry and the general relation of poetry to the spoken language.

What is Meant by Quantitative Poetry.

English poetry is based on accent, *i. e.* on a regular succession of accented and unaccented syllables, grouped by twós or threes.

The versification of

This is the forest primeval, the murmuring pines and the hemlccks,

depends entirely upon this artistic alternation of stressed and unstressed syllables, and the same is true of all ordinary English verse. This basis of English poetry, moreover, is a result of the very nature of the English language. Like all languages of the Teutonic group, our English speech is strongly stressed; we pronounce our words with an energy typical of the race.

Latin verse, on the other hand, like Greek, was based on quantity. Recent discussion, it is true, has tended to show that the native Latin verse, as exemplified by the Saturnian measure, was governed by stress; but however that may have been, it is certain that, from the time Greek metres began to be introduced at Rome, — from the time of Ennius, — Latin verse was quantitative like Greek; a line of Latin poetry consisted of an orderly and harmonious arrangement of long and short syllables, *i. e.* of syllables which it took a long or short time to pronounce. This basis of Latin poetry again, as in the case of English poetry, is strictly in conformity with the character of the spoken language. For Latin apparently, in the classical period, was not a strongly stressed language. Had it been, it is quite inconceivable that the long environing vowels should not have been shortened in such words as *ēvītābātur* and scores of others like it in which the Latin language abounds. *Cf.*, *e. g.*, a Latin *inēvītābile* with English *ĭnévĭtăble*. Strong stress has a tendency to reduce every long pre-tonic and post-tonic syllable to a short one. In other words, strong stress is absolutely inconsistent with the quantitative phenomena of the Latin language.

Now it is precisely this slightly stressed character of the Latin language that explains to us the character of Latin poetry. Stress was so weak as to constitute an inconspicuous feature of the spoken word. Quantity, on the other hand, was prominent in the spoken word. Hence quantity and not stress naturally came to be the basis of verse.

Latin a Weakly Stressed Language.

Theoretically, now, this quantitative Latin poetry may seem sufficiently simple, were it not for the so-called *ictus*, a feature to which our traditional prosody uniformly gives a prominent place. What was ‘ Ictus.’
this ictus? It is usually defined as stress accent. With a single exception to be noted below, it is invariably thus defined, so far as I am aware. Yet I question whether there is a particle of legitimate evidence, internal or external, in support of this view. The conception of ictus as stress accent seems to me to have its foundation solely in the practical assumption that Latin poetry was, like English and German poetry, really accentual. I say ‘ practical assumption.’ It would, of course, be absurd to maintain for a moment that theoretically the quantitative character of Latin verse has ever been denied. Yet so long as Latin is pronounced with absolute disregard of vowel quantity, as it necessarily is by the so-called English method of pronunciation, and as it habitually is in Germany to my certain knowledge, or with disregard of syllabic quantity, as it usually is even where the Roman pronunciation is nominally followed, so long is it inevitable that any theoretical recognition of the truly quantitative character of Latin verse should be totally clouded by the impulse toward securing a rhythmical effect by means of stress. By a pronunciation which yields *gērō, ingēnium*, and thousands more of the same sort, on the one hand, and *fīlius, vĭs, etc.*, on the other, a quantitative verse is as impossible as would be an accentual verse in English, were we to misplace the regular word-accent. It is no exaggeration to say that were we to accent Longfellow's line as follows:

This ís the forést prímeval, the murmúring pines,

the result would be no whit worse than is inevitably necessary by any system of Latin pronunciation which fails scrupulously to observe the quantity of every vowel and of every syllable. A neglect of quantity was inevitable under the English pronunciation of Latin; it is inevitable under the pronunciation of Latin current in Germany. Neglect of quantity leaves nothing except accent as a basis for a metrical effect, and naturally leads to an accentual reading of Latin verse, which brings with it the conception of ictus as a stressed syllable. Yet this conception seems to me demonstrably false, for the following reasons:

1. So far as we know, no language is ever forced to an artificial pronunciation when adapted to the service

Reasons for Rejecting the Accentual Theory of 'Ictus.' of poetry. It is irrational to conceive any such adaptation. The poet simply takes the choicer words of familiar speech and employs them in their ordinary equivalence with their regular pronunciation. He must do so. For his appeal is to the many, not to a select handful who may have been initiated into the secret trick of his versification; hence he must use words in the pronunciation familiar to his auditors or readers. Otherwise he can make no appeal. His art consists, on the mechanical side at least, in arranging words in such a way that the poetic form is obvious to the meanest observer who knows the words by ear or eye. Can any poetry be cited in any language of which this is not true? Is it then not absurd to assume that in Latin poetic form consisted in employing words with gratuitous stress accents unknown in the ordinary speech? Can we conceive of an *atavís*, a *regibús*, a *Trojaé*, a *canó*, or a thousand other equally grotesque hermaphrodites that we are compelled to father by this theory? And is it credible that poetry so inconceivably artificial should have been tolerated, not to say admired, by such sober-minded persons as the Romans?

2. The view that *ictus* was stress is to be rejected because it involves the assumption of a second basis for Latin verse. We have already noted that Latin verse is quantitative, *i. e.* a dactyl is a long time followed by two short times. But if ictus is stress, then a dactyl is a stressed syllable followed by two unstressed syllables. We should thus get two principles as the basis of Latin verse, quantity and accent (*i. e.* stress), and it seems to me impossible that there should *uniformly and regularly* have been two principles at the basis of Latin verse or any other.

3. It is nowhere hinted or implied in the ancient writers that ictus was stress. To judge from the prominence assigned to ictus in our grammars and other works on prosody, one might expect to find that the word was widely current as a technical term among the ancients. Such, however, is not the case. Among all the systematic discussions of prosody found in the Latin grammarians, I have been able to discover no definition of the term, — in fact, no mention of it as a technical term of prosody. The word does occur a few times in the classical period, but so rarely and in such context that there is no justification for regarding it as a *terminus technicus*. Thus we find it in the familiar passage of Horace, *ad Pisones*, 253:

> unde etiam trimetris accrescere jussit
> Nomen iambeis, cum senos redderet ictus
> Primus ad extremum similis sibi.

More frequently we find *ictus* in this signification combined with *digitus, pollex,* or *pes*. Thus Horace, *Carm.* IV 6, 36 pollicis ictum; Quint. *Inst. Or.* IX 4, 51 pedum et digitorum ictu intervalla signant; Pliny, *N. H.* II 95, 96, 209 ad ictum modulantium pedum. From these and similar instances (the total number, however, is very small), the natural inference is that

ictus as a metrical term primarily designated taps of the
feet or fingers, and was then transferred to denote the
rhythmical beats of verse.   Certainly there is no evidence either from the etymology of the word or from its
use in any citable case to indicate that it designated
vocal stress.

Scarcely more support of the stress theory can be derived from the use of the words arsis and thesis as employed in the systematic treatises on Latin prosody
prepared by the ancient grammarians.   These writers
give us abundant testimony, but yet an examination
of their utterances fails to reveal any definite coherent
doctrine.   The witnesses not only contradict each other;
they even contradict themselves.

I have already given three reasons why it seems to
me erroneous to regard ictus as stress: 1. Because it
involves the importation of a stupendous artificiality
into the reading of verse. 2. Because it involves a
dual basis for versification, — stress as well as quantity.
3. Because the view finds no support in any ancient
testimony.   To these three reasons I wish to add as
4. There are excellent grounds for believing that ictus
was something else than stress.   If Latin poetry was
quantitative, as its internal structure and all external evidence seem to show, then a dactyl was a long time followed by two short times, and a trochee a long time
followed by one short time, absolutely without any other
parasitic accretion.   When, now, we come to use dactyls
by the line, one part of every foot will inevitably be felt
as prominent, namely, the long syllable.   The relative
amount of time given the long syllable of every dactyl
naturally brings that long syllable into consciousness,
and especially must it have done so to the minds of the
Romans, whose nice quantitative sense is proved by the
very fact that they made quantity the basis of their

versification. Yet the long of the dactyl has no stress. It is natural for us to stress it, us whose only conception of verse is accented verse. But in so doing I believe we are simply transferring to Latin verse our own inherited verse-sense. I define ictus, therefore, not as stress, nor as accent, but simply as the quantitative prominence inherent in a long syllable. This definition applies primarily only to the four fundamental feet — the dactyl, the anapaest, the trochee, and the iambus. It does not apply to the spondee, for example, when substituted for the dactyl in dactylic verse. In such cases the *first* long of the spondee is felt as the quantitatively prominent thing in the foot, even though the second syllable of the spondee is also long. In dactylic verse, the dactylic character and feeling so dominate the line that any spondee naturally takes on a dactylic character and is felt to be quantitatively prominent in its *first* syllable, just as in the case of the dactyl itself. So in iambic measures, where the tribrach or dactyl is substituted for the iambus, the quantitative prominence inherent in the long syllable of the iambus is felt as transferred to the two final shorts of the tribrach or the dactyl.

'Ictus' Nothing but Quantitative Prominence.

This conception of thesis or ictus receives no little support from the positive testimonies of the Roman grammarians. These writers in their defini- Support for tions of arsis and thesis repeatedly call atten- this View. tion in unambiguous phrase to the essentially quantitative character of these concepts. In this, their agreement is conspicuous.

To those who may cherish a scepticism as to the tangible reality of 'quantitative prominence,' Empirical I would only say that that phrase need ap- Consider- pear shadowy to no one who will actually read ations. one thousand lines of Latin aloud *with absolute fidelity to vocalic and syllabic quantity.* My own revolt against the traditional view of ictus has been purely and solely empirical. It was simply because by faithful practice in accurate reading my ear quickly grew sensitive to quantitative differences, that I was forced to believe that, as quantity was the basis of Latin verse, so ictus was only quantitative prominence. This conclusion, I say, was first forced upon me empirically, and the theoretical formulation was entirely subsequent to, and solely the result of, my actual oral experience in reading Latin. No one, in my judgment, can approach this subject in a candid spirit who has not first taken the pains to acquire the habit of exact pronunciation of Latin vowels and syllables. Even in this country, where we have nominally adopted the quantitative pronunciation of Latin, we have still much to learn in this matter. Our shortcomings are so pronounced, and bear so directly upon the theoretical aspect of the question at issue, that I shall here venture to recapitulate some of them.

First, we habitually neglect vowel quantity. One cause of this is the vehement stress which (in accordance with our English-speaking instinct) we regularly **Points in** put upon the accented syllable. The word **which our** *ēvītābātur*, for example, contains four succes-**Pronunciation** **of Latin is** sive long vowels. Yet in ninety-nine cases **Defective.** out of a hundred, the penultimate syllable is so strongly stressed that the first three vowels are pronounced short. In Latin poetry the result of such pronunciation is to wreck the quantitative character of the verse as effectively as if in English we were to misplace the accents on successive syllables. How much poetic form would appear in Milton's opening line of Paradise Lost, were we to pronounce ' Óf man's first disóbedíence,' for instance? Besides destroying vowel quantity as a result of over-stressing the accented syllable, we habitually neglect it in hundreds of other instances where there is no such disturbing factor. By some strange fatality the *-ĭs* of the genitive singular is commonly pronounced *-īs*, while the *-īs* of the ablative plural as regularly is heard as *-ĭs;* while the number of such pronunciations as *păter, āger, nīsī, quŏd, quĭbus, ingēnium* is simply legion. No one who pronounces Latin in that way can expect to feel the quantitative character of a Latin verse, and is in no proper frame of mind to give the quantitative theory dispassionate consideration; for one or two false quantities destroy as completely the quantitative character of a verse of Latin poetry as would one or two misplaced accents any English verse.

Even more serious than our neglect of vowel quantity is our neglect of syllabic quantity. The shipwreck resulting from neglect of vowel quantity occurs chiefly in *open* syllables, *i. e.* in syllables whose vowel is followed by a single consonant, which always belongs to the following vowel, thus leaving the preceding syllable open. In such syllables the quantity of the vowel is always identical with the quantity of the syllable, so that a false vowel quantity involves the quantity of the syllable as well. In closed syllables, on the other hand (*i. e.* syllables ending in a consonant), an error in vowel quantity does not affect the quantity of the syllable. I may pronounce *vēndŏ* or *vĕndŏ*. In either case the syllable will be long. Hence in closed syllables an error in vowel quantity does not destroy the quantity of the syllable, and so does not interrupt the quantitative character of a Latin verse. But the syllable must be actually closed in pronunciation; *else where the vowel is short, the syllable will be left open, and will be metrically short*, destroying the verse. It is precisely here that we err so frequently and so fatally

(margin note: Neglect of Syllabic Quantity.)

in our reading of Latin verse. We do not close the syllables that ought to be closed and were closed by the Romans. The commonest class of words where we commit this error are those containing a geminated consonant — words of the type of *ges-serunt, ac-cipio, at-tigerat, ter-rarum, ap-parabat, an-norum, ad-diderat, flam-marum, excel-lentia, ag-gerimus.* These words we habitually pronounce in prose and verse alike, as *gĕ-serunt, ă-cipio, ă-tigerat, tĕ-rarum, ă-parabat, ă-norum, ă-didit, flă-meus, excĕ-lentia, ă-gerimus.* Words of this type are extremely frequent in Latin. I have counted forty-five in the first hundred lines of Virgil's *Æneid, i. e.* the pronunciation described destroys the quantitative character of the Latin verse at forty-five distinct points, often twice in the same verse.

Nor is this all. In other combinations in the interior of words we are often guilty of quite as serious errors. In English, besides *muta cum liquida,* there are many other consonant combinations with which in stressed syllables we show a regular tendency to begin the syllable. This is especially true of the combinations *sp, sc(k), st, squ;* also *scl, scr, str.* This tendency of our vernacular speech naturally affects our pronunciation of Latin words in which these combinations occur. The *s* of such combinations properly belongs with the preceding vowel, in order that the preceding syllable may be closed and so made phonetically long; yet we frequently (almost invariably, according to my observation) join the *s* with the consonants of the tonic syllable. I refer to such pronunciations as *ă-spér(r)ima, i-stíus, tempĕ-státibus, corŭ-scábat, mĭ-scúerat, magĭ-strórum, ă-sclépias, ă-scrípsit, quĭ-squíliae.* My own students often exhibit a tendency to combine even *ct, pt, ps* with a following accented vowel, and produce short syllables in such words as *volŭ-ptáte, ă-spĕ-ctórum, ĭ-psíus.* Where the accent rests on the vowel immediately preceding these combinations, the liability to error is very slight.

There are yet other cases in which error is frequent, if not habitual. Unstressed syllables whose vowel is followed by *r+* any consonant are particularly liable to be made phonetically short in those portions of the country where the *r* is neglected. This is especially true in the eastern part of the United States, where *pŏ(r)-tárum, tĕ(r)-minorum, etc.*, represent the prevailing utterance. The combination of *m* or *n* also with a following explosive in unstressed syllables frequently is so treated as to shorten syllables phonetically long. The process by which this is accomplished is not yet clear to me. Observation, however, has taught me that in such words as *imperator, intendo* the first syllable is frequently made short; whether by omission of the nasal, by pronouncing a short nasalized vowel, or by a short *nasalis sonans* (*n̆*), I do not undertake to say. The fact, I believe, is beyond question. A careful and distinct enunciation of the nasal, however, will obviate all difficulty in cases of this sort.

There is only one other class of cases to which I shall call attention, namely, the unconscious *liaison* of final *s* after a short vowel with the initial consonant of the following word. Where the following word begins with *s, p, c, t, v, m, n, f, etc.*, and where the connection of sense is close, this *liaison* is in my experience frequent. It is not surprising that it should be, for we habitually join a final *s* of an unstressed syllable in our own speech with a following *s, c, t*. Examples in Latin are: *urbĭ sporta, capĭ scanem, urbĭ svici*. A case that puzzled me for a time was Juv. III 53 carus erit Verri, as read by a student. The fourth syllable sounded short to my ear, and it was only after repeated readings that I discovered that the reader was really dividing: *carus erĭ-tVerri.* I do not say that this *liaison* is invariable. It is certainly frequent, and, where it occurs, must vitiate the quantitative effect of the verse.

These common errors in reading Latin must be clearly understood, if they are to be remedied. It is by no means an impossible matter to acquire an exact quantitative pronunciation. It takes time and pains and considerable oral practice. I do not believe that it requires a particularly sensitive ear. By practice in rigidly exact reading, the quantitative sense is not slow in coming; but without that exactness it cannot come and cannot be expected to come. He who has once developed the quantitative sense will, I am confident, feel no need of any artificial stress.

In this connection the words of Madvig are well worth pondering (*Latin Grammar,* § 498, N.): "We **Madvig's** should also guard against the opinion which **View.** is generally current; namely, that the ancients accentuated the long syllable (in the arsis) and distinguished in this way the movement of the verse (by a so-called verse-accent, *ictus metricus*), and consequently often accentuated the words in verse quite otherwise than in prose (*e g.* Arma virumque canó Trojaé qui primus ab oris; Ítaliám fató profugús Lavinaque venit), which is impossible; for the verse depends on a certain prescribed order and form of movement being distinguishable, when the words are *correctly* pronounced. In our own verses we do not accentuate the syllables *for the sake of the verse*, but the syllables which are perceptibly distinguished by the accentuation in prose *form verse* by being arranged to succeed each other in this way. In Latin and Greek (where even in prose pronunciation the accent was quite subordinate, and is never named in speaking of rhetorical euphony, while on the other hand the difference of quantity was distinctly and strongly marked), the verse was *audibly distinguished* by this very alternation of the long and short syllables." So far my assent with Madvig is complete. He goes on: "But as it is not possible for us, either in prose or in verse, to pronounce the words according to the quantity *in such a way* as the ancients did, we cannot recite their poetry correctly, but are forced in the delivery to give a certain stress of voice to the arsis, and thus make their verses somewhat resemble ours. It should, however, be understood, that it was different with the ancients themselves (until the last century of their history, when the pronunciation itself underwent modifications)." These words of Madvig were written in 1847 — over half a century ago. At that time it is not strange that he should have denied the possibility of our reading Latin verse quantitatively with substantial accuracy. But before the end of his life, it is likely that Madvig relinquished this part of his earlier opinion.

As regards word-accent in the reading of Latin verse, I believe that it retained its full value; for as I have maintained that in poetry words are used **Word-** with their ordinary prose values, and are **Accent.** pronounced without addition of foreign elements, so I believe that they were pronounced without subtraction of any of their elements. But we have already seen that the Latin accent was slight. It was precisely that fact which led the Romans of the classical period to make quantity the basis of their verse. Assuming, now, that the word-accent was very slight, what wonder that, with quantity predominant in the verse and *in the Roman consciousness*, such slight word-accent as existed was felt as no intrusion? An analogous situation reveals itself in our English verse. Our verse is primarily accentual, and yet each syllable has its quantity, and shorts and longs mingle harmlessly with accented and unaccented syllables. Why should not the reverse have occurred in Latin just as simply and just as naturally?

To sum up, then: Latin poetry is to be read exactly like Latin prose. Latin was primarily a quantitative **Summary.** language in the classical period and is to be read quantitatively. The Latin word-accent was relatively slight as compared with that of our strongly stressed English speech, and is therefore to be carefully subordinated to quantity both in prose and poetry. Ictus was not a metrical term current among the Romans, nor was there anything corresponding to it in the quantitative poetry of the Greeks. The term is purely modern. We first imported the conception of stress from our modern speech into the quantitative poetry of the Greeks and Romans, and then imported the term 'ictus' to cover it. But just as the conception of artificial stress in Latin poetry is false, so the term 'ictus' is superfluous. Θέσις was employed by the ancient Greek writers on metric to designate the prominent part of every fundamental foot, and is still entirely adequate to cover that conception.

It remains to say a word with regard to elision, the rule for which, as stated in our Latin grammars, is in **Elision.** substance as follows: " A final vowel, a final diphthong, or *m* with a preceding vowel, is regularly elided before a word beginning with a vowel or *h*." The exact nature of this elision, as observed by the ancients in reading Latin verse, is still very uncertain. The Romans may have slurred the words together in some way, or they may have omitted the elided part entirely. In practice, the latter procedure is probably the wiser one to follow.[1]

---

[1] The writer has frequently been favoured by prominent advocates of 'slurring,' with practical illustrations of the method of reading recom-

In actual reading it will be well to bear in mind the four following fundamental principles:

1. Observe -the quantity of each syllable scrupulously, taking care to observe the proper division of the syllables, joining the first of two successive consonants with the preceding vowel, and so closing the syllable. Some Rules for Reading.

2. Make the word-accent light; subordinate it carefully to quantity.

3. Endeavour to cultivate the quantitative sense, *i. e.* to feel the verse as consisting of a succession of long and short intervals.

4. Do not attempt to give special expression to the ‘ictus’ in any way. The ‘ictus’ (which is only quantitative prominence) will take care of itself, if the syllables are properly pronounced.

The conception of ‘ictus’ here advocated is not as yet generally accepted by classical scholars; but teachers are nevertheless urged to put it to the test of experience. A fuller exposition of the view may be found in a paper by the author in the *American Journal of Philology*, vol. xix. p. 316 ff., parts of which have been quoted in this chapter. In vol. xx. p. 198 ff. of the same periodical will be found some criticisms of my views, and at p. 413 ff. will be found my reply. But whatever be the view with regard to ‘ictus’ no one

---

mended by them; but these experiments have invariably seemed to result in producing more syllables than the verse demands. For example, in a verse like

Vix a-de|ō ag-nō|vit,

the second foot has inevitably taken the form ◡ _ _, where slurring was attempted, while in a verse like

Tan-dem | cor-ri-pu|it sē|sē atque i-ni|mī-ca re|fū-git,

the fourth foot, by slurring, has become ◡ _ ◡ ◡ ◡.

disputes the soundness of what has above been urged with regard to observing scrupulously the quantity of each vowel and of each syllable, and it is predicted that a faithful observance of quantity will bring an empirical justification of the soundness of what has been set forth concerning the nature of ' ictus.'

If there be one argument in favour of retaining the Roman pronunciation of Latin, it is that by that pronunciation faithfully observed one may reproduce the quantitative character of ancient Latin poetry. But it is only by faithful observance of the quantity of every vowel and every syllable that this can be done. So long as the Roman pronunciation is retained, this accuracy ought to be striven for. But even when it is attained, it is doubtful whether the achievement supplies a sufficient justification for maintaining the Roman pronunciation of Latin. Beautiful as is the correct reading of Latin poetry, I cannot feel that it is worth the price which we must pay for it, particularly when one reflects upon the extremely small number of those who ever acquire a pronunciation of even approximate quantitative accuracy.

Relation to the Roman Method of Pronunciation.

CHAPTER VII

SOME MISCELLANEOUS POINTS

Roman History — Comparative Philology — Etymology — Illustrative Material : Books — Maps — Photographs — Casts.

a. *Roman History.* Much excellent work in this subject is undoubtedly done in the schools. Nor is there any lack of good text-books in the field. Yet the knowledge of Roman history brought to college by the average freshman is something lamentably meagre and defective. Students are often ignorant of the commonest facts of Roman history. I have frequently asked my freshmen such elementary questions as 'Who was Clodius?' 'What was the issue that brought on the Punic Wars?' only to meet with blank faces at the benches before me. Nor are the chronological conceptions of students for this period of history what they ought to be. I was once giving a course of lectures to juniors and seniors in one of the historic New England colleges now well along in its second century. My subject was the topography and monuments of ancient Rome. As my auditors were all men of classical training and classical interests, I naturally took certain things for granted. In this spirit, I naturally referred with confidence to such historic characters as Augustus, the Flavian emperors, the Antonines, Constantine, *etc.* Yet it took me but a short time to see that something was wrong. By the eyes of my students, I could see that I was not striking home.

When I came to quiz them on the matter which I had
presented with all the clearness in my power, I found
they had gained no adequate conception of the elementary survey of the successive architectural eras of Rome
which I had endeavoured to characterize. In the
endeavour to secure a ποῦ στῶ, I put the question,
'When did Augustus reign?' '500 A. D.' was the
response from the first man I asked. As this reply
failed to meet approval, another student volunteered an
estimate. '1500 A. D.' was the answer, as I turned to
him. On another occasion I was lecturing on the history of Roman literature. My theme was Roman
tragedy in the days of the Republic. My opening sentence ran something like this: 'Roman tragedy was a
close imitation of Greek tragedy, that literary glory of
the Periclean Age.' Then, in accordance with my somewhat informal manner of lecturing, I paused and put,
to the first student whose eye I caught, the question:
'What was this Periclean Age and when was it?' The
student was a young woman in her senior year, who was
specializing in Greek and was writing a thesis in that
department. My query, however, was too much for her.
She could only say that she had heard of the Age of
Pericles, but was unable to locate or characterize it.
These two cases are, of course, extreme ones, yet a long
experience in three great American universities per-
suades me that they are somewhat typical. Ignorance
is not often so pronounced as in the instances just cited,
and, when it is, it is probably confined to a small minority
of a class. Yet classes, as a whole, certainly cannot be
trusted to know the fundamental events and tendencies
of Roman antiquity which the instructor of college freshmen ought to be able to take for granted as a permanent
possession of all his students.

With institutions, political, religious, and social, the

student is almost sure to be even less familiar. He has either no conception or a false one with regard to the different elements of the Roman political organization. Senate, consul, ædile, quæstor, censor, prætor, tribune, *imperium, comitia centuriata, comitia tributa, etc.,* — all these are apt to be but empty names. The notion that these magistrates and bodies were a part of the working machinery of the Roman state seems to have eluded the bulk of the students who come to college. Much less are such students able to give any precise statements of magisterial or legislative function and prerogative.

I am, therefore, compelled to feel that the work of the secondary school in Roman history falls far short of what ought to be realized. Nor do I speak primarily as a college teacher, to whom ignorance of the fundamental facts and tendencies of Roman antiquity cannot fail to be a serious handicap in every college course in Latin. I speak quite as much from a sense of what the Latin pupils of the secondary school — to say nothing of any others — ought, as pupils of Roman antiquity, to know, and to know well, whether they go to college or not. A minute and detailed knowledge will not of course be expected; it will not be possible either. But some things are possible, are achieved in England, France, and Germany, and ought to be not only expected but actually realized in the United States. These things are ·

What Ought to be Expected.

1. A clear conception of the different periods of Roman history, particularly with reference to constitutional development, territorial expansion, and internal social and economic problems. These periods are, in the main, sharply differentiated and strongly characterized. They are also relatively few in number.

Periods.

2. A knowledge of the great characters of Roman

history. Fabricius, Curius, Camillus, Decius, Cincin-
natus, Scipio, Marcellus, Pompey, Cicero,
Great Men.
Cæsar, — even the last two of these, — are
unfortunately often nothing but familiar names — some
of them are not even that — to the mind of the average
student. I think it is not too much to demand that the
pupil know their personality and carry in his mind some
record of their positive achievements.

3. Some knowledge of dates. I am well aware that
a mere parrot-like capacity to reel off dates is no evidence of a knowledge of history, and that a
Chronology.
very ordinary intellect is frequently capable
of memorizing such details without appreciating the
facts with which they are connected. Yet in spite of
this possible (not frequent) perversion of study, there
are many dates that every student ought to know. It is
a safe statement to say that if an event is important, its
date is important. The founding of Rome, the expul-
sion of the kings, the great landmarks in the strife
between the orders, the Cornelian law, the Hortensian
law, the Decemvirate, the Licinian Rogations, the war
with Pyrrhus, the battle of Zama, the destruction of
Corinth, the Social War, the strife of Marius and Sulla,
the assassination of Cæsar, the battle of Actium, —
these and the like are great events of whose chronological location in the course of Roman history no pupil
should be ignorant. When a student tells me that
Cicero was born 300 B. C., I cannot accept as valid his
plea that he never had the faculty for learning dates. I
see at once that he has never had any adequate conception of Roman history.

4. Lastly, I feel that the secondary student of Roman
history ought to have some orderly and sys-
Institutions.
tematic knowledge of Roman institutions.
I do not, of course, presume that he shall be familiar

with every detail of the working of the Roman constitution and with the functions and prerogatives of the scores and hundreds of minor officials. But I do claim that he ought at least to understand the Roman constitution in its broad lines. He ought to know what the Senate, and magistrates, and assemblies were, what powers they had, how they did their work. He ought to understand also the imperfections of the constitution, and how and why it proved inadequate to the needs of the later Republic.

Is the foregoing too much to ask? I cannot think it is, or that secondary teachers will judge my demands excessive. One thing, however, is certain. Nothing approaching it is now realized in our secondary schools as a body, or in any considerable proportion of them. Furthermore, could any such knowledge be assumed in the graduates of secondary schools, it would mean a veritable revolution in the possibilities of college teaching, though the improvement is urged not in the interest of the colleges but of the schools themselves.

b. *Comparative Philology.* There is an undoubted fascination to most pupils in tracing the origin of words, their development of meaning, and their cog- Comparative Philology. nates in other languages. There is also a valuable historical training imparted in the conception of the various Indo-European languages as originally members of a single group, as descended in fact from a common parent. Yet it is doubtful whether it is advisable in the secondary school to press very far in pursuit of these matters. Fascinating as is the comparison of such words as Greek καρδία, Lat. *cor*, English *heart*, German *Herz;* Greek (ὀ)δόντ-ος, Lat. *dens;* English *too(n)th;* German *Zahn;* yet the study of such equations is not properly the function to any extent of either Greek or Latin instruction in the secondary school. The function of such instruction is to convey to the pupil first a knowledge of the language, next of the literature, and lastly, so far as possible, of the civilization of the ancient Greeks and Romans. For none of these purposes is a knowledge of Latin in its relations to the Indo-European parent-speech or to the other Indo-European languages indispensable. It can do no harm now and then to show the correspondence in several languages of cognate words, and to point out the historical significance of such correspondence; but to make much of this seems to me a serious mistake, for the reason that such work inevitably diverts attention from the essential purposes of Latin study in the school. And so when I see young teachers, fresh perhaps from the enthusiasm of university studies, inculcating in secondary pupils the subtleties of Grimm's law, of Grassmann's and Verner's laws, of Ablaut and *nasalis sonans*, I cannot help deploring their misdirected energy. These philological matters are important in their place, but I cannot believe that that place is the secondary school.

c. *Etymology.* The tracing of words to their origins within the limits of the Latin language itself is an exercise of much more importance, — one, in fact,

Etymology.

which cannot be neglected. To a large extent, of course, the origin of words is obvious. The pupil does not need to be told that *amabilis* comes from *amo*, or *potentia* from *potens*. With regard to other words help is necessary, and it is cause for regret that many of the manuals to which the pupil naturally refers for information on these points are so inadequate and so antiquated. This is particularly true of the standard lexicons and dictionaries of Latin. All of them are culpably behind the times. The same is true of most of the "word-lists" which often accompany editions of school classics. The vocabularies of our standard editions of Cæsar, Cicero, and Virgil have in recent years been greatly improved, and are now fairly representative of our present knowledge in the field of etymology.

d. *Illustrative Material.* This I shall treat under the successive headings of Books, Maps, Photographs, Casts. Illustrative Material.

BOOKS. The number of books needed for reference in the library of the secondary school is not great; yet some books are practically indispensable. I shall undertake to enumerate the Books. most important.

Lexicons. In the way of lexicons, Harper's Latin Dictionary (American Book Co., New York) is, with all its deficiencies, still our best Latin Dictionary. This work does not mark hidden vowel Lexicons. quantities; but the vowels are carefully marked in an abridgment of the same book: C. T. Lewis, Elementary Latin Dictionary. New York, American Book Co.

Grammars. Besides the Latin grammar used as a basis for the ordinary class-room work, it is well to have in the school library one or two of Grammars. the larger and completer *Latin Grammars.* Gildersleeve's Latin Grammar (New York, University Publishing Co.) edited by Lodge is unexcelled for this purpose. Bennett's Latin Language (Boston, Allyn & Bacon) will also be found a useful work on points of pronunciation, orthography, hidden quantity, accent, origin of inflectional forms, growth of syntactical constructions, *etc.*

For Synonyms there is the work of Doederlein, Handbook of Latin Synonyms. Andover, Mass. W. F. Draper; also Shumway, A Hand-book of Latin Synonyms. Boston, Ginn & Co. The lexicons also by their definitions give valuable assistance in distinguishing differences of meaning in synonymous words.

Antiquities. Under this head, the best single book is the recently revised edition of William Smith's

Dictionary of Greek and Roman Antiquities. London, John Murray; Boston, Little, Brown, & Co. 2 vols. Other works are:

Harper's Dictionary of Classical Literature and Antiquities. New York, American Book Co.
Seyffert. Dictionary of Classical Antiquities. London, S. Sonnenschein & Co. ; New York, Macmillan Co.
Rich. A Dictionary of Roman and Greek Antiquities. London and New York, Longmans, Green, & Co.

All of these are dictionaries arranged on the alphabetical plan. Books of a different arrangement are:

Abbott, F. F. Roman Political Institutions. Boston, Ginn & Co.
Ramsay. A Manual of Roman Antiquities. London, Griffin ; New York, Charles Scribner's Sons.
Gow. Companion to School Classics. London, Macmillan & Co. (Ltd.) ; New York, The Macmillan Co.
Hill, G. F. Illustrations of School Classics. London, Macmillan & Co. (Ltd.) ; New York, Macmillan Co.

For the narrower field of private life may be noted:

Preston & Dodge. The Private Life of the Romans. Boston, Benjamin H. Sanborn & Co.
Fowler, W. Warde. Social Life at Rome. London, Macmillan & Co. (Ltd.); New York, The Macmillan Co.
Abbott, F. F. Society and Politics in Ancient Rome. New York, Charles Scribner's Sons.
Becker. Gallus, or Roman Scenes in the Time of Augustus. London and New York, Longmans, Green, & Co.

There are also several publications of plates which are well worthy of a place in the school library:

Cybulski, S. Bilderatlas, and Tabulae quibus antiquitates Romanae illustrantur. Leipzig, Koehler.
Baumeister, A. Bilder aus dem griechischen und römischen Altertum, für Schüler zusammengestellt. Munich, R. Oldenbourg.
Schreiber, Th. Atlas of Classical Antiquities. London, Macmillan & Co. (Ltd.) ; New York, Macmillan Co.

Topography and Archæology. Recent years have been rich in works on the topography and remains Topography and Archæ-ology. of Rome and-Pompeii. The best books are:

Platner, S. B. Ancient Rome. Boston, Allyn & Bacon.

Middleton, J. H. The Remains of Ancient Rome. London, A. & C. Black; New York, Macmillan Co.

Lanciani, R. The Ruins and Excavations of Ancient Rome. London, Macmillan & Co. (Ltd.); Boston, Houghton, Mifflin, & Co.

Mau, A. Pompeii: Its Life and Art. London, Macmillan & Co. (Ltd.); New York, Macmillan Co.

Geography. In the field of geography, the most convenient books are William Smith's Dictionary of Greek and Roman Geography. London, John Murray; Geography. Boston, Little, Brown, & Co. 2 vols.; or the same author's Classical Dictionary of Biography, Mythology, and Geography. London, John Murray. This last is an abbreviation and combination of two of Dr. Smith's larger dictionaries. These, however, are somewhat out of date. Recent and of the very highest authority is Kiepert's Ancient Geography. A useful little manual is Tozer's Classical Geography. London, Macmillan & Co. (Ltd.); New York, American Book Co. The best classical atlas is that of Kiepert. London, Williams & Norgate; Boston, Benjamin H. Sanborn & Co.

History. Every school library should contain the standard Roman histories: History.

Mommsen. The History of Rome. London, Macmillan & Co. (Ltd.); New York, Charles Scribner's Sons. 4 vols.

Merivale. History of the Romans under the Empire. London and New York, Longmans, Green, & Co. 8 vols.

Mommsen. The Provinces of the Roman Empire from Cæsar to Diocletian. London, Macmillan & Co. (Ltd.); New York, Charles Scribner's Sons. 2 vols.

Ferrero, G. Greatness and Decline of Rome. New York, Putnams. 5 vols.

Gibbon. The Decline and Fall of the Roman Empire. London, Methuen & Co. 7 vols.; New York, Macmillan Co. 4 vols.

Besides these standard works, a number of volumes in the Epoch Series are of very great value, presenting, as they do, the chief facts and features of important eras in condensed form. Especially to be noted are:

Ihne, Early Rome; Merivale, The Roman Triumvirates; Capes, The Early Empire; also Capes, The Age of the Antonines. All of these are published in London and New York by Longmans, Green, & Co.

Smith's Dictionary of Greek and Roman Biography and Mythology (London, John Murray; Boston, Little, Brown, & Co. 3 vols.), though now somewhat antiquated, is still an excellent work.

Smith's Classical Dictionary (Biography, Mythology, Geography), an abbreviation of the larger dictionaries, is also entirely adequate for all ordinary purposes of reference.

Roman Literature. Not much is needed here, and this little is fortunately accessible in the excellent **Roman** manual of J. W. Mackail: Latin Literature. **Literature.** London, John Murray; New York, Charles Scribner's Sons. Other admirable books are J. W. Duff, A Literary History of Rome. New York, Charles Scribner's Sons; H. N. Fowler, History of Roman Literature. New York, D. Appleton & Co.; W. C. Lawton, Introduction to Classical Latin Literature. New York, Charles Scribner's Sons. Excellent notices of the Latin writers may also be found in Smith's Dictionary of Greek and Roman Biography and Mythology, or in the shorter Classical Dictionary (Biography, Mythology, and Geography) of the same author.

Mythology. The fullest works of reference are either the larger work of Smith, Dictionary of Greek and Roman Biography and Mythology, or the smaller **Mythology.** Classical Dictionary of the same author already noted. Of smaller works may be mentioned:

Guerber, Helen. Myths of Greece and Rome. New York, American Book Co.

Gayley, Charles M. Classic Myths in English Literature. Boston, Ginn & Co.

Murray, A. S. Manual of Mythology. New York, Charles Scribner's Sons.

Harrington and Tolman. Greek and Roman Mythology. Boston, Benjamin H. Sanborn & Co.

Roman Sculpture. In this field we now have the admirable work of Eugénie Strong, Roman Sculpture. London, Duckworth; New York, Charles Scribner's Sons.

Bibliographical. A suggestive little book is Harrington, Helps to the Intelligent Study of College Preparatory Latin. Boston; Ginn & Co. Useful, **Bibliographical Helps.** too, is the List of Books Recommended for a High School Classical Library by the Michigan Schoolmasters' Club. Ann Arbor, Sheehan & Co.

MAPS. A few good maps hung upon the wall or suspended from rollers are a practical necessity for effective Latin teaching. One needs a map **Maps.** of the ancient world, also special maps of at least Italy, Greece, and Gaul; if possible, also a good topographical map of Rome and vicinity. The foregoing are ample for ordinary needs, but they ought to be in constant requisition. The best maps are those prepared by Kiepert and published by D. Reimer, Berlin.

PHOTOGRAPHS. These are now fortunately so cheap as to be within the reach of all schools. A judicious selection of photographs of famous classical **Photographs.** localities, famous buildings, or famous works of art does much to brighten the school-room and to add reality to the subject matter of the authors read. For a suggested list of photographs, see p. 331.

CASTS. So, too, a few casts of the famous portrait busts of distinguished Romans are often a **Casts.** desirable addition to the class-room. Like photographs, they are effective in lending vividness to a study of the past.

CHAPTER VIII

THE PREPARATION OF THE TEACHER

REFERENCES.

Russell, J. E. German Higher Schools. New York and London:
Longmans, Green, & Co. 1899. Chapter xviii. "The Professional
Training of Teachers."

Bolton, F. E. The Secondary School System of Germany. New
York: D. Appleton & Co. 1900. London: Edward Arnold. Chapter ii.
pp. 55–119.

THUS far no mention has been made of what must be
admitted by all to be the most vital element in the organization of the secondary school, namely, the teacher.
I shall make no attempt to sketch the requisites in the
way of character and of personality which must be
sought in the efficient teacher, whether of Latin or
any other branch.   Nor shall I call attention to the
importance of that capacity to give instruction which
seems to me inborn and as impossible to impart as
health or personal beauty.   I shall speak only of the
academic training desirable for the man or woman who
presumably possesses these first requisites of character,
personality, and talent for teaching.

In the preparation of our teachers is to be found
perhaps the weakest point of American edu-

Our American Training of Teachers Defective. cation.   An investigation of the causes for
this might be interesting and profitable, but
it is out of place here.   The fact, I believe,
is incontestable that we are far behind the great

nations of Europe — Germany, France, England, Norway, Sweden, Austria, Switzerland, and even Russia — in the loftiness of our conception of the teacher's function and in the seriousness of our preparation for the teacher's duties.

A better sentiment is now manifesting itself, and it is to the credit of our best educational leaders that they are keenly conscious of our shortcomings and are straining every energy to remedy them. Yet the task is so large, and its importance as yet so far from being generally appreciated, that it certainly cannot be superfluous to call attention here to our great deficiencies in the training of our teachers of Latin.

Let us look a moment at the preparation of the Latin teacher of the German secondary schools, the *Gymnasien*. In the first place, such a teacher has studied Latin for nine years and Greek for six years at some *Gymnasium*. This work extends ordinarily from the ninth or tenth to the eighteenth or nineteenth year. During this period the pupil reads, with a thoroughness unknown to us in America, substantially the following authors and works: Nepos, Cæsar (*Gallic War*, i-vii), Ovid (*Metamorphoses*, selections), Virgil, (*Æneid*), Cicero (seven Orations and selections from the Letters), Livy (i, xxi, xxii), Horace (*Odes*, i-iv, selections; *Epodes*, *Satires*, *Epistles*, selections), Tacitus (*Annals*, i, ii; *Histories*, i; *Germania*). Besides this there is an extensive amount of private reading in Sallust, Livy, Curtius, Cicero, and other authors. The language, too, receives constant attention not only in the minute study of the grammar, but also by way of writing Latin. In this latter exercise a wonderful facility is gained by the students of the higher classes of the *Gymnasien*. I have witnessed students in the highest

Preparation of German Teachers.

Course of Study in the Gymnasium.

class translate two solid pages of continuous German into Latin within thirty minutes. This was an oral exercise, and the German was not closely modelled on any original Latin, as is often customary with us. I remember well the fine disdain of the rector of this particular school, when I asked him whether this was a review lesson.

With these attainments in Latin and with corresponding attainments in Greek as the result of a six years' study of that subject, the student comes to the university at the age of eighteen or nineteen to specialize more closely in his chosen field. Yet up to this time, he has not devoted himself exclusively to classics; these have been the chief and most exacting studies of the gymnasial course, but mathematics are pursued through quadratic equations, solid geometry, and plane trigonometry; much attention is paid to the German language, literature, and history; French is pursued for several years; natural science, including natural history, physics, and chemistry, is pursued two hours a week for the entire nine years; writing, drawing, singing, and gymnastics are also included; English and Hebrew are elective. Such is the liberal foundation of the young man of eighteen or nineteen who leaves the *Gymnasium* for the University, and who, I assume, is intending to fit himself for the career of a teacher of
University Study.
Latin in German secondary schools. Arrived at the university, he devotes himself almost exclusively to the study of the classical languages, literatures, and civilizations. He takes courses in historical Latin grammar, in historical Latin syntax, on Roman literature, Roman history, epigraphy, private antiquities, political antiquities, archæology, metric, palæography, Roman comedy, *etc.*; he becomes the member of one of the seminaries and devotes days to preparing a paper

on perhaps only twenty lines of a Satire of Horace, endeavouring to constitute the text with scientific precision and to interpret the passage, in the light of all accessible information, in the most thorough and accurate fashion. His courses in Greek are similar in character. Besides this, he must take some work in philosophy, ancient or modern, and in the science of education.

The minimum period of residence for those preparing to become teachers is legally three years, but in practice the period is more often four years, or even five. When he has finished his period of study, the candidate presents himself for the trying ordeal of the teachers' examination, without passing which no one can secure a license to teach.

The Examination for Teachers.

This examination involves (1) a searching test of the candidate's knowledge of the classics; (2) a knowledge of philosophy (psychology, logic, ethics) and the science of education; (3) a familiarity with the German language and literature; (4) a knowledge of the doctrines of his religion.

"The examination is both oral and written. The written test comes first, and consists in the writing of elaborate essays on themes assigned by the commission. One theme is on some topic in philosophy or pedagogy, and is designed to test the candidate's knowledge of the philosophical basis of pedagogy and didactics, and of the development of educational thought. . . . If the applicant has published something of note, as, for instance, a dissertation for the degree of doctor of philosophy, it may be offered as a substitute for one of the essays. Essays that deal with a classical language must be written in Latin; with the modern languages, in French or English, as the case may be. . . . Six weeks are allowed for the preparation of each essay, and the commission is empowered to grant an extension of six weeks, — making twelve weeks in all, if necessary, on the subject." [1]

This written examination, if satisfactory, is followed by an oral examination before a specially appointed examiner. If both the written and oral tests are successfully met, the candidate receives a certificate authorizing him to teach.

"The intending teacher, even with his certificate in his hand, has yet other gauntlets to run. The certificate
The Probe-Jahre.
of itself confers no right to teach. Something more than general culture and minute scholarship is required. It is safe to say that Germany owes more to the pedagogical training of her teachers than to any other factor in their preparation. It is the professional spirit, which every German teacher feels, that differentiates him from his species in other countries, and this spirit is the result chiefly of his pedagogical training." [2] Accordingly the German candidate is obliged to spend two additional years of apprenticeship even after he has passed the rigid teachers' examination. The first of these two years is spent in a *Seminarium*, where the intending teacher receives special advanced instruction in the practical problems of the secondary school. The second year is devoted to actual instruction (only seven or eight hours a week) under the supervision of some experienced teacher.

Such is the preparation of the German teacher who is to go into the secondary school and give instruction in the beginning Latin work, in Nepos, Cæsar, Cicero, Virgil, *etc.* Contrast with this rigid and exacting course

---

[1] Russell, *German Higher Schools*, p. 359 *f.*
[2] Russell, *German Higher Schools*, p. 363.

of training the conditions prevalent in our own country! In the first place, teaching with us does not rank as a profession. As a result, the body of teachers is recruited largely from the ranks of recent college graduates, who resort to teaching as a makeshift while they are accumulating the means to pursue their special preparation for medicine, the law, or something else; or from young women who turn to teaching as a respectable occupation during the period they spend between the completion of their education and marriage. Even among the small number of those who enter the vocation of Latin teaching deliberately with the intention of making it their life work, few are at all adequately equipped for their tasks. Many of them have never been to college at all. Some few have had one or two years of undergraduate study of Latin. Fewer have made it a serious study throughout their course, while the number of those who have had a year or two of graduate study is so small as to constitute practically a vanishing quantity in the great sea of poorly equipped teachers of the subject.

Without good teachers, it must be impossible to have good teaching, and we shall never have good teachers of Latin or anything else (except as exceptions to the prevailing mediocrity) until we set as a first requisite a *lofty standard of knowledge of the subject to be taught.* Force of character, magnetic personality, pedagogic skill, are all necessary in their way, but the man or woman who possesses all of these and who is not saturated with the most thorough knowledge of the subject he or she has to teach is incapable of making the teacher that we have a right to demand in our secondary schools, not merely in Latin but in other branches as well. In my judgment, the greatest defect in American education to-day is the prevailing superficiality in the attainments of American teachers.   They do not know their subjects. At least they do not know Latin as well as they ought in order to teach it even with a moderate degree of success.   There are noble exceptions to this sweeping statement, which is meant only to characterize the general field of Latin teaching.   Nor would I pass judgment on the mass of the incompetent.   They are almost without exception men and women of character, of serious and earnest purpose, and faithful, often to the detriment of their health, in the performance of their tasks.   They are, nevertheless, endeavouring to achieve the impossible, — to perform a work involving the employment of large resources, without ever having secured the necessary preparation.   They are victims of a system which nothing but a quickening of the public conscience, local, state, and national, can alter.   But the change is inevitable.   It will not come in a moment; it is now in progress, however, and the devoted teacher should be the one above all others to give comfort and support to this forward movement, for it will give to the teacher new ideals, new life, and new dignity.   It is to be hoped that the time is approaching, and is not far distant, when teachers in the American secondary schools, like those in Germany, will, as a result of their completer preparation for their profession, not merely be better teachers, but will also, as a result of their enthusiasm for Latin and their devotion to it, be numbered among the ranks of those who by their labour shall, as investigators, add to the sum of our knowledge of classical antiquity.   In Germany valuable work of this kind is constantly emanating from the teachers of the secondary schools.   A number of the very ablest classical productions in that country have come from this source.

Our Teachers not themselves Responsible for the American System.

To be specific, it may be well to sketch briefly the range and degree of knowledge that may be fairly expected of the teacher of Latin.   First of all, **A Fair** the teacher must have an exact knowledge of **Demand.** the Latin language, for the language is the indispensable instrument with which the pupil works in his study of Latin.   How wide must this knowledge of the language be on the teacher's part?   What should it embrace? Will a thorough mastery of some approved manual of grammar suffice?   Far from it!   The teacher should be above any one book.   He must be familiar with many works of divergent views.   In practical teaching he will meet, or ought to meet, incessantly with problems covering the whole range of the linguistic field, some suggested by his own study and experience, others suggested by his eager pupils.   If these problems are to be met and solved, instead of being brushed aside in indolence or by artful evasion, the teacher must know the means available for their solution.   Does some question of inflexions come up, — the vocative of *deus;* the perfect of *eo?*   He must know the manuals that afford the fullest and freshest information.   Is it a question of spelling, — *quom* vs. *cum* or *quum; Juppiter* or *Jupiter?*   It is not enough to accept the statement of a grammar, however excellent; the teacher must know the sources and be able to gather the evidence for himself.   Is it a question of pronunciation, as of *v, ph, th, æ?*   Or of quantity, as in *victoria, jussus?*   Or of syntactical theory or practice?   Or some other of the important linguistic questions which are perpetually pressing for answer?   In every case the teacher ought to know the literature of his subject and be able to draw his own independent conclusion in view of the available evidence.

But while the language must be put first and foremost in the equipment of the adequately prepared teacher, there are many other fields in which he must be more than a tyro. Some special knowledge of ancient geography should be his, — particularly some knowledge of the topography of ancient Rome. The historical disciplines, too, have a large claim to make, which cannot safely be ignored. Under this head come not merely political history, but the allied disciplines of philosophy, mythology, and the history of literature. Again we have the broad domain of Roman antiquities, — political, private, religious, and legal, a knowledge of each of them being practically indispensable. Some knowledge of the nature and methods of textual criticism, too, must the teacher have before he can properly understand the condition in which the ancient texts have come down to us and the spirit in which their modern interpretation should be approached. That the prospective teacher also should have read widely in the field of the classical literature will of course be taken for granted, and that his familiarity with Latin is such that he can interpret any ordinary passage of simple prose without extensive recourse to lexicon or commentary.

The foregoing demands by no means exhaust the possibilities of the teacher's preliminary training. I have designedly omitted many important branches, such as the Italic dialects (Oscan and Umbrian), epigraphy, palæography, along with the various departments of archæology, such as architecture, sculpture, pottery, painting, numismatics, to say nothing of others. I have simply outlined the " irreducible minimum " which it seems to me the teacher must have in order adequately to meet the legitimate demands which will be made upon him in the conscientious performance of his daily duty. One other addition, however, must be made, namely, a knowledge of Greek. The teacher of Greek may perhaps do without Latin, but the Latin teacher cannot do without Greek. All Roman civilization is so dominated by Greek influences and Greek ideas, that the person ignorant of Greek is incapable of understanding and interpreting to others the significance of Roman life and thought.

When our Latin teachers have something like the equipment I have described we shall no longer merit the reproach of a recent critic,[1] who declares that the majority of our high-school teachers are hardly fit to teach in a primary school, and the majority of primary teachers are just enough educated to fill a salesgirl's place in a millinery store.

Obviously such training as I have described involves no small outlay of time and means. It involves specialization in Latin throughout the college course, and it involves probably at least two years of severer specialization in classics after graduation. We may be slow in attaining the standard indicated, but it is bound to come, and until we reach it, or something approximating it, we cannot honestly claim that we are doing our whole duty by the pupils of our secondary schools.

One word as to "methods." It seems to me that in our study of pedagogy we are often apt to overrate the importance of these. As I understand it, the Limitations of science of education aims at two things: first, "Methods." to give the history of educational theory and practice; secondly, to lay down certain fundamental psychological principles applicable to all teaching. That it should prescribe a definite and mechanical scheme for imparting instruction in Latin or anything else would be preposterous. Teaching is the very reverse of anything mechanical; it is simply constant skilful adaptation to the momentary problem in hand. This problem varies

---

[1] Professor Münsterberg in *Atlantic Monthly*, May, 1900.

with the subject and the minds with which the teacher is brought in contact. It is an unusual accident if precisely the same situation confronts the same teacher twice within any reasonable interval. There may be "methods" for reducing ores, for making steel, for treating measles and sore eyes, but the human mind is no such constant factor as even the least constant of these things I have mentioned. It recognises no universal solvent or prescription. In other words, teaching is an art demanding the fullest knowledge, the fullest judgment, the fullest skill; it is not intellectual quackery. Young teachers, I believe, cannot too carefully treasure this truth.

CONCLUDING NOTE

IN the foregoing pages I have endeavoured to discuss seriously the leading problems of secondary Latin education as they now present themselves in this country. Inspired by profound convictions as to the abiding worth of Latin, I have naturally felt also a deep solicitude for the study. With this feeling I have spoken plainly on those points where current tendencies and current practice have seemed questionable or unwise. I have not hesitated to avow my belief that most of the changes which have characterized the study of Latin in our secondary schools in the course of the last twenty-five years have worked, and, so far as they are still operative, are working to the distinct detriment of the study. The Roman pronunciation, the prevailing type of beginner's book, the bulky grammar, the newer method of teaching Latin composition, the insistence on the subjective method (direct interpretation) in the early stages of the study, — all these have long seemed to me to mark serious errors of educational theory and practice. That scores of devoted teachers who have likewise given conscientious thought to the same problems cherish opposite views on all of these questions, I am, of course, aware, as my extended consideration of their views in the foregoing discussion amply shows. It is for practical teachers in the light of their reason and experience to determine where the truth lies. To promote its ultimate determination has been the sincere purpose of this volume.

The friends of Latin should soberly consider that the study is now on trial as never before. The attacks against it are not merely reactionary, nor do they proceed alone from the prejudiced or the ill-informed. They represent in many instances the deliberate convictions of serious students of the problems of education, — convictions which it is idle and wrong to ignore. If the study is to retain its position as a permanent part of the school curriculum, it can do so only by the positive results it shows itself capable of producing. Whether these shall commend themselves to educators will depend not upon any theoretical claims or advantages of the study, but upon wise and efficient instruction.

THE TEACHING OF GREEK IN THE SECONDARY SCHOOL

BY

GEORGE P. BRISTOL, A.M.

PROFESSOR OF GREEK IN CORNELL UNIVERSITY

The Teaching of Greek in the Secondary School

INTRODUCTION

THE AIM OF GREEK STUDY IN THE HIGH SCHOOL

A selective bibliography for use in framing classical programmes for secondary schools, compiled by Isaac B. Burgess, is to be found in THE SCHOOL REVIEW, vol. v. pp. 625–635. It contains a carefully arranged list of articles bearing on the subject of Greek in the high school. The classification of the subject matter of these articles there made is as follows: I. Facts as to the present condition of Latin and Greek in American schools. II. Foreign secondary schools. III. Relation of Greek and Latin to the modern languages and to the courses of the grammar schools. IV. Specific suggested programmes. V. Psychology and method. VI. Miscellaneous facts and arguments bearing on the classical programmes of secondary schools.

THAT the position of Greek in the public high school at the present time is not a settled one will, I think, be granted. The attacks upon it are too frequent in number, and too varied in their character to permit its defenders to rest secure. It seems to me that this condition is due in large measure to the relation in which the public high school in many sections of the country stands to the older academy. An important function of these academies was the preparation of boys for college. The admission to college was based partly upon a knowledge of Greek, and the door was barred against the student who could not offer at least something in this subject. But gradually the boy without Greek found his way into

Position of Greek now.

college, though not at first by the main entrance. First a side door was opened to him, and if he passed through college without a knowledge of Greek, his diploma indicated this fact by showing a different degree. But after a while the " regular course " and the Bachelor of Arts degree were not limited to the student of Greek. Latin was longer required, but at the present time, though not so largely as is the case with Greek, has ceased to be indispensable to a college course and to what is called somewhat indefinitely a " liberal education."

This is the present state of things with which we have to deal, and this state of things has disposed of one argument for the study of Greek in the high school, *viz.*, that it is necessary to enable a pupil to enter college. The case of Greek must be defended on its merits. Unless there is value enough in its study for the student who does not get beyond the high school to justify its retention, Greek will ultimately disappear from the curriculum of the *public* high school. Of the *private* high school it is not possible to speak with certainty. It contains a much larger proportion of students who are looking forward to a college course, and for this class Greek, even when not required at the college of their choice, is apt to be regarded in the light of a college course in it. But I believe that we shall not be able to hold permanently the prominent place for Greek in secondary education which it has occupied unless we can successfully maintain two points: first, that the study of Greek gives results worth having; and, secondly, that these results cannot be reached in any other way. The study of Greek means hard and prolonged labour. There is no " thirteen weeks in Greek," with a laying by of the subject at the end of that time. Two years of continuous study is the minimum period recognised. Are the benefits derived therefrom commensurate with the work?

I assume that two objects at least are to be gained by the study of Greek in the secondary schools: first, to enable a student to acquire the ability to read a Greek text with the help of grammar, dictionary, and an edition of the author read containing some commentary and some helps on the more difficult passages. Further, to read a considerable portion of one author and something at least of another. Secondly, to gain such knowledge of the principles underlying the formation and inflection of words in Greek as will enable him to understand those principles in their application in Greek itself, and in their large and ever-increasing use in the vocabularies of the various sciences, and in the vocabulary of science common to all educated English-speaking people.

Two Objects in High School Study of Greek.

Under the first of these two heads, by the words "ability to read," I do not mean the ability to stumble through a sentence and to get the general drift of the thought merely — I mean that complete knowledge of the structure of the Greek sentence, which detects the shifted emphasis of a changed word order, which distinguishes between the meaning of attributive and predicate position in the sentence, which notes carefully the various balancing particles and so grasps the proper relations of the various words in the clause, and of clauses in the sentence. I mean a feeling for those delicate shadings in expression and in composition which make a Greek sentence a model of art. To acquire this knowledge means careful study and close attention to many little (*i. e.* minute) things. And it is just at this point that the study of Greek is often and violently attacked. This petty detail is considered in many quarters as of very slight or even of no value. We are told that the " Greek spirit," is the great thing to be gained; "why, then, should one waste the pupil's time with

Ability to read Greek.

struggles over accents, over particles with minute differences of meaning?" I say at once that this appreciation
The "Greek   of the "Greek spirit" is the greatest thing of
Spirit."   all. It is the goal toward which all should
strive. But it is not to be reached by any superficial
study of the various forms of art in which it found
expression. This very Greek spirit consisted, in part at
least, in a faithful attention to details, and it is in an
equally faithful attention to these details that we shall
see and appreciate it ourselves. It is given to a Keats
to grasp this spirit by intuition, but for the most of us
Hesiod's words hold true:

> τῆς δ' ἀρετῆς ἱδρῶτα θεοὶ προπάροιθεν ἔθηκαν
> ἀθάνατοι· μακρὸς δὲ καὶ ὄρθιος οἶμος ἐς αὐτήν.

Much is said and much is written on this point. I
quote the following statements which appeared not long
The Example ago in a journal of sound views in general,
of Macaulay because they seem to me to illustrate well a
very common attitude toward this subject. The writer is
arguing against the present methods of teaching the
classics, and in the course of his article says: "Everybody remembers what a prodigious lot of Latin and
Greek Macaulay read on his outward voyage to India
and while at Calcutta. He wrote from Calcutta in 1834:
'I read much and particularly Greek, and I find that I
am, in all essentials, still not a bad scholar. . . . I read,
however, not as I read at college, but as a man of the
world. If I do not know a word, I pass it by, unless it
is important to the sense. If I find, as I have of late
often found, a passage which refuses to give up its meaning at second reading, I let it alone. I have read during
the last fortnight, before breakfast, three books of Herodotus, and four plays of Æschylus.' It is perfectly
evident that Macaulay had some use and joy of his clas-

sics ' as a man of the world,' and it is notorious that not one American college-bred man in a hundred has that easy-going familiarity with Latin and Greek which he had. Is the discipline of half-knowledge gained by the drudgery of the grammar and lexicon in the old way so precious and upbuilding that it must be forever set above thorough knowledge and mastery? It is not the course of instruction that needs revising, but the methods of teaching."

The passage quoted from Macaulay is found in Trevelyan's *Life and Letters of Lord Macaulay*, vol. i. p. 376. In connection with it should be read the remaining pages of the volume. I wish to insert here one sentence further. Macaulay says (p. 379) : " I think myself very fortunate in having been able to return to these great masters while still in the full vigour of life, and when my taste and judgment are mature. Most people read all the Greek that they ever read before they are five and twenty. They never find time for such studies afterward till they are in the decline of life ; and then their knowledge of the language is in a great measure lost, and cannot easily be recovered." This sentence follows directly the statement that the blessing of loving literature as he loved it had been the chief means of keeping him from sinking under the heavy blow of domestic bereavement, and that chief among all his books were his Greek authors.

It seems to me that this argument on the proper method of teaching the classics in so far as it seeks to base on the example of Macaulay proves **What Macaulay's Case really means.** exactly the opposite of what it is intended to prove. I assume that it was intended to prove that, since Macaulay read as a man of the world, skipping a word now and then, or neglecting even a whole sentence, so it would be profitable for a boy to be trained in this way to read his Xenophon or his Cicero. But in fact Macaulay read like a man of the world, and was able so to read, because he had back of him long years of careful reading in school and in college. It was the power and the knowledge gained in these years of toil which enabled him to secure in after life the pleasure he so dearly loved and prized. I venture a citation or two from his letters home while at school. When thirteen he writes: " I do Xenophon every day and twice a week the Odyssey, Latin verses twice a week. We get by heart Greek grammar or Virgil every evening." This on week days. " On Sunday," he says a little later, " we learn a chapter in the Greek Testament, without doing it with a dictionary, like other lessons " This, or something like this, lasted for five years, only to be followed when he went up to the University by an amount of reading in the classics which would astonish an American college graduate, a college man even who had made the classics his specialty. No, if any argument is to be drawn from the case of Macaulay, so often cited, it is an argument for thorough work from the start and for a longer continuance of these studies than is now common.

But let me say frankly that I do not believe that in the three years (to say nothing of a shorter period) of preparatory study, the average pupil can gain the power, so often claimed and so often (apparently) demanded, of " reading Attic prose at sight." I am not convinced, however, that this power or ability is the ultimate test of the value of the study. What this study *can do*, and what this study rightly applied and rightly directed *ought to do*, is to give a habit of accuracy in reading the text; I mean, in seeing all there is of a word because all of it — prefix, root, and suffix — must be taken into account in determining the exact meaning it carries with it. The very strangeness of the

Necessary Limitations in Study.

forms will compel this searching analysis of them. That carelessness in reading of our own language is all too common among pupils in our schools, is a common complaint of teachers. A lack of training in exact observation and in exact statement is too frequently observed among men of college education, and I believe that much of it is due to careless habits of youth and of school. I do not wish to be understood as saying that the study of Greek is the only discipline which gives, or which can give, this training in accuracy, but that this training is one of the results of the study rightly followed.

Another result of the study of Greek is the acquaintance with some of the best of the world's literature. Not to press the question as to the literary value of Xenophon's *Anabasis*, which is, I believe, greater than is often admitted, the student in a three years' course can make the acquaintance of Plato in addition, or of some other prose author, and even in the minimum of two years he can get a considerable amount of Homer. This is no mean achievement if viewed from the standpoint of the literary gain alone. But all the while the drill in translating has been forcing him to think on the means of expression in the two languages, and by the delicate shadings in the Greek it should have compelled an equally careful consideration of the expression of the same thought in English.

The second of the two main results attainable in the school study of Greek is the ability to understand better the great number of modern scientific (in the widest sense) terms in English. I think there can be no difference of opinion as to the desirability of this result. If we except the study of the Law, whose vocabulary is largely English, or English with Latin elements, there is not one of the learned professions the vocabulary of which does not include an immense stock of words derived from the Greek, or formed at least from Greek elements. But it is often asserted that this knowledge can be obtained by studying just enough Greek to be able to recognise these elements or these words. I am inclined to doubt the efficiency of this amount of study of Greek for the end proposed. I doubt if the understanding of the compounds is much clearer than it would be if the words were looked up in an English dictionary, and their elements learned mechanically therein. I doubt it for this reason — learning a foreign word is an act of arbitrary memory, and the word will in all probability be forgotten unless by seeing it frequently in reading its meaning and form have become thoroughly fixed in the student's mind. It is only by seeing a word many times and in various associations that it becomes a familiar acquaintance. I think that reading is absolutely necessary to the fixing of a vocabulary.

So I think that the second of the two ends I have assumed above is reached in close connection with, and

Conclusion.

through the means of the first. In the following chapters I shall have constantly in mind this proposition. The great aim of the study of Greek in the high school is to gain the power to read Greek, and to read as much Greek as can be done with care in the time given to its study. In doing this many lessons will be learned in related lines, — in history, in art, in the problems which faced the Greeks as individuals and as organized in society. All of these manifestations of the activity of the Greek mind are intensely interesting and valuable for study, but the language in which they brought so much of their thought to expression must remain the primary object of attention in the school period of study.

CHAPTER I

PRONUNCIATION

REFERENCES.[1]

Blass, F. The Pronunciation of Ancient Greek. Translated from the third German edition by W. J. Purton. Cambridge, University Press. 1890.

This is the best work on the subject. It gives a history of the controversy in modern times about the pronunciation of ancient Greek, and states with sufficient fulness the evidence upon which the method now generally followed in schools is based. Every teacher should have access to it, and should read it carefully. The large Historical Greek Grammar of Jannaris, Macmillan & Co., 1897, furnishes an elaborate argument for the " Modern Greek method," but it is not a book from which a teacher in the high school can derive much practical assistance. A most instructive and valuable contribution to our knowledge of certain points in the pronunciation of Greek consonants was made in 1896 by J. J. Hess in an article dealing with transcriptions of Egyptian words in the Greek alphabet in the second century A. D. It is in *Indogermanische Forschungen*, vol. vi. pp. 123-135. A statement of the case for the modern Greek pronunciation in EDUCATIONAL REVIEW, vol. i. p. 265, by G. C. Sawyer. Also in vol. iv. p. 492, by MacMullen, and vol. v. p. 481, by J. S. Blackie. A reply to these in vol. vi. p. 379, by G. M. Whicher. It may safely be said that the best authorities do not accept the theories of those who would have us accept the modern Greek pronunciation on the ground that it represents faithfully the pronunciation of the fourth or fifth century B. C. It is possible to make out a case for the modern Greek pronunciation, but not upon *that* basis. See B. I. Wheeler on *The Question of Language-Standard in Modern Greece*, AMERICAN JOURNAL OF PHILOLOGY, vol. xviii. p. 19.

---

[1] I have not attempted in these references to give anything like a complete list of works on the various topics, or even always of the most important. My aim has been in this, as in the rest of my work, to help the teacher to the most simple and direct works bearing on this subject. I have always preferred English books and articles in journals to those in foreign languages when it seemed possible.

15

H. W. Chandler. A Practical Introduction to Greek Accentuation. Second edition. Oxford, Clarendon Press. 1881. A work of great usefulness. Gives rules for the accentuation of the various categories of words, and a very large number of illustrative examples, with an index of words grouped according to their terminations.

Benjamin I. Wheeler. Der Griechische Nominalaccent. Strassburg, Trübner. 1885. A valuable study of the historical development of the Greek accent.

WITH the first lesson in Greek, as in any language, we are confronted by the question of pronunciation. It is The Question of supreme importance, and it cannot be is Funda-mental. avoided. For pronounce we must, rightly or wrongly, and it is just as easy to start in the right way as in any other, while such a start saves much labour later on, and makes possible an accuracy not otherwise attainable.[1]

Language is speech, not writing. As most of our teaching is by talking to one another, so the words we Speech and use must be exact in form, if we are to be Writing. understood and to understand in return. The ear must be trained as well as the eye. The written letters and words are merely a means of making clear through the medium of sight the real words, *i. e.* sounds. It is all important, then, that these real words should have a fixed relation to their eye symbols, the written words. In Greek this relation is a simpler one than in English, for, excepting the varying quantity of the sounds denoted by *a ι υ*, each sound has one written symbol and one only. Conversely each written symbol denotes only one sound. In English the sound is often no clew to the spelling, and the reducing of unaccented

---

[1] Some excellent observations on the necessity of a correct habit in pronunciation and of the early forming of that habit may be seen in THE SCHOOL REVIEW for February, 1900, on page 88. They are contained in a report to the Association of Colleges and Preparatory Schools of the Southern States of a committee on Programme of Studies, and are by Chancellor J. H. Kirkland of Vanderbilt University.

vowels to a uniform value makes it much more difficult to keep ear symbol and eye symbol correlated in memory. For instance, a spelling of the Greek word στρατηγός as στρατιγος, lately noticed by me, gives clear proof of failure in pronouncing to distinguish η and ι when not accented. This is common enough in English, as may be seen in such words as *teachable* and *visible*, whose middle syllable is sounded like the *u* in *but*. For Greek, as for Latin, however, it is entirely wrong. If one of the results of the study of Greek is to train the eye in accurate observation in reading, it ought to do as much for the ear in the real reading, *i. e.* speaking.

Language is constantly changing. Our own language shares this principle of change in common with all others, ancient and modern. This change, though constant, is so gradual that Constant Change in Language. we usually fail to take note of the minute variations, and it is not until in a given word, or in a group of words, the difference in sound has become so marked that we are struck by it, that we speak of a difference in dialect. For instance, think of the varying pronunciation in English of the word *bath*. Between the extremes *bawth* and *baath* lie a large number of actual sounds given the word in various parts of the country. Denoting one of the sounds above indicated by *a* and the other by *z*, it is evident that we may have a large number of intermediate sounds each of which differs from its nearest related sound by a very small difference. It is only the trained ear that recognises the divergence of one of them from the next in the series, while the great difference between *a* and *z* would strike even the most uneducated listener. These changes are constantly going on in all living tongues, and we detect them by careful attention, and by training our ears to recognise the " correct " sounds, as we hear them spoken, and by imitating these alone. For languages no longer spoken this is impossible, and so the rules for pronunciation have not the same degree of certainty as in the case of languages now in common use.

Further, if we apply the same system of pronunciation to widely separated periods of a language, it is evident'

But not in the Writing of it. that it cannot be equally true for all of these periods. The written symbols when once fixed are hard to change. As time goes on, however, they are interpreted differently, they are translated into different ear symbols, and so they are not really the same words. For example, we spell our words in English mostly as they were spelled in the sixteenth century, but we know that the sounds they represent are not the same sounds which they then represented; that is, the words (sounds) are not the same words now as then, though the eye symbols of them are the same. This eye picture of a word is like the photograph of a friend taken long ago. We recognise the features as those of our friend, but we know that it is not the picture of the man as he now looks.

For a language, then, whose literature covers a period of hundreds of years, no one system of pronunciation can be right. The English of Shakspere's time did not sound as we make it sound in reading his plays to-day. In the case of Greek, as of Latin, we must for the sake of uniformity, that we may understand one another, choose the pronunciation of some one period in the history of the language, and then apply this to all other periods. This is the only practical solution of the problem.

The pronunciation adopted for ancient Greek is that **Theory and Practice in Pronunciation.** believed to have been followed by the Athenians about the year 400 B. C. In practice, however, this is commonly considerably modified, with the object of getting rid of some sounds which are strange to our ears, and with a view to ease in actual use. It seems to me wiser to admit frankly our departures from what is theoretically correct, and to defend them on the ground of practicality, than to spend too much effort in an attempt to reach the ideally perfect. I shall speak of the points in pronunciation which seem to me to be the most important in teaching the reading of Greek, and shall begin with the sounds of the vowels. First and chiefly, I regard it of the utmost importance that the student should learn the vowels *a ε ι* in their " European " values, and should always speak of them either by their Greek names ἄλφα, ἒ ψιλόν, ἰῶτα, or by repeating the sound itself, *ah, eh, ih.* The sounds connected with these symbols are about the same in Greek, Latin, French, and German, and there is an immense practical advantage in having their treatment uniform. I believe it a mistake in oral spelling of Greek, or of any foreign language, to use the English names for the letters. *E. g.,* spelling out to a student the letters *t-i-s-i-s* would undoubtedly lead him to write τίσις, but the reverse conclusion in his mind as to the pronunciation of what he had written could, if logical, only be false. Secondly, the sound of short *o, ὂ μικρόν,* is important. The difficulty in the pronunciation of this sound lies in keeping the short quantity of the sound and at the same time distinguishing it from *a.* In the United States " short *o* " as in *hot, lot, etc.,* is practically an *ăh.*[1]

The first of these two words, for example, does not often differ from the German word *hat.* The older and truer value of *ŏ* is still heard in the speech of some people, though rarely. It may be reached approximately

---

[1] See O. F. Emerson, History of the English Language, p. 209.

by shortening the vowel sound in the word *law*. Thus, *law, lawt, lăwt* (= *lot*). This vowel sound is of very frequent occurrence in Greek, and is of great importance in word formation and inflection. From the start effort should be made to have the student distinguish it from *a*. Another vowel sound often not marked with sufficient care is *υ*. The grammars give its value with practical unanimity. It should be given the sound of German *ü*, French *u*, in all cases when it is not found as the second element of a diphthong. In the diphthongs, *αυ, ευ, ηυ*, it retains its older value of the Latin *u*. This is like English *oo* in *boot*, though not long in quantity. Care taken in sounding this vowel at the outset will prevent the formation of a habit which leads to the sounding of φεύγων and φυγών alike as *fewgōne*. *η* is almost without exception given the value of English *a* in *ba-bel*, though the true sound is nearer that of *a* in *babble*. In English we represent the bleating of sheep by *baa*. Cratinus, a poet of the fifth century B. C., represented it by βῆ βῆ. There are two reasons based upon convenience in use for giving this latter value; first, the clearer view thereby gained of the shifting between *η* and *a* in the first declension; second, the avoiding of confusion with the sound of the diphthong *ει*.

The Sounds of the Diphthongs. αι, αυ. Each vowel has its own sound, and the two are combined in one syllable: λαῖμα, as English *Lima;* αὖτε, as in Latin *aut*, and like English *out;* *ευ* = English *eh-oo*. There is no exact English equivalent for this diphthong, but an effort should be made to give the sound as accurately as can be, and particularly to avoid pronouncing it in such a way as to make the sounds of *ευ, ου, υ* all equal to English *you*. If this habit of confusion is allowed, there is sure to result hopeless confounding of such forms as ἔφευγον and ἔφυγον, λούω and

The Diphthongs. ει and ευ.

λύω, and others. ηυ is not very common. The sound would be something like English *äouch* or *abäout.* ου is monophthongal and = English *oo* in *boot.* ει is like the same letters in English *eight.* There were two different sounds represented by this diphthong. First, a true diphthong in such words as λείπω, στείχω. This ει interchanges in word composition and inflection with οι and ι. *E. g.,* λείπω, λέλοιπα, λοιπός, ἔλιπον; στείχω, στοῖχος, στίχος. Second, a "spurious" diphthong — really not a diphthong at all — formed by the contraction of two ε sounds into one. *E. g.,* ἐ-φίλε-ε becomes ἐφίλει. The cases of ει in Greek in which it arises in this way are very numerous, and justify, I think, the pronunciation indicated above. The phenomena of vowel contraction and of compensative lengthening are made plainer, and the rules governing them are rendered easier of comprehension and are better retained by the use of this pronunciation. " ε-ε becomes by contraction ει " (pronounced as *ai* in *aisle*) is an arbitrary statement with no possible vocal illustration, but " ε-ε becomes ει " (pronounced as in *eight*) is easily illustrated and remembered.

The Consonants. These present fewer difficulties and there are fewer points of disagreement among teachers in their pronunciation. I note a few points of importance. ζ should not be sounded like *dz* in *adze,* but like z simply, or like *zd.* Compare, for example, 'Αθήναζε (for 'Αθηνασ-δε) and οἰκόνδε, Μέγαράδε. The aspirates φ, θ, χ, were true aspirates; that is, they were sounded approximately as in English *uphold, pothook, blockhead.* In their pronunciation, however, they are commonly treated as spirants, and are given values which they assumed much later in the history of the language; that is, they are sounded like English *f, th* (as in *thin,* not as in *this, that*) and,

Consonants.
The Aspirates.
ζ.

though not so regularly, like German *ch* in *machen*. I believe that this method is advisable, though it is certainly not historically correct, for by it π and φ, τ and θ, κ and χ are differentiated and distinguished, and the relation between many English derivative words and their Greek originals is not obscured. Compare, for instance, the immense number of compounds into which φίλος enters as a component part. In speaking of the mutes and of their classification I think the terms " labial," " dental," and " guttural" (or " palatal ") are the best.

The Accent in Pronunciation. There is still the large question of the accent. Theories as to the minor prob-

Accent. Dif- lems of the Greek tones need not occupy the
ficulties in time of the teacher. Two points are, however,
Practice. important. The accent should be placed in pronouncing where it is put in writing the words, and an effort should be made to keep the true quantity of the vowels. *E. g.*, φίλος and σῖτος, though both have the accent on the first syllable, differ in the quantity of the first vowel. σῖτος = English *seé-toss*, while φίλος = English *fĭ-loss* (*i* as in *fit*). Another frequent confusion which I have noted is between such words as δρᾶμα (= *drah-ma*) and γράμμα (= *gramma*). The first syllable is long in both of them, but in the first this length is due to a long vowel, and in the second to the doubled consonant. It is very hard to avoid lengthening short

Accent and vowels under the accent in such words as
Vowel κακία, and to keep the proper quantity of the
Quantity. long and unaccented vowel. This word is usually sounded *ka-keé-a*, and not, as it should be, *ka-kĭh-ah*. This habit tends to prevent the feeling for the quantitative principle of Greek poetry, or to very largely obscure the perception of the principle. See further discussion of this point in Chapter IV. The dis-

tinction between the circumflex and the acute can be illustrated in English. Compare the difference in sound in the word *how?* If spoken as a direct question, it is circumflexed. As, " *Go and do this!*" " *Hôw?*" But compare " *I did not tell you to do it in that way.*" " *Hów then?*" Enforce the time element in speaking and in reading Greek. Call attention to the speech of children, which is far more musical than that of their elders. In learning Greek words for the first time the accent should be learned as an integral part of the word. *Some* accent the word must have when spoken, and the right one can be learned as well as a wrong one. The suffix of a word is, of course, not the natural place for us to put the accent, but it *can* be put where it belongs, and *should* be put there from the very outset. Time spent here is well expended, and is a saving of more **Value of** labour later on, and of labour which can then **Practice for** **Eye and Ear.** far less easily accomplish the result aimed at if it can accomplish it at all. Reading out loud, committing to memory short sentences and reciting them slowly, and with distinct efforts to indicate the tones and the quantities of each syllable, are excellent exercises. The more the time that can be given to oral instruction at the start, the better the results. The teacher should call for the pronunciation of words by the students in various ways. First, let the teacher himself pronounce the word, and call upon one or more of the class to repeat it. Secondly, take some simple words, and, pronouncing them, have the class write them down. Gradually increase the number of words so used until a short sentence has been formed. A third modification of the exercise may be made by the teacher's writing down the words exactly as the student pronounces them, and then calling attention to errors. Try to make the members of the class critics of one another. Impress upon them the necessity for a large amount of practice outside the class-room. A new language with its strange sounds and forms cannot be made familiar by devoting one hour only per day to its study and practice. Eye and ear should be trained together, and the greatest possible amount of practice be secured. This question of acquiring a proper pronunciation involves no choice between methods of further instruction, and is equally important for all further instruction and study.

Enclitics and Proclitics. These are capable of receiving ample illustration in English where they are in con-

Enclisis.
Illustrations from English.

stant use. E. g. *Give him the book*, or *give him the book*, and *give him the book*; *Téll me* and *tell mé* may serve to show enclitics in English. Proclitics are furnished by the definite and the indefinite article. The main point is to show the student that what looks strange and what is described by unfamiliar names and in new words is really something simple in its nature and a matter of every-day use.

There is hardly any portion of the field of Greek studies in which there is so little unity in practice as in

The Pronunciation of Proper Names.

the writing and speaking of Greek names. One meets *Aeschylus, Aischylos, Aischulos, Aiskhulos,* and with varying pronunciation, *Eschylus, Eeschylus, Aischulos,* and possibly other variations. *Socrates* appears as *Sokrates,* and *Aesop* looks strange enough as *Aisopos. Aristotle* appears almost always in this recognised English form, but *Plato* meets us as Plat*on*, and this form is spoken either *Playtōne* or *Plah-tōne.* It is not reasonable that such confusion should continue.[1] In defence of these strange forms it

---

[1] A protest against the prevailing lack of uniformity in this matter may be seen in the EDUCATIONAL REVIEW, vol. vii. p. 495, by John M. Moss.

is urged that we should reproduce the Greek word as nearly as possible. This might be urged for the spelling *Klearkhos,* but not for pronouncing this with the accent on the second syllable, for in the Greek alphabet it is Κλέαρχος. Nor is *Kleárkhos* a help to the correct writing of the Greek form, since χ is commonly transliterated by *ch.* Against this way of writing Greek names in Roman letters may be urged **Names have an Historic** that our English literature is full of such names **Form in** **English.** which have come to have familiar forms, and that these forms may be considered as genuine English words, almost as recognised translations of their Greek originals. Further, it seems to me that this method is rarely carried out consistently by its advocates. In fact, some of them say that names which have acquired a familiar form in English writers should not be changed. Well, here is just the point of uncertainty, for who shall say that this or that name has acquired such a form? Why should *Aristotle* be left untouched, but *Plato* changed to *Platon?* The only defensible method to my mind is that generally adopted for dictionaries of biography in English, for cyclopædias, and other works of reference of a similar kind. According to this method, the Greek names are written in the Latin form, and are then spoken with the English sound-values of these letters, but with the Roman accentuation. In actual usage, some exceptions, affecting the quantity chiefly, are made. The importance of this matter and the slight attention given it in grammars and beginners' books justify a statement of these principles here.[1]

---

[1] In but one of the Greek grammars most commonly used, and in one only of beginners' books, so far as I know, is any attempt made to explain these principles of transliteration.

TABLE OF EQUIVALENTS

Greek Alphabet	Latin Alphabet
a, ε, η, ι, o, ω	a, e, i, o
υ	y
αι	ae
ει	ī (e)
οι	oe (oi)
αυ	au
ευ	eu
ου	u

But -ος and -ον as endings of nouns of the second declension are represented by -*us* and -*um*, and -οι, ending of the plural of the same declension, by -*i*. For the consonants it will be sufficient to note

$$\kappa = \text{c} \qquad\qquad \dot{\rho} = \text{rh}$$
$$\zeta = \text{z}$$
$$\xi = \text{x} \qquad\qquad \gamma\gamma = \text{ng}$$
$$\theta = \text{th} \qquad\qquad \gamma\kappa = \text{nc}$$
$$\phi = \text{ph} \qquad\qquad \gamma\chi = \text{nch}$$
$$\chi = \text{ch} \qquad\qquad \gamma\xi = \text{nx}$$
$$\psi = \text{ps}$$

Some examples will illustrate these rules of transliteration.

Ἀλκμήνη,	Alcmene.	Ἀθήνη,	Athene.
Εὐρώτας,	Eurotas.	Εὐρυδίκη,	Eurydice.
Ἑρμῆς,	Hermes.	Δέλτα,	Delta.
Πλοῦτος,	Plutus.	Νικίας,	Nicias.
Νίκαια,	Nicaea.	Αἴγισθος,	Aegisthus.
Αἰγίς,	Aegis.	Οἰδίπους,	Oedipus.
Βοιωτία,	Boeotia.	Δαρεῖος,	Darius.
Αὐτόλυκος,	Autolycus.	Εἰρήνη,	Irene.
Βυζάντιον,	Byzantium.	Δελφοί,	Delphi.
Μίλητος,	Miletus.	Ξάνθος,	Xanthus.
Χάρων,	Charon.	Χλόη,	Chloe.
Ψυχή,	Psyche.	Ἄγκυρα,	Ancyra.
Ἄγγελος,	Angelus.	Σφίγξ,	Sphinx.

Rules ?for the Pronunciation of the Latinized Forms.
These are condensed from the rules given in Walker's
English dictionary, and were, so far as I am
able to discover, first formulated by him and Walker's Rules for
published in 1791. They may well claim, then, Pronouncing these Forms.
to be accepted by all, as they merely formu-
late what was the usage of his time, because representing
principles which have been followed for at least one
hundred years, and which are well known and thoroughly
established. I see no hope for uniformity on any other
basis than this:

1. Every vowel with the accent on it at the end of a
syllable is pronounced, as in English, with its first long
open sound: thus, *Philomé'la, Ori'on, Pho'cion, Lu'cifer*
have the accented vowels sounded exactly as in the
words *mé'tre, spi'der, no'ble, tu'tor*.

2. Every accented vowel not ending a syllable, but
followed by a consonant, has the short sound, as in English: thus, *Man'lius, Pen'theus, Col'chis, Cur'tius* have
the short sound of the accented vowels, as in *man'ner,
plen'ty, col'lar, cur'few*.

3. Every final *i*, though unaccented, has the long
open sound.

4. Every unaccented *i* ending a syllable not final, as
that in the second of *Alcibiades*, is pronounced like *e*, as
if written *Alcebiades*.

5. The diphthongs *ae* and *oe*, ending a syllable with
the accent on it, are pronounced like the long English *e*,
as in *Caesar, Oeta*, as if written *Cee'sar, E'ta*. They are
pronounced like the short *e* when followed by a consonant
in the same syllable.

6. *Y* is exactly under the same predicament as *i*. It
is long when ending an accented syllable as *Cy'rus*, short
when joined to a consonant in the same syllable as
Lyc'idas; and [sometimes] long [and sometimes short]

when ending an initial syllable not under the accent. *Lycur'gus* is pronounced with the first syllable like *lie*. Present usage treats all cases as long, so that I have modified Walker's rule as indicated by the bracketed words.

7. *E* final, either with or without the preceding consonant, always forms a distinct syllable, as *Penelope* (four-syllabled). But whenever a Greek or a Latin word is anglicized into this termination by cutting off a syllable of the original, it becomes then an English word, and is pronounced according to our own analogy. Thus, *Hecate* pronounced in three syllables when in Latin and in the same number in the Greek word Ἑκάτη, in English is contracted into two. [This holds for Shakspere, but is against the present usage.] Κρήτη has become in English *Crete*. Συράκουσαι similarly is *Syracuse*, while *Thebes* and *Athens* have received the English plural sign *s*.

The Consonants.

1. *C* and *g* are hard before consonants, and the vowels *a, o, u*. They are soft before *e, i, y*, and the diphthongs *ae* and *oe*.

2. *T, s*, and *c* before *ia, ie, ii, io, iu, -yo*, and *eu* preceded by the accent, change into *sh* and *zh*. Ἡσίοδος, *Hesiodus, Hezhiod*. But where the accent is on the first of these two vowels, the consonant preserves its sound pure. So Μιλτιάδης, *Miltiades* pronounced *Milti'ades*, like *satiety*.

3. *Ch* before a vowel is like *k*.

4. *Sche* beginning a word is like *sk*.

5. *Ph* followed by a consonant is mute. Φθιῶτις, *Phthiotis* sounds as *Thio'tis*.

Rules for the English Quantity of Greek and Latin Proper Names.

1. Words of two syllables, with one consonant in the middle, have the long sound of the first vowel whatever its quantity may be in the original: thus, Λύσις, *Lysis*, is pronounced *Ly'sis*, although υ in the Greek is short. Similarly *Cha'rēz*, Greek Χάρης (ᾰ); *Mē'non*, Μένων. Walker's Rules for English Quantity

2. Words of three syllables with the accent on the first, and with but one consonant after the first syllable, have that syllable pronounced short, let the Greek or Latin quantity be what it will. — Exception. When the first syllable is followed by *e* or *i followed by another vowel*, the vowel of the first syllable is long unless it be the vowel *i* or *y*. Examples: Τήλεφος, *Telephus*, *Tel'ephus;* Οἰδίπους, *Oedipus*, *Ed'ipus*. Examples under the exception are Βορέας, *Boreas, Bo'reas;* Λᾰμία, *Lamia, Lā'mia;* and of *ι* and *y* under this condition, Νῑκίας, *Nicias, Nish'ias;* Λῡδία, *Lydia, Lyd'ia*.

3. The general tendency is to shorten every accented antepenultimate vowel or diphthong (the term *antepenultimate* is used to denote any vowel preceding the penult of the word) unless followed in the next syllable by *e* or *i* and another vowel. In this case the quantity follows the exception to Rule 2.

The accent is determined by the rule for Latin words. If the penult is long in words of more than two syllables, it receives the accent. If the penult is short, the accent is placed on the antepenult. and for Accent.

CHAPTER II

THE BEGINNING WORK

REFERENCES

For the matters treated in this and the following chapters, the teacher who commands the use of German will find many suggestions and much help in various numbers of the *Lehrproben und Lehrgänge aus der Praxis der Gymnasien und Realschulen*, Halle, 1885, and still continued in monthly numbers. In general, also, reference may be made to the treatise by Dr. P. Dettweiler in *Handbuch der Erziehungs und Unterrichtslehre*, edited by A. Baumeister, vol. iii., Munich, 1898, and to the article *Griechisches Unterricht* in vol. iii. of *Encyklopädisches Handbuch der Pädagogik*, edited by Rein, Langensalza, 1897. See also the bibliography indicated on p. 8 f.

Books for First Readings.

Moss, C. M. A First Greek Reader with Notes and Vocabulary. Boston, Allyn & Bacon. 1900.

Colson, F. H. Stories and Legends. A First Greek Reader, with Notes, Vocabulary, and Exercises. New York, The Macmillan Company. 1899.

As auxiliary to the work in the earlier stages, T. D. Goodell's The Greek in English is valuable. The author takes pains to point out in a very clear manner the way in which Greek words and stems are used in coining terms in modern English.

THERE are two distinct methods now represented in books for beginners in Greek. One of these, and the one more generally followed at present, aims to present an amount of material " which can be completed in two terms, and which will properly prepare pupils for the rapid but exact reading of a book of the *Anabasis* during the last third of the year." The books written on this plan contain all the necessary grammar material, and their use permits the postponement of the direct use of the grammar until the reading

Two Methods now in Use.

of a text is begun. For this method the claim of simplicity is made, and justly. The student is not obliged
to make use of more than one book at the start. It is
certainly simpler for him to have selected for his use
the portions of the grammar which he needs. In fact,
I think it might be said that this is but a further and
reasonable step in the process of reduction of amount
by which the " school grammar " is made from a complete grammar of the language. Whether this simplification is wise or not, is another question. If Greek
were the first foreign language studied, I think there
could be little question as to its desirability. But as a
matter of fact, the boy beginning Greek has already had
at least one year of work in Latin. In this year of study
he must have learned the use of a grammar, and the
way to get from it the help he needs in any particular
place.

The books of the second type involve the use of the
grammar from the outset. In them references are
made at the beginning of each lesson, or section, to the
portions of the grammar needed for that lesson. Each
lesson is furnished with a vocabulary of the words used
in it, and contains sentences for translation from Greek
into English and *vice versa*, much like the books of the
class first mentioned. This method has an
advantage in that it trains the student from **Value of
knowing how**
the first lesson to use the grammar, and the **to use the
Grammar.**
grammar is the book which must be con-
stantly in his hands during his first two or three years
of reading. I think this a very considerable advantage.
Most teachers know by experience how helpless students are when in beginning the reading of a text they
are compelled for the first time to refer to the grammar for rules and for paradigms. Now, if this habit of
referring directly to the grammar is formed at the be-

ginning, the labour of the early lessons is not very much increased. The teacher's advice and help in learning the use of the grammar removes many difficulties. The student gains in this way gradually and surely the familiarity with the arrangement of material in the grammar which is absolutely essential to satisfactory progress. The difficulties of this plan are more numerous at first, but I believe time is gained in the end. By this method, too, one avoids the feeling of discouragement so often brought about by the apparent " beginning all over again" in grammatical study.

The choice of a method, however, is of far less importance than the thorough mastery of the method he is using by any teacher. The age of the members of a class is an important factor. The number of students in a class is also of importance, as it determines the amount of personal drill which each individual can receive.

The Teacher is greater than any Method.

The secret of success in the first year's work in Greek does not depend upon method one half so much as upon the teacher. I wish to point out the matters upon which I think emphasis should be laid, and whose importance is not in any way dependent upon the method followed. As regards various short cuts to a knowledge of Greek, or of reading Greek, by whatever names they are called, — " natural method," " inductive method," " gate," etc., — I will say once for all that I have no faith in them. As I have said, and as I firmly believe, the teacher is greater than any method, and I willingly admit that in the hand of an able and thorough teacher any particular method may be made to yield first-rate results. I believe, however, with equal firmness that it is the individuality of the teacher that is the efficient factor in the result, and not the virtue of the method he employs.

(a) *The First Paradigms of Conjugation.* The best

verb to start with is a pure verb of three syllables like κελεύω. This is easier to pronounce than λύω, for ῡ is not an easy sound. It affords in the first **The best Verb** aorist a better opportunity of noting the **for the Start.** normal accentuation of imperative and infinitive. *E. g.* κέλευσον and κελεῦσαι, are more helpful to a student than λῦσον and λῦσαι. The latter suggest that all verbs are accented in these forms on the penult, and further that the infinitive of the first aorist (a very common form) should always have the circumflex. κελεῦσαι does not suggest this last inference, because the graphic designation by the diphthong ευ is less misleading. The present and imperfect indicative of a few verbs and their present infinitive forms (it is a mistake to postpone the infinitive to a much later time) should be thoroughly memorized. These forms should be analyzed both orally and in writing: thus, έ-κέλευο-ν, έ-κέλευε-ς, έ-κέλευε. This should be continued until the pupil is able from any stem given him to speak and write correctly the forms called for.

In inflection, the dual forms of verbs and nouns are best omitted altogether. The best beginners' books recommend this omission now, though none **Omission of** of them, so far as I know, has taken the **Dual Forms.** logical and desirable step of omitting dual forms from their paradigms, or of placing them *after* the plural forms or printing them in smaller type. Dual forms are not necessary for the beginner's book, nor should he be given exercises containing them. When met with in reading, and this will not be a frequent occurrence, they can be explained by the teacher, if this is not done in the notes on the passage. I doubt if the dual had ever acquired a place in beginners' books were it not for the fact that there are a few examples of it in the opening sections of the *Anabasis*.

It is best to add to the forms of two or three pure verbs those of one or two verbs representing severally a stem ending in a labial, a dental, and a pala- tal mute. This means, in addition to κελεύω (βασιλεύω, πιστεύω, *etc.*), πέμπω, λείπω; πείθω, ψεύδω; λέγω, φεύγω; or others of similar formation. The advantage gained by the introduction of these mute stems lies in the fact that in forming their future forms the pupil has an opportunity to see the changes produced by the addition of ς. These changes are so important in the inflection of both verbs and nouns that they are best introduced at a very early moment. The details of the development of the verb inflection — *i. e.,* how to combine the successive steps in the inflection of verbs and of nouns — may well be left to individual judgment, or to the method of the book in use

Proper Se- quence of New Forms.

There is one practice, very common indeed, which seems to me a great mistake, *viz.,* introducing the forms of the perfect at an early stage in the pupil's progress. The student should be taught that the present (with the imperfect), the future, and the aorist are the tenses most used. With these he should be made thoroughly familiar before going to any others. He should not be given the forms of the perfect until he has learned that in Greek the aorist is oftener than the perfect the equivalent of the English perfect. The perfect tense may be, and I think should be, ignored or postponed until the student has become familiar with the turning of such English phrases as *having done, having said, having made* into Greek aorist forms. If the perfect be brought in too early in the lessons, confusion results in the student's mind. Furthermore the perfect is not so very frequent in use as to justify giving it an equal place with the aorist in beginners' lessons. In the first book of the *Anabasis*

The Perfect not to be taught too early.

there are not thirty occurrences of forms of the active
perfect, counting both first and second perfect forms.
Of these, too, nearly one half are from the two verbs
οἶδα and ἵστημι.

See further remarks on this subject in Chapter V.

(b) *The Declension of Nouns.* I regard it as settled
beyond dispute that the study of the declensions in Greek
should begin with the second, or -o, declen- Begin with
sion. It is simpler and presents fewer -o Declension
varieties of forms. To make the difficulties connected
with the accents easier, the first lesson should consist of
paroxytones only. Both masculine and neuter and group
examples may be chosen. This will give according to
sufficient words for exercises, — *e. g.* λόγος, Accent.
νόμος, βίος, φίλος, ὕπνος ; τόξον, ἔργον, δένδρον. This
group requires no change in the place of the accent or
in its kind. The second group may include proparoxy-
tones which involve a change in the place of the accent
but not in the kind of accent used. Thirdly, the pro-
perispomena, involving change of kind of accent, but
not of its place ; and lastly the oxytones. I should favour
devoting one lesson to each group, not leaving this until
the principles involved are thoroughly mastered. Adjectives may be given in connection with each group.
If this is done, care must be taken to introduce those
only which are identical in accentuation with the nouns
of that particular group. So with ἵππος, *etc.* may be
given ὀλίγος, νέος, μόνος, but not μικρός, *etc.* Application of
With the material now in hand — the second Forms learned.
declension of nouns ; the present and imperfect indicative and the present infinitive of several verbs ; the
simpler prepositions ἐκ, ἐν, εἰς, ἀπό, πρό ; the forms ἦν,
ἦσαν, ἔφη, καί, γάρ, μέν, δέ, οὐ — I should urge the most
thorough drill in forming sentences orally and in writing.
I would not let a pupil proceed another step until he can

write these forms correctly from dictation, and can repeat them when heard by him. Each teacher will be
the best judge of the mastery obtained by his class, and
can increase the number of exercises here at will.[1] Time
spent here will prove to be time saved later. There is
scope for considerable reading with the forms of the
second declension alone. See, for instance, the reading
exercises introduced in the early lessons of Sandys'
First Greek Reader and Writer, or in Forman's *First
Greek Book*.

Three groups are necessary in taking up the first de-
clension: 1. stems in $\bar{a}$; 2. stems in -η; 3. stems in $\breve{a}$.

The Forms of First Declension. The all-important rule is the following: a is
retained in the case terminations throughout
the singular if preceded in the nominative by
ϵ, ι, ρ, and in the accusative singular if the accent of the
nominative shows that the a is short in quantity. See
the statements and examples in the grammars. The exceptions may be neglected at this stage. Contract
nouns of declensions one and two I should postpone to
a later time. Feminine nouns of the second declension
and masculine nouns of the first declension should
come next, and then a halt in studying noun declension
until the present middle and the future and first aorist
active of verbs have been thoroughly mastered and
made the subjects for much practice in writing and in
speaking.

At this point the inflection and use of ὅς, οὗτος, ἐκεῖνος,

Demonstrative Pronouns. and αὐτός with perhaps ὅδε should be taken
up and made the basis of drill as with nouns.
The subsequent order followed in the development of forms may very well be left to in-

---

1 "An Experiment in Greek Teaching," by Mary Whiton Calkins,
EDUCATIONAL REVIEW, vol. vii. p. 80, may prove suggestive to teachers
who wish to introduce something in the way of drill in pronunciation and
in knowledge of a vocabulary.

dividual judgment. I think the battle will have been won at this point, if absolute thoroughness has been maintained.

(c) *The Development of Syntax.* The main thing to be kept in mind is the securing of familiarity with the most frequently used forms of expression. What these are in the earlier weeks of reading will naturally depend upon the author or work chosen for the first reading. In our schools this is now, almost without exception, Xenophon's *Anabasis.* A most valuable help to the most important facts of syntax in the *Anabasis* is a book by Artur Joost, entitled *Was ergiebt sich aus dem Sprachgebrauch Xenophons in der Anabasis für die Behandlung der griechischen Syntax in der Schule?* Berlin, 1892. In connection with the book should be considered Professor Gildersleeve's review of it in the *American Journal of Philology.* I quote here from Joost's conclusions on some of the weightier matters, pages 337 ff. ·

Importance of Knowledge of Normal and Common Usage.

"The following constructions must be taken up at an early time and constantly discussed and practised.

" 1. In declension the placing of attributive phrases between the article and the noun, or after the noun with repetition of the article; the possessive and partitive genitive (ὁ τοῦ φίλου υἱός, οἱ ἀγαθοὶ τῶν ἀνθρώπων, τῶν σοφῶν τις). The prepositions ἐκ, ἐν, εἰς, σύν, ἐπί with the accusative, πρός with accusative in local use, διά with genitive of place, κατά with accusative of place, περί with genitive and equal to *about, concerning,* παρά with genitive, ἀπό of place, διά with accusative, ἐπί with accusative of person to indicate hostile purpose, *against.* The dative of the agent, the dative with εἶναι or γίγνεσθαι of possession. The dative of manner, of time, of cause, with verbs compounded with σύν. The 'accusative of extent of time or space,' the accusative of reference (limitation), double accusative with verbs of making, etc. The use of the article for the possessive pronoun. The omission of the article with the noun in the predicate. Such uses of the adjective as ἀγαθόν τι, οὐδὲν καλόν.

" 2. In treating of pronouns the syntax of the relative must receive early and particular attention, in its ordinary use as relative and also as introducing indirect interrogative sentences. Further the use of the article as pronoun, and with modifying genitive, and in other phrases without a noun added.

" 3. In verb syntax, the passive construction with ὑπό and the genitive must be illustrated early. εἰ in simple (logical) conditions, ἐπεί and ἐπειδή with imperfect and aorist indicative are very important, and equally so ὥστε with the indicative, and ὅτι and ἐπεί used in causal clauses. Attention must be paid to the subjunctive with ἐάν (ἤν), and with ὅπως, ἵνα, ὡς. The optative uses of most importance are those of indirect statement, in indirect question and the potential use with ἄν. Further, the optative in final clauses after a past tense. The infinitive with ἔφη is all important, and further its use with δεῖ, δοκεῖ, ἔξεστι, in result clause with ὥστε, with ἱκανός and similar adjectives. Attention must be given to the infinitive with βούλομαι, ἐθέλω, and κελεύω, and to the future infinitive with verbs of hoping, promising, and the like. The participle, first of all in the present, then in the aorist, is to be carefully studied and copiously illustrated by writing exercises. The following are the more important uses: Participles in the nominative, representing a subordinate clause, which are to be translated by a conjunction with finite clause, temporal and causal. Participles both with and without the article which represent a relative clause, and are so to be translated. The object participle of indirect statement with words of perception and sight, and also ὅτι clauses in the same use. The participle with τυγχάνω, and the future participle, with and without ὡς, to express purpose."

I wish to add or enlarge upon a few points which my own experience has shown me are of great importance. First of all, the essential difference in attribu- Importance tive and predicate position. This should be of Word-illustrated in writing and orally by such position. phrases as αἱ ὁδοὶ ἦσαν μακραί. These words may easily be extended by the addition of τῆς νήσου, and then ἐν τῇ νήσῳ, as attributive limitations of the nominative. I should lay special emphasis on the second type of attributive phrases — *i.e.* a preposition with a case, οἱ ἐκ τῆς νήσου ἄνθρωποι — because I find so often a com-plete failure on the part of the student to recognise the collocation and dependence of the words in such sen-tences, and consequently a failure to grasp their meaning. It should be made the subject of practice from the out-set. Teach the pupil to read out loud, grouping the associated words closely together in his enunciation, and have him write a large number of them, making all the possible combinations of the words given him. The ob-ject is to train his eye to take in the whole group at a glance, and to pronounce it in such a way as to indicate its unity in thought. The fact that an English relative clause may be so expressed — *the men who were in, etc.* — must be shown and illustrated by examples. Thucydides, Book I. chapters 101–103, affords, in the phrase οἱ ἐν Ἰθώμῃ, or οἱ ἐκ Ἰθώμης, some good models for this.

Keeping the words already chosen for a model sen-tence, this may then be extended by the Building up addition of predicate adjectives connected by a Model μέν–δέ; for example, αἱ ὁδοὶ ὀλίγαι μὲν ἦσαν, Sentence. μακραὶ δέ. Then a sentence should be given with the

scheme of double clauses from the start, as, τῶν στρατι-
ωτῶν οἱ μὲν κακοὶ ἦσαν, οἱ δὲ ἀγαθοί, or οἱ μὲν στρατη-
γοὶ. . . . οἱ δὲ στρατιῶται.   Make as many different
combinations of sentences as possible to illustrate these
two ways of using μέν . . . δέ.   Note that in one of these
the subject is common to both clauses, while the predicate words are contrasted.   In the other there are two
subjects standing in a contrasted relation to each other.
μέν . . . δέ clauses are not necessarily mutually exclusive.
They are often, strictly speaking, not paratactic at all.
Don't be afraid of spending too much time on this point.
It is of the highest importance.   Next come clauses with
γάρ and οὖν.   The meanings and the proper place in the
clause of these words should be carefully explained and
illustrated.   Then let the students add clauses involving
their use to the model sentence.   So this will grow by
the judicious selection of clauses to be added to it.   A
very few sentences may be made to illustrate all the
more important principles of position of words in a
clause and of the simpler rules of syntax.   To the three
simplest prepositions, each with one case only, may be
added πρός with the accusative, ἀπό, περί with the genitive, ἐπί with the accusative in the meaning *against*.   ἔφη
with the infinitive, and also ὅτι, *that*, should be abundantly illustrated, taking care that the ὅτι clause does
not require the optative mood.   These model sentences
should be well fixed in the pupil's mind, and made to
take the place of a constant citing of grammar rules.

It is of the greatest importance that the student should
be made familiar with the joining of clauses in various
The Joining   relations at a very early period in his course
of Clauses.   in Greek.   The majority of beginners' books
do not pay sufficient attention to this matter, and the
result is that students who have had drill in detached
clauses alone stand helpless before a piece of connected

writing, no matter how simple it may be. This is particularly true of the use of δέ, and of clauses with μέν
δέ. The latter method of joining clauses is very common, and I have spoken of it above. In one of the most
widely used of first-year books, I find that μέν . . . δέ,
is first used in the illustrative exercises of the sixteenth
lesson, and is there accompanied by an explanation which
seems to me to be inadequate to the full comprehension
of its value and use. That the importance of this construction is not realized by the author, seems to me to be
evident from the fact that in the first twenty-six lessons
and reading exercises it is used eight times only. In the
twenty-eighth lesson, however, there is presented as an
exercise for reading about half a page of original Greek
text. In this passage there are four cases of μέν . . . δέ
clauses, one of which is particularly unsuitable for presentation to a beginner, as it stands in a passage which is
almost universally modified by editors, because of the
peculiar position of the δέ. The net result of this must,
it seems to me, be to produce confusion in the pupil's
mind. In another beginners' book the μέν . . . δέ arrangement is first introduced in the sixteenth lesson, although
before that point a number of forms of the perfect tense,
rarely found in use, have been given. Here a footnote
to μέν refers the student to the vocabulary at the end
of the book, where the statement of its use is exceedingly vague. In forty lessons of this book, covering one
hundred pages, there are fourteen sentences with the
μέν . . . δέ construction, and of these, two are decidedly
confusing instances. Taking these two books, and they
are not bad books by any means, as typical, it seems to
me evident that this very important point is not adequately treated. This use should be constantly explained, illustrated, and made the basis for practice. It
is difficult work, at the best, to acquire a feeling for the

meaning of the particles, and this result can be reached only by a familiarity gained through much reading and many repetitions of the words.   An instructive parallel is afforded by the German *ja*.   If a boy is told that this means *yes*, and is given sentences which illustrate this meaning and use of the word alone, he must either ignore its presence in many a sentence met with in reading, or translate falsely.   See more on this in Chapter V.

(d) *Further Work in the Study of Forms.   Nouns, Third Declension.*   Begin with the palatal stems and **Other Nouns** continue with labial and dental stems, then **and Verbs.** nasal stems.   The neuter noun stems in -a (τ) and in -os (-ϵs) may follow.   Vowel stems in -ι and -υ should be postponed to the last, as they present confusing divergences from the normal scheme of inflection.

The development of verb forms may be carried out according to individual judgment or to the method of the textbook in use.   I think, however, that contract verbs should not be postponed too long.   They may well be taken up, especially those in -$\epsilon\omega$, as soon as the noun inflection calls for a knowledge of the principles of contraction.   For a convenient classification of verbs according to their forms of conjugation, the following scheme may be of assistance :

CLASSIFICATION OF VERBS

A.   Verbs with stems in -ω.   Thematic Verbs.

   1.   Pure verbs — Stem ends in a vowel.
      a.   Stems in ι, υ, or diphthong, not contracted.
      b.   Stems in a, ϵ, o.   Contract verbs.
   2.   Verbs with stems ending in a consonant.
      a.   Labial stems in π, β, ϕ. ⎫
      b.   Dental stems in τ, δ, θ. ⎬ Mute verbs.
      c.   Palatal stems in κ, γ, χ. ⎭
      d.   Liquid (nasal) stems in λ, μ, ν, ρ.

B. Verbs in -μι.

These differ in form of inflection in the present, imperfect, and second aorist, active and middle.

Further help on the question of the second aorist may be gained by noting the following list of verbs in -ω, otherwise regular in their inflection, which make aorists of the so-called *second* form. ἄγω, βάλλω, κατακαίνω, ἀνακράζω, λείπω, τίκτω, τρέπω, φεύγω. This list should be copied into the book in use, and gradually learned.

Along with the presentation of forms will go naturally the extension of syntactic uses. These are best and most surely taught by means of composition Advance in exercises. The principles made prominent Study of should be those most fundamentally important Syntax. for reading, and each new principle should be *immediately* illustrated in reading and applied in writing. Practice, and practice alone, makes perfect, and makes easy as well. A rule, or a set of rules learned, but not actually applied in use, is soon forgotten.

(e) *The First Reading.* The *Anabasis* of Xenophon may be begun at the earliest moment that sufficient grammatical knowledge has been obtained to What to make connected reading possible, or a reader read first. made up of simple selections of progressive difficulty may be taken up as a preparation for Xenophon. The choice of method here must depend upon the kind of introductory book which has been used. If it has been one in which connected reading has been carried on from the first, then by the time that the twenty or twenty-five weeks devoted to its study have been completed, the pupil is quite ready to go on with the *Anabasis* itself. If, on the other hand, the book has afforded drill in reading isolated and detached sentences only, then a book of simple prose selections is better adapted to the pupil's knowledge.　For reading matter ought never to be so difficult that some considerable amount of it cannot be covered at one exercise.　Power to read comes by reading.　A book of easy passages helps to this end.　Further, it enables the teacher to proceed from the simple to the complex.　It postpones the more difficult points in construction until the pupil has thoroughly mastered the easier ones.　It affords, too, topics in reading, each one of which is complete in itself.　This is a distinct advantage, and helps to arouse an interest in the subject matter, which is scarcely to be gained if an historical narrative, like the *Anabasis*, be broken up into very small portions.

There is a third way represented in some beginners' books which consists in introducing from the first lesson

The Question of a "Simplified" Anabasis.

words, phrases, and clauses taken from the *Anabasis*, and, as fast as it can be done, much of the narrative of the first book, with what changes in the way of simplification are needed.　For this method it is claimed that much of the reading of the *Anabasis* is anticipated and accomplished in connection with the grammar lessons.　This is certainly true in part, but I believe only in part. Sentences must often be changed from their original form and connection to avoid constructions not yet learned.　All stylistic effect is thus lost, and much of the real syntax.　To gain a real knowledge of the story as told by Xenophon, much, if not all, must be read over again, and this could be only with diminished interest.　I shall leave it to the judgment of the teacher who wishes to form an opinion on this point after presenting a passage of Xenophon (*Anabasis*, I. 7, 4), and the same as modified for use in a beginners' book.

ὅπως δὲ καὶ εἰδῆτε εἰς οἷον ἔρχεσθε ἀγῶνα ὑμᾶς εἰδὼς διδάξω. τὸ μὲν γὰρ πλῆθος πολὺ καὶ κραυγῇ πολλῇ ἐπίασιν· ἂν δὲ ταῦτα ἀνάσχησθε, τὰ ἄλλα καὶ αἰσχύνεσθαί μοι δοκῶ οἵους ἡμῖν γνώσεσθε τοὺς ἐν τῇ χώρᾳ ὄντας ἀνθρώπους. ὑμῶν δὲ ἀνδρῶν ὄντων καὶ εὖ τῶν ἐμῶν γενομένων, ἐγὼ ὑμῶν τὸν μὲν οἴκαδε βουλόμενον ἀπιέναι τοῖς οἴκοι ζηλωτὸν ποιήσω ἀπελθεῖν, πολλοὺς δὲ οἶμαι ποιήσειν τὰ παρ' ἐμοὶ ἐλέσθαι ἀντὶ τῶν οἴκοι.

As "simplified," or "adapted," this reads as follows:

Ἐγὼ δὲ εἰς οἷον ἔρχεσθε ἀγῶνα ὑμᾶς διδάξω. τὸ μὲν γὰρ πλῆθος τῶν βαρβάρων πολύ ἐστι καὶ κραυγῇ πολλῇ ἐπέρχονται· ἂν δὲ ταῦτα ἀνάσχησθε, τὰ ἄλλα αἰσχύνομαι οἷοι ἡμῖν οἱ ἐν τῇ χώρᾳ εἰσὶν ἄνθρωποι. ἐὰν δὲ ὑμεῖς ἄνδρες ἦτε καὶ εὖ τὰ ἐμὰ γένηται, ἐγὼ ὑμῶν τὸν μὲν οἴκαδε βουλόμενον ἀπελθεῖν ζηλωτὸν ποιήσω τοῖς οἴκοι, πολλοὺς δὲ οἶμαι βουλήσεσθαι παρ' ἐμοὶ μένειν.

CHAPTER III

XENOPHON AND OTHER PROSE WRITERS — THE GREEK NEW TESTAMENT

REFERENCES.

Rehdantz, C. Xenophon's Anabasis, sixth edition, by Dr. Otto Carnuth. Berlin, Weidmann. This is the edition of the Anabasis of fundamental importance for the grammatical study of the work. It contains notes in German on all of the uses of the various parts of speech as illustrated in the text, with many cross references to other passages. Its great lack is an index of words and of passages. The book should be in the hands of every teacher who can use German.

Pretor, Alfred. The Anabasis of Xenophon with English notes. Two vols. I. Text. II. Notes and Indices. Cambridge, The University Press. An excellent edition of the entire work with English notes.

White, John T. Grammar School Texts. Xenophon's Anabasis. Each Book separately, with a vocabulary to each. Very convenient for supplementary reading, or for the reading of a small amount of the Anabasis. London and New York, Longmans, Green & Co.

Rolfe, A. G. The Fifth Book of Xenophon's Anabasis with notes and vocabulary. Boston, Ginn & Co., 1897.

White, J. W., and **Morgan M. H.** An Illustrated Dictionary to Xenophon's Anabasis. Boston, Ginn & Co. An excellent and valuable work.

Blake, R. W. The Hellenica of Xenophon, Books I. and II. Boston, Allyn & Bacon, 1894.

Gleason, C. W. The Cyropædia of Xenophon Abridged for Schools. New York, American Book Company, 1897.

Phillpots and **Jerram.** Easy Selections from Xenophon. Parts of the Anabasis. The earlier pieces are "simplified." Oxford, The Clarendon Press. Same authors. Selections adapted from Xenophon. Passages from the Hellenica. Same publishers.

For the various questions of syntax, the discussions scattered through the volumes of the AMERICAN JOURNAL OF PHILOLOGY, now in its twentieth year. Many of these discussions are by the editor, Professor B. L. Gildersleeve, himself, and most of the rest by his associates or pupils. A full list of books may be found in the edition of the first four books of the Anabasis by F. W. Kelsey, published by Allyn & Bacon, Boston.

ALMOST without exception Xenophon's *Anabasis* of Cyrus is the first piece of literature taken up by the student of Greek. Therefore, while much of The First his work must be directed towards the extend- Literature. ing of his grammatical knowledge, there is a natural desire on his part to reap some fruit from the labour of the previous months, and a feeling that the time for such reaping has arrived. The reading of this work then should mean something more than a continuation of grammar work. It should bring some pleasure in a feeling of power gained, and in a consciousness of ability to get at the subject matter and to reach the thought contained in the words. To meet this reasonable wish the reading must not proceed at too slow a pace. If the introductory work has been well and truly done, a rate of advance in the reading now will be possible which will keep the student interested in the story being told and in its development.

The hour, or even, in many cases, shorter time, of the daily recitation affords a very inadequate opportunity for the treatment of the many points of in- Problem of terest which. are sure to arise each day. The the Recitation great problem, as I see the state of the case, Hour. is, " What shall be done in the recitation period and what shall be left untouched?" It is manifestly impossible to do all that the teacher sees to be done, or anywhere near all. The question is one of selection. I shall attempt to make some suggestions as direct and as specific as possible.

First. The recitation hour should not be made an hour for a daily examination alone. The teacher ought not to spend these few and precious moments Teaching entirely in questioning the pupils about things is not Examlearned at home, or even those explained ining. previously in the classroom. To devote all the time to this means to lose the finest opportunity for *instruction*, in the best sense of the word. Something in the nature of examination is necessary. But with earnest students the result sought — to know how well they understand matters previously studied, or how thorough has been their home preparation — can be reached by inviting *them* to ask questions on all points not understood. Individual difficulties thus presented will in most cases cover all the more difficult points, and the students are spared the tiresome exercise of listening to statements of what they know.

Second. *Parsing*, as commonly understood, should be reduced to a minimum. It is, if at all prolonged, a **"Parsing" kills Interest.** dreary exercise, and when applied to sentences which have been already analyzed and whose meaning has already been discovered, it is certainly a *hysteron-proteron*. Nothing so surely takes the life out of the exercise, and the interest in the work out of the pupils, and specially out of the brightest and quickest of them. *Some* explanation in class of forms and of syntactic problems there must be, but it should be confined to those that have proved difficult for the class, that have not been mastered by private study, or that have been brought out by a faulty or inadequate translation. The **Recitation must be an Hour of Progress.** student must be made to feel that the recitation hour is a time in which progress is made. So much by way of caution. Positively I suggest the following method: The first lesson to be read is taken up in class at the first exercise in the subject, and before any attempt at preparation has been made by the pupils themselves. The teacher should point out the more difficult forms and constructions, showing those which have been already met with and those which are new. In particular it is important to point out that any roots already known may be found in words that are new.

To illustrate what I mean I will take examples from the opening sections of the Anabasis. ἠσθένει. The form is in the imperfect. Why? The accent (compare ἐφίλει) shows that. Hence it has at the beginning an augmented vowel. This vowel may be α, as in ἦγον from ἄγω, or ε, as in ἤθελον from ἐθέλω. This suggests ἐσθενέω or ἀσθενέω. Possibly ἀσθενής or σθένος has been already learned. If not, σθένος may be written on the blackboard, and the others derived from it, and the English derivatives *callisthenics* and *asthenic* may be pressed into service by way of fixing the meaning of the root word. ὑπώπτευε should be first analyzed, and then the meaning of the prefix explained and illustrated by the Latin *su(b)spicio*. παρὼν ἐτύγχανε needs careful explanation, if not already familiar. In Greek the participle contains the leading or chief idea of the expression and the verb the subordinate thought. In English the expression is constructed in the reverse way. The uses of the tenses of the verb and of the supplementary participle should be explained, model sentences framed to illustrate them, and exercises, oral and written, based upon these principles. The present participle with the present or imperfect of the verb is found in three fourths of all occurrences of this idiom, and should be made the basis for illustration of it. The uses of the connecting μέν . . . δέ should be discussed. The first μέν . . . δέ are correlatives without any strong opposition implied; the second δέ is connective and nearer in meaning to *and* than to *but*. Then again μέν . . . δέ almost, but not quite, as in the first case. Then καί, emphasizing a single word and not a copulative conjunction as in the first sentence. ὅσοι, *as many as, who*, suggests the use of these correlatives. In connection with this the tables in Goodwin's Grammar, § 429, and in Hadley and Allen, § 282, should be read over and carefully

Opening Sentences of Anabasis as Illustration.

explained. Special note should be made of the difference between οὗτος and τοιοῦτος, between τοιοῦτος and
τοσοῦτος, between οἷος and ὅσος. The definite article and
its uses should receive attention. Note its omission in
Καστωλοῦ πεδίον, in effect a proper name. Cf. in English *Marshfield.* οὖν is once used, μὲν οὖν, to sum up
the story to that point; that is, it is continuative and not
equal to English *therefore.* It is once resumptive after
the digression καὶ στρατηγὸν δὲ αὐτὸν . . . ἀθροίζονται.
As many of these points as can be should be pointed out
and explained by the teacher, and the passage assigned
for recitation on the following day. When the class
meets again, this portion should be translated by the
pupils, who should be urged to modify their renderings
when faulty by repeated trials until a translation has
been obtained which shows that the pupils have mastered,
first, the meanings of the words, second, their proper
syntactic relations in the clause, and, third, the syntactic
and rhetorical relation of the clauses in the period.

Special attention should be given in this connection
to the emphasis given words by their positions in the
Order of clause. For instance, in section two of the
Words and its passage from *Anabasis*, I. 1, ἀναβαίνει, and
Importance. further the added emphasis of the καί before
στρατηγόν, and the extending of the relative construction by an independent clause. Then, last of all, a careful reading of the Greek text with special attention to
the pronunciation of the words so as to show their
mutual relations, and to bring out the meaning clearly
by good enunciation. There is just as much difference
between good reading and bad reading in Greek as in
English. Then repeat the process of the day before on
a new portion of the text. I should not advise the
pupil's undertaking at first new passages of text before
these have been considered with the teacher. Unlearn-

ing and relearning takes more time than learning, and though the progress of the class may be slower in this way for a while, I believe that through increased certainty the ultimate gain is considerable.

An occasional rapid review of a chapter or of some larger portion of the narrative which is complete in itself, is of great value in aiding the pupil to get an idea of the subject matter and of the movement of the story.

It may frequently seem best not to include an entire book of the *Anabasis* in the first reading, but to make omissions. The selection of these must be left to the judgment of the teacher, and he will be guided in making the omissions by the capacity and the cleverness of the particular class in question. Some classes will be able to read the first four books without any omissions, while with others it may be best to omit some of the more difficult portions at the first reading, reserving them for study later on. In book one, a considerable part of chapter two and much of chapter four may be omitted on the first reading. Chapter six is episodic, and may be postponed without interrupting the story. The same is true of chapter seven. With regard to chapter nine, so often viewed by students as a bugbear, I should say read it at the first time. It marks the close of the first great division of the history, and Cyrus does not figure in the subsequent narrative.

In book two I should recommend the omission of chapter six. I do not believe that it is of an importance commensurate with the difficulties it presents to the student with no further preparation for it than he has gained in reading the story which has preceded it. Enough has not been told about the generals to make these analyses of their characters of particular interest, and the facts, if they are considered important, can be obtained with far less labour.

Two, or possibly three, books should be read in this careful manner, and then the reading should be more

Increase in Rapidity of Reading. rapid. The range of discussion on topics connected with the lesson may be broadened, as the grammatical interpretation will naturally demand less time. This difference in treatment is recognised in the plan recommended by the Committee of the American Philological Association, and is a thoroughly reasonable one. No slovenly or inaccurate habits in translation should be tolerated at any point in the course, but correct habits ought to be fixed by this time, and so a more rapid rate of progress be possible without sacrifice of accuracy. The subject matter increases in interest, in my opinion, from the beginning of book three. From this point Xenophon becomes the central figure of the story. His account of his joining the expedition, of his dream, told at the beginning of book three, and of the reorganization of the army and the choice of new generals is interesting and instructive. The last named shows us the army as a typical self-governing political community with its attendant individual insubordination and independence of thought and speech. The long speech of Xenophon, III. 2, 8–32, may be considerably cut down in length. From this point the story is full of exciting scenes and situations. Book four gives much interesting information about the manner of living of the tribes the Greeks met with on the northward march. The terrors of a winter in the highland and mountains of Armenia have never been better described. The passage at the end of the first chapter and the beginning of the second may be left out. It is hard to understand, and the facts may easily be summarized. So book four is brought to an end at a fairly rapid rate, and with it comes the end of the normally prescribed reading in prose of the three-year course in the high school.

The question arises frequently, however, " What further reading is to be recommended when there is still
time for the purpose? " For time there will
often be. Many classes, especially small
classes, will finish ahead of the usual time.
Others will have extra time gained by taking an additional half-year or year for preparation for college, or
may find leisure because they are ahead in other studies.
The answers given to this question are four: First,
selections from one or more of the other works of
Xenophon, — the *Hellenica* or the *Cyropædia*. Second,
something of Plato. Third, selections from Lysias, or
another of the Attic orators. Fourth, portions of Herodotus. In favor of some further reading in another
work of Xenophon, it may be said that his style has
been mastered, and that a wider vocabulary can be
obtained by the reading proposed. This may be granted
and still not be convincing. It is often the subject of
complaint that the student comes up to his college work
with a very limited vocabulary. Another work of Xenophon will not materially aid in removing the ground of
this complaint. For the choice of the *Hellenica* it may
fairly be said that the subject matter is of importance,
and that some valuable knowledge of history may be
gained by its study. No such argument can be urged
for the *Cyropædia*, however, nor can I think it of sufficient importance to justify the devoting to it of precious
time.

That some of the easier portions of Plato may be
taken up with profit seems likely. I cannot speak from
any actual experience in school work in this
author, but I know that, as freshmen in college, students never fail to become interested
in him. Some book of selections may be taken to furnish the reading matter, or one of the easier dialogues
may be chosen.

The *Protagoras* is admirably adapted for the first readings in Plato. It can be arranged by some omissions so as to furnish no very great difficulties. As an example of Socrates' habit and manner of giving a serious turn to the most trivial remarks, and of introducing themes of the highest importance in an unexpected manner and in an unlooked for connection, it is unsurpassed. Besides this there is the live question introduced at the beginning, " What is the end of education, and what kinds of education are there? " This is a particularly fit theme for the last year of school work, and of positive value for the man who does not go to college as well as for the prospective collegian. The beautiful myth of the creation of man and of the organization of society is not hard reading, and it is certainly very suggestive and stimulating to further study in this wonderful author. Another practical advantage in the reading of the *Protagoras* lies in the fact that the vocabulary of the earlier chapters is admirably adapted for drill in prose composition. Other short and easy dialogues sometimes chosen are the *Lysis*, *Menexenus*, and *Laches*. I do not myself think the *Apology af Socrates* is suitable for the first introduction to Plato. It contains many difficulties. It is a defence of a life of peculiar activity, and it is better understood and more thoroughly appreciated later in the course, when more has been learned of this life and of the habits which are the subject of the defence. Various other minor works proposed for the purpose of additional prose reading I do not discuss, because I think that the time of the student should not be claimed for writings of little historical or literary value. The amount of Greek he can and will read is very limited at best. All save the finest should be excluded from consideration.

The plan of taking something from one of the orators

is not so easily judged. There are great advantages in reading from Lysias, for instance. He is a recognised master of a simple and attractive style. His **Portions of** vocabulary is a valuable one, particularly for **the Orators.** further work in the orators, and much of the subject matter is of great interest, as it deals with Athenian private and public life. But the narratives must be separated from the argumentative portions of his speeches, owing to the difficulties in thought presented by the latter. The two are often so interwoven that this separation is almost impossible, or if made produces a text which is incomplete and fragmentary. This scrappiness is an all too frequent result of selections in Greek reading, and should, I think, be avoided as far as possible.

The fourth plan, and the one which has the official endorsement of the American Philological Association, proposes Herodotus for reading in this place **Herodotus.** in the course. So far as style and subject matter are concerned, he is an ideal author for the purpose. I think, however, that the introduction of a third dialect of Greek into the high school is entirely indefensible. It can but add a confusing element to the student's ideas and knowledge of Greek forms. The Homeric dialect has diverted the student's attention from the Attic, but that we suffer for the greater gain in a literary way. The acquaintance with, and the ability to handle, the Attic forms is too important, however, to be subjected to further hazard.

If Herodotus is to be read at all in the preparatory course, I should prefer to follow an English custom and have the text *atticised* throughout. The objections to this seem to me to be of less weight than the damage otherwise done to the student, who is at this time trying hard to attain to a certainty in the recognition of grammatical forms.

Preferable to any of the plans mentioned is, in my judgment, that of reading the remainder of the *Anabasis*, More of the or, at least, large portions of it, and for these Anabasis. reasons: First, the reading done, both in college and in school, is, at the best, very fragmentary. Consider the latter as commonly done. First, of one author about one half of one work, the *Anabasis*. Then, a small portion, not more than one fourth at the outside, of one poem, the *Iliad*. This portion of the poem is not sufficient to carry through to its conclusion any one of the developments of the story suggested in the part that is read. This is the usual acquaintance with Greek literature which the boy possesses when he enters college. There again too often the same fragmentary nature of this Greek reading is continued. So it does not seem to me wise to add to the school reading another small fragment of a work like Herodotus' history. Second, the entire setting of any *new* work must be learned, while with the *Anabasis* and with its author, who in the later books is the chief actor, the students are already acquainted. Third, the subject matter of Books V.–VII. of the *Anabasis* is of much interest. This is especially true of Book V. Here the personality of Xenophon comes out with distinctness. The descriptions of the various inhabitants of the north coast of Asia Minor, of their manner of living, and of the life and home of Xenophon himself in later years, — all this is interesting, and it is told in a language not at all difficult. If less than the whole seven books of the *Anabasis* must be the limit, I think that Book V., at least, should be read. This reading can be done by the student with more ease and with more rapidity than a new work or a new author. Therefore it will be read, I believe, with more pleasure and profit.

There will be a sense of satisfaction in the completing

an entire work, and in the increasing ability to read with less labour in the use of the dictionary. I add a few words about the vocabulary of the fifth book Special of the *Anabasis*. Xenophon's *Anabasis*, Book Advantages V., contains about two hundred and fifty in this. words which have not been used in Books I.–IV. Thirty of these are contained in one passage, a few sections in length. More than one fourth of them are new prepositional compounds of verbs already met with in the earlier books. To the understanding of these the lexicon is hardly necessary, if the meanings of the prepositions have been carefully studied. Other new words are of common occurrence in Greek works to be read later, and an acquaintance with them is a direct advantage. Such words are αἷμα, ἁλώσιμα, ἀνάθημα, ἄποικος, ἀσφάλεια, ἀφροσύνη, βίαιος, γέλοιον, διάνοια, δικαστής, ἔνδοθεν, ἔμπορος, ἔντιμος, ἔξοδος, εὐπορία, καθάπερ, κοίλη μισθοφορά, νόσος, πόθεν, πρόξενος, στήλη, φόρος, φορτίον, ψῆφος. These two classes, of which the second might be extended, comprise one third of the whole number of new words met with in Book V. These considerations seem to me worth careful weighing when deciding the main question of *what next?* It may be added also that this book describes the march of the Greeks through a country which is at the present time of much interest in many ways.

The Greek New Testament. Few, if any, schools make systematic provision for instruction in the Greek New Testament. I do not believe that it can Desirability be crowded into the curriculum, which is of Instruction now over full. But I do think that a wide- in Greek New awake teacher would often be able to get an Testament opportunity to spend perhaps an hour a week with his students, and to start them in this time in the reading of some of the easier portions of the New Testament in their original form. Once started, they could, and, I believe, would, follow up the reading by themselves. If this can be accomplished, there will be a double gain therefrom. First, the student will gain some knowledge of the Scriptures in Greek. I regard this as desirable. In fact, it seems to me that the present ignorance of the Greek New Testament on the part of people who have had a " classical education " is little short of a disgrace. It may be said that the college is the place where this branch of Greek literature should be read. As a matter of fact, it is not read there to any great extent, nor by any considerable number of students, even in those colleges in which instruction in it is offered. I venture the statement that very few, outside the number who may be looking forward to a course of study in a theological seminary, choose this. More's the pity! Few pieces of literature are more impressive or more charming in their simple and straightforward earnestness. But these books are more to us than literature. Stripped of all theological interpretation, they present the first literary message and the first history of the religion professed by most of the civilized world. Acquaintance with these books may be begun at an early period in the student's work in Greek. I would advise urging upon every student who has begun to read Xenophon the purchase of a Greek New Testament. Let him carry this with him to church always and follow in it the reading of the Scriptures. Besides affording him a knowledge of the text, this habit will assist him not a little in his school work in Greek. His vocabulary will be increased, and his familiarity with Greek made greater. I have refrained from presenting any arguments based on religious considerations, but I believe that the careful study of the Greek text will prove superior in moral effect to numerous homilies on the value of the lessons taught therein.

I add the titles of some books which will be helpful in this field. The best available edition for the whole of the New Testament is that of Wescott and Hort. It is published by The Macmillan Company, both with and without a lexicon by Hickie. The same text is to be had, without lexicon, of The American Book Company, New York. Both of these editions contain matter of importance for the text in a supplement, which is condensed from a larger work by the same authors.

A very handy edition of the text is Novum Testamentum Graece, edited by D. E. Nestle, Stuttgart, 1898. This edition may be had of any importer of German books at a small cost. It is quite a marvel of condensation, containing marginal references and text variations. The typography is excellent. The type itself is rather thin-faced, however. There are some good maps at the end of the book, which is by far the best cheap edition of the text.

Good editions of the several books of the New Testament may be had in the Cambridge Greek Testament for Schools and Colleges. Each volume contains the Greek text, with copious notes and analyses of contents, etc. The Gospels, Acts, and the Epistle to the Romans may also be had in separate volumes in White's Grammar School Texts.

The best lexicon of New Testament Greek is by Professor Joseph H. Thayer (New York, The American Book Co.). It is one of the most complete dictionaries for the field it covers which have ever been made.

Hickie's lexicon, mentioned above, is also published separately.

The best grammar of the New Testament Greek is by Professor Friedrich Blass. It is to be had in English, translated by H. S. Thackeray, or in the original German, Göttingen, 1896. It is not a grammar **for** beginners in Greek, but its use presupposes some knowledge of classical Greek.

Burton, E. D. W.   Syntax of the Moods and Tenses in New Testament Greek (Chicago: The University Press).   An excellent book in the field it covers.

Huddilston, J. H.   Essentials of New Testament Greek (London and New York: Macmillan, 1895).   A book for beginners in Greek.   Based entirely on the grammar of the New Testament usage, its aim is to provide the shortest method for acquiring sufficient knowledge of the language to read the New Testament in Greek.   It can be used without a teacher, if need be, and is a thoroughly good book.   It contains also a selected bibliography of works on the New Testament.

CHAPTER IV

HOMER

REFERENCES.

A. Language, Antiquities, Literary Questions.

Gehring, A. Index Homericus. Leipzig, 1891. Indispensable to every teacher who wishes to make a first-hand study of the poems.

Ebeling, H. Editor. Lexicon Homericum. 2 vols. Leipzig, 1885. The largest and most complete work. It is valuable for a library of reference, but rather expensive for individual ownership.

Autenrieth, G. A Homeric Dictionary. Translated by R. P. Keep, and revised by Isaac Flagg. The American Book Company, New York. The most convenient small work of the kind, though not always accurate. Its small cost places it within the reach of every teacher, and every student in school who intends to pursue Homer in college should be urged to buy it.

Monro, D. B. A Grammar of the Homeric Dialect. Second edition. Oxford, 1891. The standard grammar of the language, including forms and syntax.

Jebb, R. C. Homer: An Introduction to the Iliad and the Odyssey. London and Boston. An exceedingly useful book, whose purpose is "to furnish, in a compact form, a general introduction to the study of Homer. The four chapters into which it is divided deal respectively with four aspects of the subject: (1) The general character of the Homeric poems, and their place in the history of literature; (2) their historical value, as illustrating an early period of Hellenic life; (3) their influence in the ancient world, and the criticism bestowed on them in antiquity; (4) the modern inquiry into their origin." These are matters about which every teacher of Homer should know. They are treated in this work with the brilliancy and grace which are so characteristic of the author's work.

Cauer, P. Grundfragen der Homerkritik. Leipzig, 1895. A good presentation of the various phases of the " Homeric question " or questions.

Buchholz, E. Die Homerische Realien. 3 vols. Leipzig, 1871–1885. An extended and, in the main, satisfactory treatment of the " antiquities " of the poems.

Helbig, W. Das Homerische Epos aus den Denkmälern erläutert. 2d ed. Leipzig, 1887. An attempt to illustrate the various descriptions of clothing, armour, etc., in the poems by means of archæological material.

Reichel, W. Ueber Homerische Waffen. Vienna, 1894. An attempt to illustrate the descriptions of armour in Homer by means of the Mycenæan remains.

Lang, Andrew. Homer and the Epic. Longmans, Green, & Co. London and New York, 1893. A general discussion of the " Homeric question " from a literary and conservative point of view. Lang argues for the unity of authorship.

Leaf, Walter. A Companion to the Iliad. Macmillan & Co. London, 1892. Like the last-named work, a discussion of the Homeric question. Leaf believes the Iliad is an enlargement of an earlier and shorter poem.

Geddes, W. D. The Problem of the Homeric Poems. London, 1878. In addition to a discussion of the subject, the book contains a statement of the history of the discussion.

Much matter of a similar nature is to be found in some of the editions named below.

B. Editions.

Monro, D. B. Homeri Opera et Reliquiae. Oxford, The Clarendon Press, 1896. A beautiful text edition, on India paper, containing in one octavo volume all of the Iliad, the Odyssey, and the Homeric Hymns. It costs $3.50, and is a real treasure.

Christ, W. Homeri Iliadis Carmina sejuncta, discreta, emendata. Prolegomenis et apparatu critico instructa. The poem is separated into forty shorter songs, whose comparative age is indicated by four different kinds of type in printing the text. The Prolegomena are of much value.

Leaf, W. The Iliad edited with English Notes and an Introduction. 2 vols. London, Macmillan & Co., 1900, 1903. A fine library edition. The notes are largely critical and exegetical. The introduction to the second volume contains a table of arrangement of the various books in the supposed order of their composition. This table is a valuable analysis of the contents of the poem.

Ameis, K. F., and Hentze, C. Homers Ilias für den Schulgebrauch erklärt. Teubner, Leipzig. The best, and it is very good indeed, edition with German explanatory notes. An appendix contains detailed discussions of particular passages, with the citation of a vast number of books and pamphlets. It is published in eight different parts, each of which contains three books of the poem, and to each of these there is a corresponding part of the appendix. New editions are constantly appearing, and this fact makes it one of the most valuable of aids in the study of the poem. There is an edition of the Odyssey by the same editors, and identical in plan and scope.

Henke, Oscar. Die Gedichte Homers. Part 1, the Odyssey. Part 2, the Iliad. A finely printed, large, clear text for German schoolboys. Teachers may derive much help from the arrangement of the subject matter of the poems, and in particular from the results of pedagogic experience shown all through the book. Published by Teubner. Leipzig.

C. Translations.

Chapman, George. 1616. A convenient edition is that of R. Hooper, in Temple Classics, London, 1898. **Pope, Alexander.** 1720. Available in many editions. **Cowper, W.** 1791. **Bryant, W. C.** 1871.

Way, A. S. 2 vols. London, 1886, 1889. A translation into spirited hexameters.

The above mentioned are verse translations. The following are prose versions of merit.

Of the Iliad: **Lang, Leaf, and Myers**, London, 1883, and **John Purves**, London, 1891.

Of the Odyssey: **Butcher and Lang**, London, 1882, and **G. H. Palmer**, Boston, 1884.

THE arguments for and against the study of any part of the Homeric poems in the high school have often been stated, and there is nothing to be gained from a discussion of them. On the one side there is good reason for objection to the intro- The Case for Homer in the High School. duction into a short course of study in Greek of a form of that language so different from the form which is made the basis of grammatical description and practice that it is almost a new tongue. On the other side, the pleasure to the teacher and the pupil alike in the reading of Homer must rightly be given considerable weight. More than one teacher of Greek has said to me, " If I could n't teach Homer, I should n't care to go on with my classes." For the student who is going to keep on in a college course in Greek, it may fairly be urged that a better acquaintance with prose writing will enable him to read poetry with more rapidity, with greater ease, and with a deeper appreciation. For the student who does not go to college the school course must afford an opportunity to get some knowledge of Homer. We

18

must accept the situation and proceed upon the theory that some portion of the *Iliad* or the *Odyssey* is to form a part of the high school course in Greek.

The field of Homeric study is so vast, and the various problems connected with it are so numerous, that the The Problem first question the teacher must meet and of Selection. answer is that of selecting what he will empha-size, and of deciding what must be passed by. The reasonable answer seems to me to be, first of all, the poem itself. It makes no possible difference to the young student beginning this reading whether the *Iliad* is a unit or a collection of poems. He will not be troubled by confusion, real or fancied, of motive, or by forms which are " unhomeric." His difficulties are far simpler ones than these, or others like them. His diffi-culties consist in the strange forms of inflection, the novel uses of syntax, the separation of the parts of compound verbs, and so on. Not until he has mastered all these and has read a considerable portion of the poems, should problems of textual or literary criticism be suffered to disturb his appreciation. *Sympathetic study and inter-pretation* are the things which will make this, his chief literary study in school, of lasting value and enjoyment.

First of all, in my judgment, comes the reading of the text in an accurate and true rhythmical fashion. If Reading of the the student has already learned to read his Homeric Text. *Virgil* in this manner, there will be no great difficulty with the Homer. If not, then time enough must be devoted at the start to master the rhythm of the verse. The Homeric verse is easier to read than the Latin. The elisions of vowels are nearly all made in the text as printed, and vowels do not have to be crowded out or slurred in pronunciation. Again, the vowels whose signs are doubtful in quantity are fewer than in Latin verse. *a*, *ι*, and *υ* are usually short. In the first two hundred verses of the first book of the *Iliad*, there are twelve cases of ā (not counting inflectional syllables) in which the accent as printed does not show the quantity, or the vowel is not in the first syllable of the verse. Of these the word λαός furnishes five, and ᾿Απόλλων four. The remainder is made up of ἀρητήρ twice, and the rare word πολυάϊκος. ῑ is met with under similar conditions twenty-two times, of which ἀτῑμάω furnishes four, and ὀί̈ω three. ῡ is found eighteen times in the two hundred lines. Of these θῡμός, seven times, and λῡ́ω, three times, make up more than one half.

A careful noting of these facts will be a great help, and save much uncertainty. An examination by the teacher of the passage to be read will enable him to select the more important words from this point of view for memorizing by his pupils and for practice in pronunciation. The mechanical analysis of the Mechanical
Aids in this. verse will often afford much help in getting the quantity. As the verse is made up of dactyls and spondees exclusively, — barring the final foot in the verse, which may be a trochee, — it is evident that one short syllable will never be found standing alone in it. That is, the succession of syllables – ∪ – (a cretic) cannot occur. Further, it is equally plain that three successive short syllables, ∪ ∪ ∪, cannot occur. Two long syllables must be followed by a third long. So a scheme like the following may be used in determining the quantity of syllables which to the eye are doubtful. Let *x* represent the one uncertain in quantity. In the combinations – *x* – and – ∪ ∪ *x*, *x* must be equal to . In –*x* ∪ and – ∪ *x*, *x* must be equal to ∪. I have found this a saving of time in discussing quantity in Homeric verse. Care is necessary, however, that the pupils do not get the idea that this explains the *cause* of the quantity, and not merely the fact. Explanations of metrical difficulties of a special nature will be found in the notes to any good school edition. One phenomenon of rather frequent occurrence is the shortening of a diphthong, *when final in a word*, before the initial vowel of the following word. *E. g.* Iliad A 18, καὶ ἄλλοῐ ἐυκνήμιδες 'Αχαιοί. Note that the αι of 'Αχαιοί is not so treated.

This shortening may be illustrated in English, approximately, by the fuller sound of the letters *oy* in *enjoy* or *enjoyment*, for instance, than in the participle *enjoying*. Other examples, like *employ, employment, employer ; cry, crier, crying*, will suggest themselves to the teacher or even to the bright pupil. The teacher may show, too, that ω is like *oo*, and that in such a line as τὴν δ' ἐγὼ οὐ λύσω, Iliad A 29, it may be considered that the second of these *o* sounds has been elided.

When the quantity of all the syllables has been settled in a verse or verses, and the proper division into feet Rhythmical has been made, the reading aloud should be Reading. thoroughly practised in perfect time. By perfect time I mean $\frac{4}{4}$ time, that is, with its unit formed by a measure that has four beats and can be used as a march movement. In theory nothing can be simpler than this analysis, but in practice it is difficult, because of the confusion caused in the application of these terms of Greek metrical systems to English poetry, in which the principle of rhythm is entirely different. English "dactylic" verse is not in the least like Greek dactylic verse. The English dactyl is represented by the same signs, − ◡ ◡, but it depends entirely upon stress for its effect and not upon quantity. It is really in $\frac{3}{4}$ time. The tendency on the part of English-speaking students, and teachers too, to carry this method of reading into the Greek hexameter is almost irresistible. But the true quantitative rhythmic effect can be obtained by patient practice, and especially if it be insisted upon from the very beginning, so that a false habit is not formed. To illustrate this method, I give a verse with the time marked

$$\underline{1\,2}\ \ \underline{3\,4}\ \ \underline{1\,2}\ \ \underline{3\,4}\ \ \underline{1\,2}\ \ \underline{3\,4}\,\underline{1\,2}\ 3\ 4\ \underline{1\,2}\ 3\ 4\ \underline{1\,2}\ 3$$

πολλὰς δ' ἰφθίμους ψυχὰς Ἄιδι προίαψεν

or, in musical notation,

It will be of assistance in learning this way of reading if each syllable in the accented part of the foot be said in a higher tone. This makes it easier to be certain of the time given to the ictus syllable. The hardest part of this method, and the point in which I have found the most difficulty in practice, lies in securing the proper time for the unaccented long syllable of a spondee. For example. in the verse given the -λᾱς of πολλάς, the -φθῑ of ἰφθίμους, and the ψῡ of ψυχάς. The student invariably inclines to shorten these and all similar syllables and so to revert to $\frac{3}{4}$ time. Reading the verses while marching, or, better yet, reciting them from memory, is one way of improving the rendering of them. Or let the class in concert recite while the teacher beats time himself, or selects a leader from the class to do this.

When the class has acquired the ability to divide properly the verses into feet, and to read them in strictly correct time, the students should be taught **Reading with** to bring out the meaning of the lines by care- **Expression.** fully distinguishing and separating the words. While a pupil reads, or recites the verses, let the teacher, without looking at the text, try to pick out the words. In the line above, the student, with his attention fixed upon

the feet and upon reproducing them, will probably divide in this way:

πολλὰς | δ᾽ ἰφθί | μους ψυ | χὰς ῍Αι | δι προί | αψεν

making a distinct pause at the end of each foot, and
none between the words themselves. Call attention to
the fact that there is no such word as μουςψυ or χαςαϊ.
It cannot be too often emphasized that this poetry was
composed for recitation, not for reading; and that it
was to be understood by hearing. The only way to
reproduce the effect and to get any adequate idea of
the artistic form is to imitate this process of reciting as
best we may. This same principle must be borne in
mind in discussing the cæsural pause of the verse. It
should be an aid to the understanding of the poet's
meaning. Therefore what is closely joined in thought
should not be separated by it. Nor is it always of the
same weight. Compare in this respect the line given
with line five, or lines eight and nine with each other.
The very common habit of making a complete break in
the third foot of the verse, quite irrespective of the sense
required, should not be tolerated.

The interpretation of the text which has been so
studied, should be, on the teacher's part, a first-hand
Interpretation interpretation as far as possible. I would
of the Text. urge the teacher, with the help of Gehring's
Index, to follow the uses of any given Homeric word
through as many passages as possible, and in this way
form his own idea of the precise meaning and use of the
word, and of the most adequate English word to replace
it in translating. A teacher who has done this has a
command of the text which cannot be obtained from the
vocabularies alone, and can be much more confident of
his knowledge and much clearer in explanation to the
A Typical   class. Further, the students should be en-
Example.   couraged to make a similar study for them-

selves, after they have followed their teacher through the steps of the process in a few examples. I shall try to give an illustration of what I mean.

Iliad A 111–115 reads as follows ·

οὕνεκ᾽ ἐγὼ κούρης Χρυσηίδος ἀγλά᾽ ἄποινα
οὐκ ἔθελον δέξασθαι, ἐπεὶ πολὺ βούλομαι αὐτὴν
οἴκοι ἔχειν. καὶ γάρ ῥα Κλυταιμνήστρης προβέβουλα,
κουριδίης ἀλόχου, ἐπεὶ οὔ ἑθέν ἐστι χερείων,
οὐ δέμας οὐδὲ φυήν, οὔτ᾽ ἀρ᾽ φρένας οὔτε τι ἔργα.

Here the problem is to distinguish in verse 115 the meanings of δέμας and φυήν. The notes in school editions and the vocabularies most used show a wide difference of interpretation. If the editions of Keep and of Seymour are both represented in the class, it may happen that one pupil reading according to Keep translates *not in figure nor in stature.* Another, however, quotes Seymour's note " δέμας, *not in build.* This probably refers to her stature, since the Greeks always associated height and beauty."[1] Now this is confusing. *Figure* and *stature* are not the same thing, and it is hardly possible that the same Greek word meant either one at pleasure. If now to meet the difficulty thus presented we look into other books for help, we find that Autenrieth's dictionary gives as equivalents for δέμας *frame, build,* and for φυή *growth, form, physique.* This is not specific enough to be of much assistance. Leaf, in his edition of 1886, says in his note on the passage: " The distinction of δέμας and φυή is not quite clear. From phrases like δέμας πυρός it would seem natural to take

---

[1] Seymour refers further to line 167 in support of this idea, but it seems to me that that particular passage, if lines 168 and 169 be read, is not a good one for his purpose. Of the correctness of his statement there can be no possible doubt, for *Homeric* times at least.

δέμας as *outward appearance* generally; φυή as *growth*,
i. e., stature. But this latter meaning belongs to δέμας
in E 801. Perhaps we may render *stature and figure*
with about the same degree of vagueness." But Leaf
and Bayfield, in their edition of 1895, translate *neither*
Help from the *in favour nor stature.* So there seems to be
Poem itself. no settled opinion as to the meaning of either
word. Now if, as the next step in the process, we compare *Iliad* B 56–58,

$$\theta\epsilon\hat{\iota}\acute{o}\varsigma \ \mu o\iota \ \acute{\epsilon}\nu\acute{\upsilon}\pi\nu\iota o\nu \ \hat{\eta}\lambda\theta\epsilon\nu \ \text{"}O\nu\epsilon\iota\rho o\varsigma$$
$$\grave{\alpha}\mu\beta\rho o\sigma\acute{\iota}\eta\nu \ \delta\iota\grave{\alpha} \ \nu\acute{\upsilon}\kappa\tau\alpha\cdot \ \mu\acute{\alpha}\lambda\iota\sigma\tau\alpha \ \delta\grave{\epsilon} \ \text{N}\acute{\epsilon}\sigma\tau o\rho\iota \ \delta\acute{\iota}\omega$$
$$\epsilon\hat{\iota}\delta\acute{o}\varsigma \ \tau\epsilon \ \mu\acute{\epsilon}\gamma\epsilon\theta\acute{o}\varsigma \ \tau\epsilon \ \phi\upsilon\acute{\eta}\nu \ \ddot{\alpha}\gamma\chi\iota\sigma\tau\alpha \ \acute{\epsilon}\acute{\omega}\kappa\epsilon\iota,$$

we find φυή used, and a third word, εἶδος, added, while
μέγεθος is used in place of δέμας. This change of word
is a help to the understanding of δέμας. Additional light
is thrown on the meaning of δέμας by *Iliad* E 801,

$$\text{T}\upsilon\delta\epsilon\acute{\upsilon}\varsigma \ \tau o\iota \ \mu\iota\kappa\rho\grave{o}\varsigma \ \mu\grave{\epsilon}\nu \ \ddot{\epsilon}\eta\nu \ \delta\acute{\epsilon}\mu\alpha\varsigma,$$

and by *Iliad* Γ 226,

$$\grave{\alpha}\nu\grave{\eta}\rho \ \acute{\eta}\acute{\upsilon}\varsigma \ \tau\epsilon \ \mu\acute{\epsilon}\gamma\alpha\varsigma \ \tau\epsilon,$$
$$\ddot{\epsilon}\xi o\chi o\varsigma \ \text{'}A\rho\gamma\epsilon\acute{\iota}\omega\nu \ \kappa\epsilon\phi\alpha\lambda\acute{\eta}\nu \ \tau\epsilon \ \kappa\alpha\grave{\iota} \ \epsilon\grave{\upsilon}\rho\acute{\epsilon}\alpha\varsigma \ \ddot{\omega}\mu o\upsilon\varsigma.$$

From these passages it seems that μικρός and μέγας
used with δέμας indicate that the latter word refers to
stature. That μέγας means *tall* may be seen by *Iliad*,
Γ 167, μείζονες κεφαλῇ ἄλλοι ἔασι, *a head taller.* There
are two passages in the *Odyssey* which give us some
help on this point: *Od.* ε 211–218, where Calypso says,
in comparing herself with Penelope:

$$o\grave{\upsilon} \ \mu\acute{\epsilon}\nu \ \theta\eta\nu \ \kappa\epsilon\acute{\iota}\nu\eta\varsigma \ \gamma\epsilon \ \chi\epsilon\rho\epsilon\acute{\iota}\omega\nu \ \epsilon\ddot{\upsilon}\chi o\mu\alpha\iota \ \epsilon\hat{\iota}\nu\alpha\iota$$
$$o\grave{\upsilon} \ \delta\acute{\epsilon}\mu\alpha\varsigma, \ o\grave{\upsilon}\delta\grave{\epsilon} \ \phi\upsilon\acute{\eta}\nu, \ \acute{\epsilon}\pi\epsilon\grave{\iota} \ o\ddot{\upsilon}\pi\omega\varsigma \ o\grave{\upsilon}\delta\grave{\epsilon} \ \ddot{\epsilon}o\iota\kappa\epsilon\nu$$
$$\theta\nu\eta\tau\grave{\alpha}\varsigma \ \grave{\alpha}\theta\alpha\nu\acute{\alpha}\tau\eta\sigma\iota \ \delta\acute{\epsilon}\mu\alpha\varsigma \ \kappa\alpha\grave{\iota} \ \epsilon\hat{\iota}\delta o\varsigma \ \acute{\epsilon}\rho\acute{\iota}\zeta\epsilon\iota\nu.$$

Odysseus replies to Calypso, lines 215 f:

οἶδα καὶ αὐτὸς
πάντα μάλ'. οὕνεκα σεῖο περίφρων Πηνελόπεια
εἶδος ἀκιδνοτέρη μέγεθός τ' εἰσάντα ἰδέσθαι·
ἢ μὲν γὰρ βροτός ἐστι, σὺ δ' ἀθάνατος καὶ ἀγήρως.

In these two passages we find δέμας and φυή finally replaced by μέγεθος and εἶδος. These words are definite enough in root and meaning to warrant the rendering *stature* and *form* or *figure* for them and for δέμας and φυή as well. Homer has a definite picture in his mind in all of his descriptions, and it will not answer to call this picture "vague" because its details are not easily discovered by us.

A second way, or perhaps a modification of the first-mentioned method, is to follow up the derivation of the word under discussion. To take a simple Help from example, the meaning of κνημίς — so frequent Etymology. in the compound ἐυκνήμιδες — may be approximately determined by the defining of κνήμη. Passages like *Iliad* Δ 147, and 519, show what part of the body κνήμη denotes. Further than this we cannot get from information furnished by the poem. κνημίς is a part of the armour and for the κνήμη. κνήμη is part of the leg between ankle and knee. *Iliad* H 41 shows that they were made of metal. The shape must be determined, if at all, by outside sources of knowledge about them. I would encourage students to make drawings to illustrate the ideas they get from reading the poem itself. It is one of the best tests of understanding a passage to try and express in graphic form its meaning. In the same line it is an excellent idea to have a pupil make an outline drawing of a man's figure, and then as the various words for parts of the body are met with in reading, fill them in on the appropriate place of the drawing. I would advise students also to make collections of the epithets used with any particular word, and so to try and gain something of the vision which the poet had of that person or thing denoted by the word. It is this clearness of vision which means everything in the power to appreciate Homer. The teacher *must* have it, if he expects to be successful in his work, and the pupils ought to gain something of it if they are to enjoy the work and to get real and lasting benefit from it. Now, just how far this or a similar method can be used to advantage in a class, must, as in so many other points, be a matter of individual judgment. Something of it can be, I think, tried in any class. I have confidence that this way of working will prevent the danger of that deadening use of a vocabulary in a purely mechanical way, and will bring the students closer to the real living poet. I shall mention the aid to interpretation gained from works of art later.

The turning of the Homeric poetry is easy, if one regards merely the story. The consequence is that it is **Translating** usually badly done by students, done worse **of Homer.** than the translating of Xenophon. Careful study which gives a firm grasp on the details of the narration is the only preparation which can make an adequate translation possible. This must be followed or aecompanied by an equally careful study of the style and manner of the narration. As a guide in this study I think that there is nothing better, after all that has been said and written, than the essays of Matthew Arnold *On Translating Homer*. Every teacher of Homer should be familiar with them, and with the conclusions therein stated, and I should advise that a summary of their contents, or the conclusions at least, be put before students at an early moment in their study of Homer. Try and get students to make direct use of these principles of

Arnold's in their own work by attempting written translations for themselves. These translations should be in prose at first, but after some experience has been gained, the student may be encouraged to make metrical versions. If this be tried, each verse of the Greek should be expressed wherever possible by one verse in English. An adequate appreciation of the rapidity of movement of the Homeric verse can best be gained in this way.

One of the best helps that I have found in trying to point out these characteristics of Homeric thought and style consists in comparing a published English version with the Greek text, and noting the excellences and defects of the rendering. *Comparison of English Versions.* This forces the student to take careful note of many little points which are apt to be overlooked. This comparison of one English version with the Greek may thus be extended so as to include the comparison of several translations, one of which might be put into the hands of each pupil. Or one may place side by side on a printed sheet three or four standard English versions. In using these it is well to take each sentence by itself, first making as close a translation as can be done in the class, and then comparing the English renderings of the same sentence with the Greek and with each other. This affords opportunity to judge how far one translator is dependent upon another for phrases.

To illustrate this method, I reproduce here four English translations of *Iliad* A 428–487

This passage is complete in itself, and affords opportunity for studying the effect of the translations in a larger way, as well as for testing them in matters of detail. I have chosen these translations because they represent different periods in the history of translating Homer into English, and because each presents well-marked individual features.

FOUR TRANSLATIONS INTO ENGLISH OF HOMER, ILIAD 431–487.

I. CHAPMAN, 1598.

Thus, made she her remove,

And left wrath trying on her son, for his enforcéd love.
   Ulysses, with the hecatomb, arrived at Chrysa's shore;
And when amidst the hav'n's deep mouth, they came to use
    the oar,
They straight strook sail, then roll'd them up, and on the
    hatches threw;
The top-mast to the kelsine then, with halyards down
    they drew;
Then brought the ship to port with oars; then forkéd
    anchor cast;
And, 'gainst the violence of storm, for drifting made her fast.
   All come ashore, they all expos'd the holy hecatomb
To angry Phœbus, and, with it, Chryseis welcom'd home;
Whom to her sire, wise Ithacus, that did at th' altar stand,
For honour led, and, spoken thus, resign'd her to his hand:
" Chryses, the mighty king of men, great Agamemnon, sends
Thy lov'd seed by my hands to thine; and to thy God commends
A hecatomb, which my charge is to sacrifice, and seek
Our much-sigh-mix'd woe his recure, invok'd by ev'ry Greek."
   Thus he resign'd her, and her sire receiv'd her highly joy'd.
About the well-built altar, then, they orderly employ'd
The sacred off'ring, wash'd their hands, took salt cakes; and
    the priest,
With hands held up to heav'n, thus pray'd: " O thou that all
    things seest,
Fautour of Chrysa, whose fair hand doth guardfully dispose
Celestial Cilla, governing in all pow'r Tenedos,
O hear thy priest, and as thy hand, in free grace to my pray'rs,
Shot fervent plague-shafts through the Greeks, now hearten
    their affairs

II. Dryden, 1697.

Meantime with prosperous gales Ulysses brought
The slave, and ship with sacrifices fraught,
To Chrysa's port: where, entering with the tide,
He dropp'd his anchors, and his oars he plied.
Furl'd every sail, and, drawing down the mast,
His vessel moor'd; and made with haulsers fast.
Descending on the plain, ashore they bring
The hecatomb to please the shooter king.
The dame before an altar's holy fire
Ulysses led; and thus bespoke her sire.

    Reverenc'd be thou, and be thy god ador'd:
The king of men thy daughter has restor'd;
And sent by me with presents and with prayer;
He recommends him to thy pious care;
That Phœbus at thy suit his wrath may cease,
And give the penitent offenders peace.

    He said, and gave her to her father's hands,
Who glad receiv'd her, free from servile bands.
This done, in order they, with sober grace,
Their gifts around the well-built altar place.
Then wash'd, and took the cakes; while Chryses stood
With hands upheld, and thus invok'd his god.

    God of the silver bow, whose eyes survey
The sacred Cilla, thou, whose awful sway,
Chrysa the bless'd, and Tenedos obey:
Now hear, as thou before my prayer hast heard,
Against the Grecians, and their prince, preferr'd:
Once thou hast honour'd, honour once again
Thy priest; nor let his second vows be vain.
But from the afflicted host and humbled prince
Avert thy wrath, and cease thy pestilence.
Apollo heard, and, conquering his disdain,
Unbent his bow, and Greece respir'd again.

    Now when the solemn rites of prayer were past,

I. Chapman, 1598 — *Continued.*

With health renew'd, and quite remove th' infection from their
    blood."

He pray'd; and to his pray'rs again the God propitious stood.

All, after pray'r, cast on salt cakes, drew back, kill'd, flay'd the
    beeves,

Cut out and dubb'd with fat their thighs, fair dress'd with doubled
    leaves,

And on them all the sweetbreads prick'd.   The priest, with small
    sere wood,

Did sacrifice, pour'd on red wine; by whom the young men
    stood,

And turn'd, in five ranks, spits; on which (the legs enough) they
    eat

The inwards; then in giggots cut the other fit for meat,

And put to fire; which roasted well they drew.   The labour done,

They serv'd the feast in, that fed all to satisfaction.

  Desire of meat and wine thus quench'd, the youths crown'd cups
    of wine

Drunk off, and fill'd again to all.   That day was held divine,

And spent in pæans to the Sun, who heard with pleaséd ear;

When whose bright chariot stoop'd to sea, and twilight hid the
    clear,

All soundly on their cables slept, ev'n till the night was worn.

And when the lady of the light, the rosy-finger'd Morn,

Rose from the hills, all fresh arose, and to the camp retir'd.

Apollo with a fore-right wind their swelling bark inspir'd.

The top-mast hoisted, milk-white sails on his round breast they
    put,

The mizens strooted with the gale, the ship her course did cut

So swiftly that the parted waves against her ribs did roar;

Which, coming to the camp, they drew aloft the sandy shore,

Where, laid on stocks, each soldier kept his quarter as before.

II. DRYDEN, 1697 — *Continued.*

Their salted cakes on crackling flames they cast.
Then, turning back, the sacrifice they sped:
The fatted oxen slew, and flay'd the dead.
Chopp'd off their nervous thighs, and next prepar'd
To involve the lean in cauls, and mend with lard.
Sweetbreads and collops were with skewers prick'd
About the sides; imbibing what they deck'd.
The priest with holy hands was seen to tine
The cloven wood, and pour the ruddy wine.
The youth approach'd the fire, and, as it burn'd,
On five sharp broachers rank'd, the roast they turn'd;
These morsels stay'd their stomachs: then the rest
They cut in legs and fillets for the feast·
Which drawn and serv'd, their hunger they appease
With savoury meat, and set their minds at ease.

Now when the rage of eating was repell'd,
The boys with generous wine the goblets fill'd.
The first libations to the gods they pour:
And then with songs indulge the genial hour.
Holy debauch! Till day to night they bring,
With hymns and pæans to the bowyer king.
At sun-set to their ship they make return,
And snore secure on decks, till rosy morn.

The skies with dawning day were purpled o'er;
Awak'd, with labouring oars they leave the shore.
The Power appeas'd, with winds suffic'd the sail,
The bellying canvass strutted with the gale;
The waves indignant roar with surly pride,
And press against the sides, and beaten off divide.
They cut the foamy way, with force impell'd
Superior, till the Trojan port they held:
Then, hauling on the strand, their galley moor,
And pitch their tents along the crooked shore.

III. POPE, 1715.

The goddess spoke: the rolling waves unclose;
Then down the steep she plunged from whence she rose,
And left him sorrowing on the lonely coast,
In wild resentment for the fair he lost.
 In Chrysa's port now sage Ulysses rode;
Beneath the deck the destined victims stow'd:
The sails they furl'd, they lash'd the mast aside,
And dropp'd their anchors, and the pinnace tied.
Next on the shore their hecatomb they land·
Chryseïs last descending on the strand.
Her, thus returning from the furrow'd main,
Ulysses led to Phœbus' sacred fane;
Where at his solemn altar, as the maid
He gave to Chryses, thus the hero said:
 "Hail, reverend priest! to Phœbus' awful dome
A suppliant I from great Atrides come:
Unransom'd, here receive the spotless fair;
Accept the hecatomb the Greeks prepare;
And may thy god who scatters darts around,
Atoned by sacrifice, desist to wound."
 At this, the sire embraced the maid again,
So sadly lost, so lately sought in vain.
Then near the altar of the darting king,
Disposed in rank their hecatomb they bring;
With water purify their hands, and take
The sacred offering of the salted cake;
While thus with arms devoutly raised in air,
And solemn voice, the priest directs his prayer:
 "God of the silver bow, thy ear incline,
Whose power incircles Cilla the divine;
Whose sacred eye thy Tenedos surveys,
And gilds fair Chrysa with distinguish'd rays!
If, fired to vengeance at thy priest's request,
Thy direful darts inflict the raging pest:
Once more attend! avert the wasteful woe,
And smile propitious, and unbend thy bow."

IV. COWPER, 1791.

So saying, she went; but him she left enraged
For fair Briseïs sake, forced from his arms
By stress of power. Meantime Ulysses came
To Chrysa with the Hecatomb in charge.
Arrived within the haven deep, their sails
Furling, they stowed them in the bark below.
Then by its tackle lowering swift the mast
Into its crutch, they briskly push'd to land,
Heaved anchors out, and moor'd the vessel fast.
Forth came the mariners, and trod the beach;
Forth came the victims of Apollo next,
And, last, Chryseïs. Her Ulysses led
Toward the altar, gave her to the arms
Of her own father, and him thus address'd.
  "O Chryses! Agamemnon, King of men,
Hath sent thy daughter home, with whom we bring
An Hecatomb on all our host's behalf
To Phœbus, hoping to appease the God
By whose dread shafts the Argives now expire."
  So saying, he gave her to him, who with joy
Received his daughter. Then, before the shrine
Magnificent in order due they ranged
The noble Hecatomb. Each laved his hands
And took the salted meal, and Chryses made
His fervent prayer with hands upraised on high.
  "God of the silver bow, who with thy power
Encirclest Chrysa, and who reign'st supreme
In Tenedos, and Cilla the divine!
Thou prov'dst propitious to my first request,
Hast honour'd me, and punished sore the Greeks;
Hear yet thy servant's prayer; take from their host
At once the loathsome pestilence away!"
  So Chryses prayed, whom Phœbus heard well-pleased ·
Then prayed the Grecians also, and with meal
Sprinkling the victims, their retracted necks
First pierced, then flay'd them; the disjointed thighs

III. Pope, 1715 — *Continued.*

So Chryses pray'd. Apollo heard his prayer:
And now the Greeks their hecatomb prepare;
Between their horns the salted barley threw,
And, with their heads to heaven, the victims slew:
The limbs they sever from the inclosing hide;
The thighs, selected to the gods, divide:
On these, in double cauls involved with art,
The choicest morsels lay from every part.
The priest himself before his altar stands,
And burns the offering with his holy hands,
Pours the black wine, and sees the flames aspire;
The youth with instruments surround the fire:
The thighs thus sacrificed, and entrails dress'd,
Th' assistants part, transfix, and roast the rest:
Then spread the tables, the repast prepare;
Each takes his seat, and each receives his share.
When now the rage of hunger was repress'd,
With pure libations they conclude the feast;
The youths with wine the copious goblets crown'd,
And, pleased, dispense the flowing bowls around;
With hymns divine the joyous banquet ends,
The pæans lengthen'd till the sun descends:
The Greeks, restored, the grateful notes prolong;
Apollo listens, and approves the song.
    'T was night; the chiefs beside their vessel lie.
Till rosy morn had purpled o'er the sky:
Then launch, and hoist the mast: indulgent gales,
Supplied by Phœbus, fill the swelling sails;
The milk-white canvas bellying as they blow,
The parted ocean foams and roars below:
Above the bounding billows swift they flew,
Till now the Grecian camp appear'd in view.
Far on the beach they haul their bark to land,
(The crooked keel divides the yellow sand,)
Then part, where stretch'd along the winding bay,
The ships and tents in mingled prospect lay.

IV. COWPER, 1791 — *Continued.*

They, next, invested with the double caul,
Which with crude slices thin they overspread.
The priest burned incense, and libation poured
Large on the hissing brands, while, him beside,
Busy with the spit and prong, stood many a youth
Trained to the task. The thighs with fire consumed,
They gave to each his portion of the maw,
Then slashed the remnant, pierced it with the spits,
And managing with culinary skill
The roast, withdrew it from the spits again.
Their whole task thus accomplish'd, and the board
Set forth, they feasted, and were all sufficed.
When neither hunger more nor thirst remained
Unsatisfied, boys crown'd the beakers high
With wine delicious, and from right to left
Distributing the cups, served every guest.
Thenceforth the youths of the Achaian race
To song propitiatory gave the day,
Pæans to Phœbus, Archer of the skies,
Chaunting melodious. Pleased, Apollo heard.
But, when, the sun descending, darkness fell,
They on the beach beside their hawsers slept;
And, when the day-spring's daughter rosy-palm'd
Aurora look'd abroad, then back they steer'd
To the vast camp. Fair wind, and blowing fresh,
Apollo sent them; quick they rear'd the mast,
Then spread the unsullied canvass to the gale,
And the wind filled it. Roared the sable flood
Around the bark, that ever as she went
Dash'd wide the brine, that scudded swift away.
Thus reaching soon the spacious camp of Greece,
Their galley they updrew sheer o'er the sands
From the rude surge remote, then propp'd her sides
With scantlings long, and sought their several tents.

Other passages suitable for this purpose are *Iliad* B 35–52, 84–100, 299–320. Any translations at hand may be used. I think that Bryant may well be studied; and Pope's translation, which is so generally prescribed now as a part of the high school course in English, will generally be available. Pope's version is instructive. A student will soon see where it is faulty, and, with a little help, will see just why it is faulty. I would **Keeping the Greek Order in Translating.** encourage translating in the order of the Greek. It will be a surprise to one who attempts it for the first time to see how closely the Homeric word order may be followed, and how good an English sentence such an order in translating will produce. Verses 601 and following of *Iliad* A may be tried as an experiment. As with the first reading and translating of Xenophon, the secret of ultimate success and satisfaction lies in slow and careful work at the start. There is no other way possible.

I have not felt it necessary to enter into details concerning the learning of the forms peculiar to the **The Homeric Language.** Homeric poems. Most of the grammars and the school editions without exception give enough material in the way of explanation in this field. They do not, however, or most of them do not, exhibit in regular paradigms the forms of declension and of conjugation.

These I would encourage the student to make up for himself in a note book, filling up the paradigms as the forms occur in his reading. For example, the first twenty-five lines of the first book of the *Iliad* afford examples of the Homeric forms for the genitive singular and the dative plural of the -o stems; of the genitive, dative, and accusative singular of the third declension nouns in -ευς.

The teacher may well point out that from the standpoint of an analytic treatment the Homeric forms are easier to understand than the Attic forms corresponding to them. βασιλῆος, for example, shows the ending of the genitive singular more clearly than the Attic βασιλέως.

Caution should be observed in putting such questions as " What is the Attic form of such and such a word? " In such a case as the genitive singular ending -οιο this does well enough, because it can be pointed out how -οιο through the stages -οιο, -οο passes into the contracted form -ου.

Homeric and Attic Forms.

But the Attic ending -ου for masculine nouns of the first declension is not derived from the Homeric ending -αο, or -εω, and to ask what this form is, or what it would be, in Attic serves only to create confusion as to the historic relations of the forms. The same holds true of the relations of the forms for the dative plural in -οισι and -οις. The latter is not derived from the former. Neither is the Attic subjunctive ending -η derived from the longer Homeric form in -ησι.

The Homeric language is best treated as an independent form, and for its understanding and comprehension there is no need of discussing its relations to other forms of Greek in literary use. If comparison of forms is undertaken at all, the teacher should exercise care to avoid such explanations as, because of their unscientific character, must be unlearned subsequently. The language must be mastered to such an extent as to make the subject matter clear. Further study in school should be directed towards getting a firm hold on the spirit of the poem, for that, after all, is the great and all-important end. This feeling of and for the real spirit of Homer will be the vital and permanent possession gained from Homeric study.

For many, perhaps for most, teachers the question as to just what parts of the *Iliad* or of the *Odyssey* he shall
What Por- choose for reading with his class is not an
tions to read. open one. The selections are fixed for him in advance, either by the curriculum of the school in which he is teaching, or by certain entrance requirements prescribed by some college or by an association of colleges. The question is one, however, well worth consideration, for upon its answer, and upon the plan followed in consequence thereof, must depend in considerable degree the success of the teaching itself. The principles which should guide one in making his selections have been very well stated by Dr. A. Lange in *Lehrproben und Lehrgänge aus der Praxis der Gymnasien und Realschulen*, No. 43, p. 48.

" As it is not possible to read all of Homer, selections for this purpose must be made, and they should be made according to the following principles:

" I. Passages whose subject matter has a high poetical value, or particularly valuable ethical contents.

" II. Passages which shall fix and hold the interest of the pupil.

" III. Passages which have a permanent value in their relation to culture and to its history; that is, which have furnished material of a permanent influence in art and literature. For example, the picture of Zeus in *Iliad* A 528 ff. :

ἦ καὶ κυανέῃσιν ἐπ' ὀφρύσι νεῦσε Κρονίων.
ἀμβρόσιαι δ' ἄρα χαῖται ἐπερρώσαντο ἄνακτος
κρατὸς ἀπ' ἀθανάτοιο · μέγαν δ' ἐλέλιξεν Ὄλυμπον.

Or that of Hermes in *Odyssey* ε 43 ff. :

οὐδ' ἀπίθησε διάκτορος ἀργειφόντης.
αὐτίκ' ἔπειθ' ὑπὸ ποσσὶν ἐδήσατο καλὰ πέδιλα,
ἀμβρόσια χρύσεια, τά μιν φέρον ἠμὲν ἐφ' ὑγρὴν

ἠδ' ἐπ' ἀπείρονα γαῖαν ἅμα πνοιῆς ἀνέμοιο.
εἵλετο δὲ ῥάβδον, τῇ τ' ἀνδρῶν ὅμματα θέλγει
ὧν ἐθέλει, τοὺς δ' αὖτε καὶ ὑπνώοντας ἐγείρει.
τὴν μετὰ χερσὶν ἔχων πέτετο κρατὺς ἀργειφόντης.

" IV. Each portion selected must be complete in itself.

" V. Passages should be chosen in which the chief characters are active, and which show the basic fabric of the poem; that is, of the *Odyssey*, passages in which Odysseus appears as chief figure, and of the *Iliad* those in which Achilles is prominent. But in the *Iliad* there are other heroes to whose deeds whole passages are devoted."

These principles of selection may be applied to both poems. For the *Iliad*, however, we must face another problem, which is this: Shall we take passages alone which carry forward the main action? Or shall we include in our selections those which contain episodes not connected so directly with the wrath of Achilles, the quarrel with Agamennon, and the results attendant thereon? In the *Iliad*

And further: Shall we, if we *do* include these episodes, take them in the order in which they come in our Homer, or treat them separately, as stories not directly connected with the main narrative? It is of interest to see how Dr. Lange's selections from the *Iliad*, made on the basis he advocates, turn out. I add, therefore, the *Iliad* as he arranges it in his scheme.

The *Iliad* is begun in the fifth year of the study of Greek, and after the *Odyssey* has been read during the two years immediately previous.

He prescribes Book I. all, II. 1–483, III. all, IV. 1–250, VI. 119–529, VII. 1–312, IX. 1–523 and 600–713, XI. 1–520, XII. 35–471, XV. 592–746. This makes a total of 4225 verses for this year of reading. It is followed in the fourth year of Homeric reading, which is the sixth in Greek study and the final year of the German gymnasium, by these passages of the remaining books of the *Iliad:* XVI. all, XVII. 1–236, 426–462, 651–761, XVIII. all, XIX. 1–214, 277–424, XXI. all, XXII. all, XXIII. 1–261, XXIV. all.   Or a total in this year of 4421 verses.   The amount covered in both these years is 8646 verses, which is more than one half of the total number of verses, 15,693, of the poem.   I will not go through the *Odyssey* in similar detailed fashion, but his total number of lines there is 5414, or less than one half the total number of 12,110 verses in

and in the   the entire poem.   In this scheme for the
Odyssey.   readings in the *Odyssey*, Books II., III., IV ,
XV., XVIII., XX., XXIV. are omitted altogether, and 79 verses only are included of Book I.   This is in striking contrast to the latest school edition of the *Odyssey* published in the United States, in which Books I.–IV. are given entire.

Returning to the consideration of the *Iliad*, it will be evident that the four thousand lines which our present

Present Ar-   programme of reading requires, may be so
rangement   chosen from the poem that they will include
of School   more of its famous parts than they do now.
Reading.
As it is, I think the student rarely gets a clear idea of the action of the poem.   The first book is reasonably clear.   Achilles' resentment, his prayer to his mother Thetis, her request of Zeus and the promise of the latter, are plainly told, and there is none of that bewildering confusion of motive which begins almost at the start in Book II.   To select from the *Iliad* such portions as would carry out the theme stated in Book I., and contain the subsequent decision of Achilles, first to send Patroclus, and then, after the latter's death, to enter the fight himself, the resulting fight with Hector, the death and burial of Hector and

the ransoming of his body by Priam, — this would give a complete story and include some of the most famous scenes of the poem. Such a plan, the details of which might be varied by any teacher according to his own tastes, or as the limitations of time permit, would have decided advantages over the plan of reading now followed. A scheme may be worked out by the aid of Leaf's arrangement in the introduction to the second volume of his edition. I do not mean to say that any theory of the " Homeric question " should be made the basis of selection. That question is not suited for discussion in school, and need not be raised. It is simply a question of selecting from a larger body of poetry a sufficient amount for the purpose in hand.

I believe the *Odyssey* is the better poem with which to begin the school work in Homer. The Greek is easier, for one thing, and the story is plainer **Advantages** and presents more variety within a limited **of the** compass of text. Books IX.–XII. may be **Odyssey.** taken first, and followed up by Books V., VI., VII., VIII., and a part of XIII. These books, in which large omissions may be made according to choice, as necessity may compel, give the story of the wanderings of Odysseus from Troy back to Ithaca. They are of especial interest in matter and manner to students reading Virgil's *Æneid*, and well suited to be studied at the same time. If this plan is followed in the preparatory course, the student who enters college will be able to read, with his increased power, a much larger portion of the *Iliad*. But the interests of the pupils who do not go beyond the school should not be forgotten, and they may sometimes be made the controlling motive in choosing between the *Iliad* and the *Odyssey*.

CHAPTER V

GREEK COMPOSITION

REFERENCES.

Sidgwick, A. Introduction to Greek Prose Composition. London, Longmans; Boston, Ginn & Co. Far too difficult a book for use in schools, but containing much explanatory matter of great value to teachers. A further work by the same author is Lectures on Greek Prose Composition, London and New York, Longmans. This, too, is full of valuable hints and suggestions.

Allinson, F. G. Greek Prose Composition. Boston, Allyn & Bacon, 1890. Contains good " Notes on Idiom and Syntax, Rules for the Cases, Rules for the Accent."

BY common agreement in the statements of all teachers whose experiences I have learned, this is the part of Subject is not Greek instruction in school which is regarded liked. with the least satisfaction by teachers themselves, and the part which gives the most meagre returns for the labour it involves. Teachers and school programs are apt to slight it, and students seek to shirk it as far as they can. And yet it ought not to prove so uninteresting. Composition is in its nature not unlike a problem to be solved. In a way it is like a puzzle to be guessed. Now, this characteristic, this containing something to be discovered, to be guessed, has always the power of attracting a student's mind. But the puzzle must not be too difficult. One tires soon of puzzles which he cannot work out to an evident answer, or of riddles which he Because it is cannot guess. At the same time the problem often too must be hard enough to furnish stimulus to Difficult. the pupil. I believe that most of the mistakes made in the teaching of Greek composition, so far as books for that purpose go, lie, first, in making the problem or problems too difficult. One passage offers often too many hard points for solution. I quote as an example a part of the first exercise set in a book on composition, a book which has some good features. It is as follows: "When, now, the Cilician queen saw the Greeks with spears atilt coming on and running with shouts toward the Persian camp, and saw the barbarians running away in fright, she fled from her carriage in great alarm. And the fear of all the barbarians was so great that even the marketmen forsook their wares and ran away. Cyrus, however, was much pleased when from his chariot he saw the brilliant discipline of the Greeks, who ran with laughter to their tents, while the barbarians feared them and were fleeing from them; for he was taking the Greeks with him that he might not be forced to wage a long war with the king, but that he might destroy his great power in one battle." The Greek text on which this exercise is based affords no example of such complex arrangement of clauses as the last sentence here seems to call for. The multiplication of difficulties produces at least two bad results: first, a discouragement on the part of the student; and secondly, a too lenient judgment on the part of the teacher of the results reached by the pupil. I can see no value at all in the writing of Greek unless the results are to be exact and are to be measured by exact standards, and by rules which are so definite that the students can understand and master them. Otherwise the exercise can result only in a half knowledge which will reveal itself in equally lax habits in translating from Greek into English.

A second cause which contributes in my judgment to the lack of success so often met with in the teaching of Greek composition is the selec- **Subject Matter.** tion of subject matter for the exercises in writing which is not connected with the Greek text being read at the same time. This habit brings up a new vocabulary of words, rarely furnishes topics of interest, and, what is the most important of all, does not afford an opportunity of comparing the exercises written by the student with the original Greek text. This method is fortunately far less common than formerly.

I think there is substantial agreement as to the object of the work in Greek composition in the school. It is to Object of "get a firmer hold on the facts of accidence, Composition. of syntax and of idiom," to enable the student to read Greek more intelligently and to translate more exactly. It is, indeed, true here that "writing maketh the exact man." The writing of Greek should, I think, be kept up continuously from the very first lesson, — a daily exercise, if possible, and at any rate, not less frequently than once a week. The work ought to be (1) simple, — that is, proportionate to the knowl edge already gained; (2) progressive in difficulty; (3) designed to cover systematically the most important parts of noun and of verb syntax; (4) be directly connected in subject matter with the reading which is being carried on at the same time.

When the student begins the reading of the *Anabasis*, and has presumably written sentences in Greek in con-Composition nection with the beginners' book he has been while Read- using, he will be ready for composition work ir g. somewhat more difficult and of a different kind. Just what will be most needed and just what he will be prepared to do, must be a matter to be settled by the individual judgment of his teacher. The question will require possibly a different answer for each class. I think one may assume that the average student will have learned by this time how to use the cases in their commoner constructions, and the moods and tenses in the less complicated forms of sentences. He must now face longer sentences in his reading, and with them the problem of arranging clauses in the sentence. This, then, suggests the first point of importance and often of difficulty.

The Articulation of Clauses. It is certainly ·true that the Greek makes use of a greater number of particles to express various relations of clauses than the English does. And yet I do not assent to the rule often given, " Always begin each clause with a conjunction or particle." Sometimes the reasons given by students for using this or that particle have reminded me of Topsy's explanation that " she must 'fess something and could n't think of anything else to 'fess "[1] I should much prefer to put it in this way· " Never use a particle unless you can give a reason why you choose the particular one employed." This joining of clauses is of the highest importance. Stylistic effect is largely dependent upon it.

Importance of Greek Particles.

The best way to study the principles involved is by careful study of a Greek paragraph or two. Let us take Xenophon's *Anabasis*, I. 1, 4, 5 as an illustration. 'Ο δ' ὡς ἀπῆλθε κινδυνεύσας καὶ ἀτιμασθείς, βουλεύεται κ. τ. λ. The first question will naturally be why ὡς ἀπῆλθε and not the participle ἀπελθών? And this question will often arise in correcting exercises. No fixed grammatical rule can be given. The meaning would, in most cases, be nearly the same. The reason lies sometimes in the general effect on the sound of the sentence. Here, for instance, it can readily

Example of Articulation.

---

[1] Since writing this sentence, I have received the following answer to a question, in an examination paper, concerning the use of τε. "τε is a word thrown broadcast throughout the Greek writing and language. It means nothing to us, but a great deal to the Greeks. Greek would not be Greek to a Greek without it."

be seen that three participles one after the other would not be euphonious, nor would the relation of the ideas expressed by the different participles be easily grasped. More weight is often given to a thought expressed by a clause with a finite verb. Compare *Anab.* I. 1, 7: Ὁ δὲ Κῦρος ὑπολαβὼν τοὺς φεύγοντας συλλέξας στράτευμα ἐπολιόρκει Μίλητον. Here the description carries us rapidly forward to the besieging of Miletus. Dakyn's translation, "Cyrus, on his side, welcomed these fugitives, and having collected an army laid siege to Miletus," does not move on to the main point with equal swiftness. Compare further *Anab.* I. 2, 4 with I. 2, 5. To enable the student to become familiar with both forms of expression, it is well to have him write both a participial clause and its equivalent dependent clause with a conjunction, for each English dependent clause. Then help him to select the one which under the circumstances seems the better in each case. The next point in this

Greek and English Word Order. sentence is the question why the order should be ὁ δ' ὡς ἀπῆλθε, and not ὡς δ' ἀπῆλθε. This difference in idiom between the English and the Greek is fundamental, and, if not already learned, should be copiously illustrated and explained. Further points for consideration in connection with this clause are: Is ὡς the most common conjunction? Ask the student to note ἐπεί used for this purpose. Is the aorist different from the imperfect? Keep a memorandum of the uses of each. What are some of the uses of ὡς? Regarding this last question on the uses of ὡς, the practice of Xenophon in the *Anabasis*, if one takes Joost's figures, is not to use it extensively in temporal clauses. The verbs denoting sense perception make up two thirds of all occurrences. The phrase ὡς εἶδον (εἶδεν) forms over one third. So, I should say, it were better not to introduce this use of ὡς in practice. It is better to give as few equivalents for an English expression or word as may be enough to get along with. The next clause with ὅπως should be compared with the first sentence of § 6, where ὅπως appears as a final particle. The translation *how that* will answer for both clauses. ἀλλά. Point out difference in use between this word and δέ, and give sentences to illustrate these uses. μὲν δή. This μέν has no δέ corresponding to it, and the fact should be noted. I. 1, 5. ὅστις δ᾽ ἀφικνοῖτο, *whoever*. Compare this word with the conditional εἰ δέ τι of I. 5, 1. Make several sentences in English with *whoever, whatever* clauses, and let each be turned into Greek in two ways, with a relative and with εἴ τις phrase. ὥστε with the infinitive. It may be as well, in choosing between the infinitive and the indicative construction with ὥστε, to allow the pupil to follow the English set for him. If the infinitive is used in the English sentence, *so as to*, then the infinitive in Greek: if in English *so that*, then the indicative in Greek. The line between the two constructions is a difficult one to draw, and I do not think it the best way of employing a pupil's time at this stage of his progress to attempt to explain such delicate questions, even if a satisfactory statement were possible.

Closely connected with the use of conjunctions and particles is the wide extension of the participle construction in Greek as compared with English. I find often that fairly good students are not familiar with this use in Greek. In setting **The Use of Participles in Greek.** sentences for translation, the teacher should call for both ways of phrasing subordinate clauses, as above suggested; and for some sentences, too, where the genitive wlll be needed as well as the nominative. In the sentence under consideration φιλοῦσα (causal) and διατιθείς (temporal) are good examples of the "imperfect participle."

Especially should it be made clear that a subordinate clause with the pluperfect in English should be rendered by the *aorist* participle. Important also are the uses corresponding to English *the men who are doing, saying, etc.*, or *those who do, say, etc.* Greek οἱ ποιοῦντες.

The uses of the various pronouns are frequently not well learned. ἐκεῖνος and αὐτός, οὗτος and ὅδε are too often confounded. The rules for their use are perfectly simple, and it must be from failure to notice their uses in reading or from lack of practice that the confusion arises. The habit of translating into English by pronouns strongly emphasized wherever they are used as the equivalents of the Greek demonstratives, will prove a great help. The English sentences given for translation into Greek should be made to show this, whether they are given to the class in writing or orally. *Anabasis*, I. 1, 4, and 5, furnish two or three good illustrations. Do not allow αὐτόν to be given emphasis in any English translation, or to be put in the emphatic place, first in its clause, in Greek. The form ταῦτα proves a stumbling-block in the way of good translation in many cases. We do not say in English *these things*, or *such things*, with any frequency. And yet ταῦτα and τοιαῦτα are exceedingly common in Greek. ταῦτα means *this* over and over again. Or we may, in cases where ταῦτα is the object of a verb, put the special meaning of the verb into the form of a noun, and then translate the verb by such a general word as *made, did, etc.* E. g. ταῦτα εἶπεν, *he said this*, or *he made this statement* (*statements*).

One other group of pronominal words needs attention — the correlatives. I have spoken of them above (page 259).

An exercise of great value consists in making a sentence for translation that contains one word in a variety

Demonstrative Pronouns (side note)

of meanings calling for a number of different words in Greek. For example, English *that* may be chosen, and a sentence like this given: " Xenophon tells us **Various** in the Anabasis *that* Cyrus collected an army **Devices for** *that* he might march against his brother. He **Practice.** did this so secretly *that* his brother did not perceive *that* plot." Or to illustrate the word *ask:* " Cyrus *asks* Clearchus to *ask* the soldiers why they *ask* for more pay." Other English words of common occurrence, and which may be profitably used for such work are these: *To*, as a preposition in various senses, as an indication of a purpose clause, before an infinitive. *Then*, which must be distinguished carefully when emphatic and temporal — in that case corresponding to τότε, and when inferential or transitional, when it is to be translated by οὖν· *Now*, to be treated in a similar way. *Would*, when used where Greek optative is required or allowed, has two distinct values in Greek. It is either conditional, or it represents a *will* of direct discourse. ˙These two uses, I have found, are very often confused in the student's mind, and consequently in his composition. Another way would be to give a number of English words in a sentence, all of which are to be rendered by the same word in Greek. The prepositions will furnish examples here. The various uses of one Greek word may be grouped together and illustrated in one exercise. The various ways of expressing one idea will prove a good theme for practice at one time. Take a sentence, for instance, which contains a clause of purpose, and let the students endeavour to express the purpose clause in as many ways as possible. The same plan may be followed for the expression of cause, of time, and so on. Other phrases often mistranslated are *he must do, he had to do, he ought to do.* Correct translation from the Greek in the first place, is the best help to right use in composition. If a student is allowed to translate δεῖ with the infinitive by *it is necessary for*, he is pretty sure to use a dative in Greek when told to express a thought by δεῖ.

The order of words in writing is always puzzling to a beginner. The Greek order is quite free, and often **Order of** corresponds to the English order in the same **Words.** sentence. The student should be cautioned against putting the verb at the end of its clause in all cases, against putting an unemphatic word first in the sentence, and against misplacing the particles used. In particular, ἄν should not be put first in its clause.[1] The proper position of attributive and of predicate words should be strictly noted and followed. For the rest, the best advice is to follow models to be found in the Greek text. Make the pupil feel that he must be ready to give a reason for the order in which he places his words, as well as for the choice of the words themselves. The really dangerous attitude toward the matter is one which assumes that it does not make any difference how it is done. If a reason cannot be found for a particular arrangement, then it is best to admit the fact plainly, but only after a reason has been diligently sought for.

In this review of some of the problems presented by this part of the teaching of Greek, I have not attempted to be exhaustive, or to do more than suggest **Teaching of** ways of meeting certain defects and difficul-**Composition** ties which I have found to be common. I **means Hard** wish to add, however, my firm conviction **Work.** that no lasting results can be secured without constant and hard labour by the teacher in correcting the exercises

---

1 I should not think it necessary to emphasize this, had I not found ἄν so misplaced in an illustrative sentence in a book on composition which is widely used.

written by the student. This should be done for every exercise given out and for each individual paper. There is no efficient substitute for this work. Allowing the students to correct their own exercises from a model sentence or sentences written on the blackboard, will not answer at all. The mistakes made are so varied that they demand individual treatment. In a class of any considerable size, I think it well, after each paper has been corrected and handed back to its writer, to take up the essential points involved in the lesson, and treat them at length with blackboard illustration. This gives an opportunity to take up and consider the misconceptions which have been discovered through the mistakes made, and allows of individual questions on any matters connected with the exercise. The information which the teacher gains in this way is of great aid in choosing the points to be emphasized in the following lessons. As a valuable aid in this work of correction, the students should be compelled to write all of their exercises upon paper specially prepared for this purpose, and put up in padded form, with a code of abbreviations of the highest value. It is called the *Greek Composition Tablet*, was devised by Professor B. L. D'Ooge, and is published by Messrs. Ginn & Co., Boston.

CHAPTER VI

GEOGRAPHY AND HISTORY

REFERENCES.

Holm, A. History of Greece, 4 vols. New York, 1896–1898. The best general history of Greece which takes account of recent investigations and explorations.

Oman, C. W. C. A History of Greece from the earliest times to the death of Alexander the Great. London and New York, Longmans, 1891.

Botsford, G. W. A History of Greece for High Schools and Academies. New York, Macmillan, 1899. A book of the highest value to every teacher of Greek history. It gives much space to the social and literary development of the people. Contains also good lists of selected books of value to teachers in this field.

Cox, G. W. Lives of Greek Statesmen, 2 vols. New York, 1886.

Abbott, E. Pericles and the Golden Age of Athens. New York, 1891.

Wheeler, B. I. Alexander the Great. The Merging of East and West in Universal History. New York, 1900.

Gardner, Percy. New Chapters in Greek History. Historical results of recent excavations in Greece and Asia Minor. London, 1892.

Harrison and Verrall. Mythology and Monuments of Ancient Athens. London, 1890. A translation of the portion of Pausanias which is devoted to Athens, with a full commentary, many figures and plans. A very valuable work.

Mahaffy, J. P. Survey of Greek Civilization. Meadville, Pa., 1896.

Jebb, R. C. A Primer of Greek Literature. New York, 1887.

Gilbert, G. Handbook of Greek Constitutional Antiquities. London, 1895.

Greenidge, A. H. J. A Handbook of Greek Constitutional History. London, 1896.

For the best works on Ancient Geography, see page 199. The works just mentioned are but a few out of a vast number which could be given. Others may serve as well. I feel sure that these will not prove disappointing.

SCHOOLS differ considerably in their ways of treating the teaching of Greek history. In some it is made a part of the duties of the teacher of Greek; History a in others it is treated as a portion of history proper Part of in general, and its teaching is assigned to the Greek Work. department of history. In their valuable report to the American Historical Association the committee (of that association) of seven criticise unfavorably the first of these two ways of teaching Greek history, and enter a strong plea for a change everywhere to the second method of dealing with this subject. They say: " In some schools the history [of Greece and Rome] remains a subordinate subject, coming once or twice a week, and even then it is often in the hands of a classical instructor who is more interested in linguistics than in history, and has had no training in historical method. . . . The perspective and emphasis within the field covered have been determined by literary and linguistic rather than by historical considerations, with the result that the chief attention is devoted to the periods when great writers lived and wrote. Too much time, for example, is commonly given to the Peloponnesian war, while the Hellenistic period is neglected." All this is undoubtedly true. The proper remedy is, I believe, not to transfer the instruction in Greek history to another department of instruction, but to insist that the teacher of Greek shall have had some adequate training in historical method as an essential part of the preparation for his work. The teacher of Greek must be familiar with the field of Greek literature, and he must have studied some, at least, of the masterpieces of that literature. In this way he has a stronger grasp of the great factors of Greek history — the life and thought of the people — than the man trained in historical method but lacking in this first-hand knowledge of Greek can possibly have. I do not think that a teacher unfamiliar with Homer could give anything like as good an impression of what the "Mycenæan civilization" means in Greek history as one to whom the *Iliad* and *Odyssey* had made Homeric life a real and living thing. A knowledge of the drama of Æschylus and of the dramatic narrative of Herodotus is essential to a clear view of the conflict between Greek and Persian. The verdict of modern historians upon the issues involved in the struggle of Athens and Macedon for the leadership among Greek states robs Demosthenes' name of much of the glory so long attached to it. I doubt, however, if a teacher who had not studied the speeches of Demosthenes could appreciate the attitude of the orator or the power he wielded over his fellow-citizens. The failure to realize this power and its results means failure to grasp the most important fact in the whole struggle.

I urge, then, that the teacher of Greek should be the teacher of the history of the Greeks, as well as the teacher of their language and their literature, and that he should be trained for this work as carefully as he is trained for work in teaching Greek grammar.

The history to be studied is the history of the activities of various Greek peoples and of different Greek states, — a history of the *Greeks*, not of *Greece*. Therefore it is of the highest importance that the student should get a correct idea of the geography of the countries inhabited by these different peoples. The student's first map of the Greek world should be broad enough to include all the lands which were the seat of Greek activity in history and in which their civilization was developed. This map should include not Greece alone — as is too often the case — but all the borders of the Mediterranean, both sides of the Ægean, the Bosphorus, and the western end of the

Importance of Correct Maps.

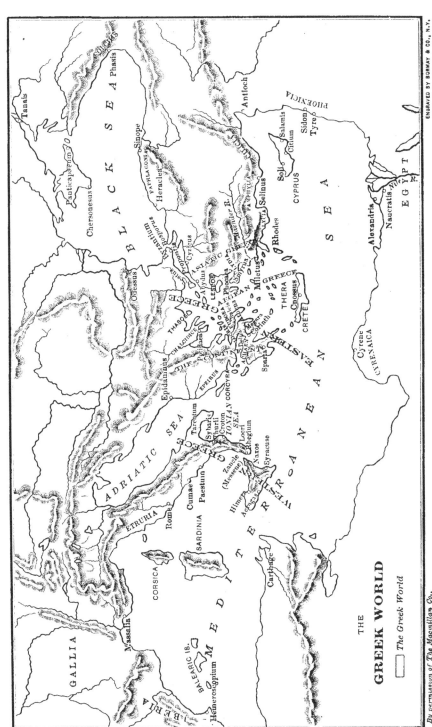

THE
GREEK WORLD

☐ The Greek World

By permission of The Macmillan Co.,

ENGRAVED BY BORMAY & CO., N.Y.

Euxine. No map of Greece can be satisfactory which does not include the Greek cities of Sicily and southern Italy, nor one which fails to show Miletus, Smyrna, Rhodes, Antioch, and Alexandria. The excellent map of the Greek world reproduced here is taken from Botsford's *History of Greece*, by the kind permission of the publishers of that volume.

On this map notice may be taken of these features, and the attention of the students called to them. First, although a considerable part of Asia is Features to be shown, that part faces westward. The Greek emphasized. settlements and cities on the Ægean coast of Asia Minor are in effect a part of Europe. Their history is a part of the history of the West, not of the Orient. Further, the various portions of the Greek world are connected more closely by water than by land. Some expressions in the language itself mark the coast as the starting-point for journeys by land or by sea. *E. g.* ἀναβαίνειν, "to go up from the coast to the interior;" ἀνάγεσθαι, "to put out to sea;" and κατα-βαίνειν and κατάγεσθαι with meanings just the opposite of these. Communication was in ancient times, and still is, easier by water routes than by land. The prevailing winds were during the season of navigation fairly regular and even, thus favouring the development of a commerce which was vital to the existence of a people much of whose land was not specially rich. "From three sides the sea penetrates into all parts of Hellas; and while it accustoms men's eyes to greater acuteness and their minds to higher enterprise, it never ceases to excite their fancy for the sea, which, in regions where no ice binds it during the whole course of the year, effects an incomparably closer union between the lands than is the case with the inhospitable inland seas of the North. If it is easily agitated, it is also easily calmed again; its dangers are diminished by the multitude of safe bays for anchorage, which the mariner may speedily reach at the approach of foul weather. The winds are legislators of the weather; but even they in these latitudes submit to certain rules, and only rarely rise to the vehemence of desolating hurricanes. Never, except in the short winter season, is there any uncertain irregularity in wind and weather; the commencement of the fair season — the safe months, as the ancients called it — brings with it an immutable law followed by the winds in the entire Archipelago: every morning the north wind arises from the coasts of Thrace, and passes over the whole island-sea. . . . This wind subsides at sunset. Then the sea becomes smooth, and air and water tranquil, till almost imperceptibly a slight contrary wind arises, a breeze from the south." [1]

Great confusion arises often in the minds of students from the different scales on which maps are made. Most maps of Greece are drawn on a rather large scale. Unless other maps which contain a larger number of countries be used for the purposes of comparison, the size of the various Greek states is apt to be much exaggerated. For example, Sicily usually appears on a map containing Italy, in whole or in part, and so seems to be much smaller than the Peloponnese, although the latter is but about four fifths its size. Again, the importance of Athens in the history of the Greek world makes the mistake of overestimating its size and the size of Attica a not uncommon one. Attica contains about nine hundred and seventy square miles, which is almost exactly the size of Warren County in New York State. The State of Rhode Island has an area of twelve hundred and forty-seven square miles. The city of Athens was

Comparative Size of Towns and Countries.

---

[1] Curtius, History of Greece, English translation, vol. i. pp. 21 f.

not a large one. It contained about two and one quarter square miles of land, or just about the area of Chelsea, Massachusetts. Every teacher can find opportunities for illustrations of this kind, and thus help his students to get a clearer idea of what they are studying.

Special maps and plans of Athens should be available, and, if possible, a plaster model of the Acropolis. Special maps for the various battlefields are Plans of to be found in many of the histories in use. Athens. They ought to be supplemented by photographs of such places, if these can be obtained. One or two views of the bay of Salamis or of the pass of Thermopylæ are worth pages of description. In the rush to get at the *facts*, usually emphasized as the all-essential points, descriptions are apt to be read hurriedly, if at all; or, if studied, to leave an impression of words rather than a real picture of the scene described. Almost anything is better than a mechanical repetition of statements from a textbook. In teaching the special geography of a locality or the topography of a town, it is always of the greatest advantage to be able to use some illustrations from the localities familiar to the students. The teacher who has his eyes open, and who is watching for such opportunities for illustration, will be pretty sure to find them, and will surely be pleased, perhaps surprised, at the results obtained by their aid.

It is manifestly impossible within the limits of the high school course to give much more than an outline of Greek history. But to do this well, and in How much such a way that the outline shall contain what can be done. is most important, most vital, most characteristic in the life of the people, requires careful training and preparation. It demands that the teacher have the necessary training in historical method, and that he possess such knowledge as will enable him to see the field in its proper relations to other portions of history and in the right perspective. The teacher should have the qualifications for this branch of his work which are demanded by the committee of the American Historical Association. He will then be able to take a careful survey of the entire field, and to arrange his plan for outlining and subdividing the work. It is of primary importance that the teacher shall have thought out his plan from the beginning to the end, and shall have settled in his own mind just what periods and just what events he intends to dwell upon. If, as is commonly the case, a textbook be used, he must understand the author's plan thoroughly. If, on the other hand, he prefers to teach by dictating the heads of subjects to his class, who are to fill in the outline thus given by reading in works assigned them, he must be convinced of the superior value of his own arrangement. Clearness of view on the part of the teacher is the first condition of understanding on the part of the student.

The following division seems to me a convenient one, and one which gives opportunity for enforcing the main Division into facts of Greek history : I. Mycenæan. This Periods. includes the earliest portion of Greek history. It is impossible to fix dates for its beginning or its close. It is made to include all the time from the first traces of human activity in the lands afterwards inhabited by Greek peoples down to about the year 1000 B. C. Strictly speaking, it is limited to the period when Mycenæ was the great state in the Greek world. To this may be given, tentatively, the limits 1500–1000 B. C. Our sources of knowledge of this period of the history of the Greeks are of two kinds: First, the statements in the literature and especially in the Homeric poems. For instance, in the second book of the *Iliad* the poet says that

Agamemnon received the sceptre of his family as a badge of authority to rule over all Argos and many islands.

The second source of knowledge concerning this period is much larger in amount, much more direct in its character, and consequently much more important. It consists in the discoveries made by archæological research and excavations. These have really revealed to us a new and hitherto unknown civilization. In the first rank stand the explorations of Schliemann and his successors in Argos and the Troad. The interest of the high school student who is reading Homer will surely be awakened for this part of Greek history. Simple problems in the relations of the archæological remains to the descriptions of the poet may profitably be assigned for solution by a class. The attempt at comparison will produce a more careful study of the Greek text and of the objects under discussion. Furthermore, this kind of illustrative material is being discovered constantly; and the questions settled or raised by each new *find* are so broadly interesting that they appeal to a wide circle of readers, and the accounts of such discoveries are published in journals of a general character. A good illustration of this was supplied by the accounts in the *New York Independent* for May 31 and June 7, and by Mr. Louis Dyer in *The Nation* of August 3, 1900, of the discoveries made by Mr. Arthur J. Evans in Crete. His explorations there, in addition to much other valuable knowledge, have thrown new light upon the question of writing in Mycenæan times and upon the early history of the alphabet. Material of this kind is more available for the use of the high school student than that which appears in archæological or philological journals merely. Its use gives a freshness to the interest in this earliest period of Greek history, a period with which the student becomes acquainted through his Homer.

The early history of the historic states, in particular Athens and Sparta, and the colonizing activity of the Athens and Greeks form the main features of the political Sparta. history of the next period, which may be limited by the year 500 B. C. and the beginnings of the wars with foreign states.

The history of this period gives ample illustration of the breaking down of the old inherited political system, and of the development in various ways towards newer forms of organization. These changes should be studied, and their causes and their results should be understood.

This is particularly important in the case of Sparta and of Athens, since these states came to represent types of government, and were in the next period of Greek history the leaders in the Greek world. Two other features of the history of this period are of much importance. First, the expansion and extension of Greek commerce over the lands of the Mediterranean. The placing of traders' posts, and sometimes, a little later, a regular colony from the mother city (μητρόπολις) at the points most desirable for trade, was the starting-point for some of the most flourishing of Greek cities. It also gave a distinctively Greek character to the life and the civilization of Sicily and lower Italy, among other countries, which they never lost in later times nor under the greatest political changes. The second point is the creative activity of the Greek mind, particularly in poetry and in philosophy. Some of the finest of Greek lyrics were written in the sixth century. The same century saw the beginnings of that philosophical activity which made Greek thought and Greek thinkers in this field famous for all time. If Herodotus is read in the school course, many of his most charming stories [1] may well be chosen for reading in connection with the study of this period of Greek history.

The third period may be limited by the years 500 and 431 B. C. In the years between these dates the Greeks established themselves firmly against the at- East and tacks of non-Greek peoples in both the East, West. where the Persians were the leaders, and the West, where the attack came from the Carthaginians.

The general term *barbarians* was applied by the Greeks to all other peoples, but the word should be avoided because it carries with it, as now used by us, wrong impressions. The better way to look at this great struggle for supremacy in the lands of the Mediterranean is as a struggle between East and West, and the form of civilization represented by each; a struggle which began long before this time, and which has been repeated in various forms many times since then, even to the present day. The struggle was successfully waged by the Greeks. They placed succeeding generations under a debt of gratitude to them, and in the first rank to Athens.

Athens made the greatest sacrifices in these wars, and Athens reaped the greatest benefits from their successful conclusion. The extension of the power of Athens during the years following the battles of Salamis and of Plataia is the second great *political* feature of these seventy years. There is no danger that too little attention will be paid to the various achievements of the "Periclean Age." In fact, the historians complain that too much time is spent on this part of Greek history. But it is in this time that Athens made some of her noblest and richest contributions to the things of the spirit.

---

[1] *E. g.*, the story of Crœsus and Solon, of Cleobis and Bito, of Arion, of Agariste.

A fourth period may be made to include the years of war between the various Greek states from 431 B. C., the

Civil Wars.   formal outbreak of the Peloponnesian war, to 338 B. C., the battle of Chæronea. This, politically considered, is a period of confusion. The earlier part of it is occupied by the contest between Athens and Sparta, with the allies of each. The success of Sparta is not of long standing before Thebes becomes the chief city of the eastern Greek world, — a place which *she* also is unable to hold. The period closes with the final triumph of the Macedonian power over the disintegrated states of Greece. In other than the political aspect the period presents many facts of the highest importance. The greatest of Greek prose writers lived during this time; Greek art reached its highest perfection, Greek philosophy its most perfect form. The intellectual life becomes more and more separated from the soldier's and statesman's life. Theories in religion, in government, were thought out and put in many cases to actual experiment. The time was in many ways peculiarly and interestingly " modern." A more general knowledge of some of the theories, especially in what may be somewhat broadly termed " the field of sociology," and of the attempts to put them into practice, might possibly prevent at the present time the repetition of the failures which then followed.

Alexander and Hellenism   The fifth period includes the time of the Macedonian empire and the Hellenistic kingdoms and cities, down to the incorporation of the last of them into the empire of Rome in 30 B. C.

Alexandria is the central place in these years, whose interest lies in the growth and extension of Greek thought over East and West. In the kingdom of the world Greece has ceased to have power, in the realm of the soul she has established her right to rule forever.

I do not attach great importance to this particular division into periods. It may not suit a single teacher. One may prefer more, another fewer divisions. I do believe, as I said above, that it is of supreme importance for the teacher to have a clear notion of what he is going to attempt before he begins the work. The least uncertainty or confusion in the teacher's mind will be multiplied many times in the mind of his pupil. As to details of method, I shall offer but a single suggestion. I believe strongly in the value of a study of biography. Wherever possible I should try to introduce it. I am not sure but the story of the Persian War would be remembered quite as well if taken in connection with the life of Themistocles, as in any other way.

I feel quite sure that the Macedonian struggle with Athens can best be understood if looked at in connection with the life of Demosthenes. The main thing — let me repeat it once more — is, first, a conviction that these actions and these thoughts of the Greeks have a value for us, that they mean something to us now; and secondly, a clear notion of what that value is and what that meaning is.

Modern Greece: Descriptions of Land and People. Some knowledge of the country of Greece as it is at the present time, and of the people and their life is a valuable help to the teacher in describing and illustrating places and events of ancient time. The most desirable way of getting this knowledge is, of course, by a visit to the country. But this is not possible for many, and recourse must be had in most cases to the accounts of travellers.

I give here the titles of some of the works best adapted to this end :

Baedeker, Karl. Greece. Handbook for Travellers. English Edition. Leipzig, Karl Baedeker; New York, Scribner. One of the well-known series of guide-books for travellers, and the best in English. It contains many maps and plans, which show both the ancient and the modern conditions, and has also a sketch of Greek history and of Greek art. It is the best book for obtaining an accurate and systematic description of the land and the buildings, and its usefulness is not limited to travellers.

Bent, J. T. The Cyclades, or Life among the Insular Greeks. London, 1885. One of the most interesting descriptions of the life of the Greek people in the districts where modern changes have affected it the least.

Tozer, H. F. The Islands of the Ægean. Oxford, 1890. Similar in theme to the one last mentioned.

Rodd, R. The Customs and Lore of Modern Greece. London, 1892. Interesting descriptions of present-day folk-lore and folk-song, with suggestions as to the connection of some of them with the ancient customs and beliefs.

Diehl, C. Excursions in Greece to recently Explored Sites of Classical Interest. London, 1893. A popular account of the results of recent investigations.

Barrows, S. J. The Isles and Shrines of Greece. Boston, 1898. A charmingly written book of travel. Perhaps the best general book of the kind within the last few years.

CHAPTER VII

MYTHOLOGY AND ART

REFERENCES.

A. On Mythology.

Gayley, C. M. The Classic Myths in English Literature. Based chiefly on Bulfinch's "Age of Fable." Accompanied by an interpretative and illustrative commentary. Boston, 1893. A most excellent work, particularly for its treatment of the mythological element in English literature.

Bulfinch, Thomas. The Age of Fable. A new revised and enlarged edition by J. L. Scott. Philadelphia, 1898. Similar to the last-named work.

Raleigh, K. A. Translator from **Petiscus, A. H.** The Gods of Olympos, or Mythology of the Greeks and Romans. With a preface by Jane E. Harrison. London, 1892.

These three are the most convenient elementary manuals in this field. The first excels in literary illustration; the third in pictorial matter, having many choice illustrations drawn purely from classical sources. The second book has a number of good illustrations, but they are taken from modern as well as ancient works of art, and hence are not so well adapted to showing the *Greek* conception.

Smith, William, Editor. A Dictionary of Greek and Roman Biography and Mythology. London, 1880. A large work in three volumes. A great work for its day, and still useful, though on many points additional light has been thrown since it was published.

Farnell, L. R. The Cults of the Greek States. Three vols. Oxford, 1898.

Dyer, Louis. Studies of the Gods in Greece. London, 1891.

Campbell, Lewis. Religion in Greek Literature. London, 1898.

These three are valuable works of reference on the archæological and the literary interpretation and expression of the Greek religious cults.

B. On Art.

Collignon, M. Manual of Greek Archæology. Translated by J. H. Wright. New York, 1886. An excellent brief work, covering the history of all forms of Greek Art.

Tarbell, F. B. History of Greek Art. Meadville, Pa., 1896. Good general survey of the entire field.

Gardner, E. A. A Handbook of Greek Sculpture. New York, 1897. Two parts. May be had separately or both in one volume. This is the latest and best short work on Greek sculpture, and well worth owning. It is well illustrated and contains a selected bibliography.

Mitchell, L. M. A History of Ancient Sculpture. New York, 1883. A large work dealing with the entire field of ancient sculpture. Somewhat behind the fuller knowledge of the present time, but an excellent book for a school library. There is an atlas of illustrations published in connection with it.

Larger and more expensive works are:

Baumeister, A. Denkmäler des klassichen Altertums. Munich, 1888. Three large volumes, splendidly illustrated. The book of pictures edited by the same man, and mentioned on page 198, is made up of selections from this work.

Furtwängler, A. Masterpieces of Greek Sculpture. Translated by E. Sellers. London, 1895. With atlas of plates.

Perrot and Chipiez. History of Art in Primitive Greece. Mycenæan Art. Two vols. London, 1894. A splendid book, finely illustrated. Particularly valuable in connection with the study of Homer.

Harrison and MacColl. Greek Vase Paintings. A selection of examples with preface, introduction, and descriptions. London, 1894. Magnificent work, but too expensive for the average teacher. A luxury for a school library.

A list of dealers in photographs is given in the Appendix at the end of this volume. I wish to commend the collection of the Messrs. A. W. Elson & Co. Their catalogue descriptive of the history of Greek and Roman art, with a list of illustrations selected by Professor F. B. Tarbell, is a valuable help in making purchases in this line.

CLOSELY connected with Greek history is the subject of Greek Mythology. The line which separates the two **Mythology** cannot always be drawn with certainty, nor **and History.** when drawn is it sure to remain stationary. Recent historical investigation has accepted as true, and hence characterizes as history, some stories which had long been considered idle tales of the ever-lively Greek fancy. In general, I believe that the tendency of the studies and discoveries of recent years has been towards confirming ancient tradition.

Our ability to prove the truth of legendary history

must always be limited by the accident which gives or withholds the information on which a judgment may be based. But in so far as the effect of these legends upon the Greeks themselves is concerned, their absolute truth or falsity is of no importance. The Greeks believed them, and acted upon the basis of this belief. It is this influence of their legends and myths upon the Greeks which makes the study of their mythology important to the understanding of the religion and the social organization of the Greek states.

Greek mythology is also of the first importance for the study of Greek art. The two were most intimately associated. Religious subjects furnished the highest inspiration to their artists, whether sculptors or poets. In temples, the finest and richest houses they could build, their artists placed the noblest images of their gods. The worship of these divinities called forth the best efforts of their poets and musicians. Not merely the person of a god is represented in the statues and reliefs, but some activity of the god, some one of the legendary events in his life and dealings with his people.

And this is, of course, the case in representations of groups of divinities. A good illustration of this principle may be seen in the figures in the pediments of the temple of Zeus at Olympia. The Apollo, for instance, which forms the central figure in the group of the western pediment is a magnificent piece of work. Its full meaning, however, can be understood only in connection with the help of the surrounding figures and the story thus represented. . So far, then, as Greek mythology deals with human beings, it is closely related to Greek history, and where it touches the deeds of gods as well as of men it finds its most perfect interpretation in Greek art.

These considerations concern primarily the understanding and interpretation of *Greek* literature and art.

Greek My-
thology in
English
Literature.
Another reason may be urged for the study
of Greek mythology, — one which will appeal
to a larger number of teachers and students,
and which may be considered stronger than
those mentioned.   It is the importance of some knowledge of the myths of the Greeks for an adequate understanding of *English* literature.   With the possible
exception of our Bible, no literature has contributed so
largely to the stock of illustration, of comparison, and
of familiar reference in the best English authors as has
the Greek. A mythological name has in many instances
in English been the source of a word, most frequently an
adjective, whose origin in its common use has become
largely obscured, or perhaps quite forgotten.   For example, the words *tantalize, vulcanize, martial, mercurial*
would seldom, I think, suggest their ultimate derivation.
In *herculean, cyclopean, delphic, saturnine* the derivation
has not been so completely lost.   Again, in figures and
comparisons, and here especially in poetry, Greek mythology furnishes no inconsiderable amount of material.
I give as illustrations the following examples chosen
from one poem:

> " The murmur of a happy *Pan*."
> " The pulses of a *Titan's* heart."
> " But some wild *Pallas* from the brain."
> " The reeling *Faun*, the sensual feast."
> " Sad *Hesper* o'er the buried sun."
> " On thy *Parnassus* set thy feet."
> " To many a flute of *Arcady*."

Lastly, Greek mythology has furnished the subject
matter for many beautiful poems in English; and, of
course, English translations from the ancient classics are

full of its creations. Granting, then, the desirability or necessity for learning something of Greek mythology, how can this be best accomplished? Un- How can Knowledge of Mythology best be gained? doubtedly the simpler stories can be most easily learned in childhood. Many children will learn them at home or in their first reading lessons. But many — I fear, an increasing number — will not. These will come to the study of their Latin and Greek largely or completely ignorant in this field. How shall they be taught? One way is by a definite lesson in a book to be learned and recited. This plan is urged by Gayley in his excellent book, already noticed. I cannot speak from experience, but am not over-sanguine as to the retention in memory of matters learned in that way apart from some association or connection with other work. The framework — the names and relations of the greater gods, for instance — ought to be carefully and exactly learned. I should think it advisable to leave much of the details to be taken up in connection with the places in the reading where references to myths or to mythological persons are found. For instance, Apollo, one of the most important of Greek gods, is spoken of in the *Anabasis* in connection with his oracle at Delphi, while in the first book of the *Iliad* he is seen visiting his wrath upon the Greeks by means of a pestilence. The two passages afford an opportunity for studying the different aspects of the cult of Apollo, and so, it seems to me, of fixing in the student's mind these essentials in a much firmer way than if they were learned out of connection with an actual observed case.

To assist this knowledge further, and to enlarge at the same time the student's acquaintance with The Reading of English Poetry. Greek themes in English literature, it is well to call for the reading of some bit of English which has the same or a similar theme. To illustrate what I have in mind, I would suggest the reading of Swinburne's *The Lost Oracle* in connection with the study of Apollo and his oracle. Tennyson's *Tithonus* will come naturally in connection with the reading of the *Odyssey*, Book V. Further material in great abundance may be found in Gayley. It is the existence of a myth as a factor in literature that is the main point to be grasped. As to attempting an explanation of the origin of a myth, I believe that is a matter to be settled by each teacher, as his judgment shall decide. Such explanations are not always certain, they are frequently confusing, and their value is secondary. It is best to treat these creations of the imagination as actual living creatures, for only so is their influence to be at all adequately grasped. There is, at best, little enough of the imaginative left in our school work.

Greek Art. "Though, as a matter of fact, most people are more familiar with classical authors as a source for in-

Importance of Greek Art. formation, the remains of art, and especially of Greek art, are, from its position in antiquity, one of the most important sources for the study of the institutions, customs, and, above all, the spirit and character of that people, and of the changes and modifications of its constitution and spirit in various localities and various epochs. It is difficult for those of our time to realize this primary and essential position held by art with the Greeks, simply because art is not to us the great reality which it was to the ancient Greeks." These sentences, taken from a distinguished contemporary interpreter[1] of Greek art, present at once in clear fashion the importance of this part of the study of Greek antiquity, and at the same time indicate the great difficulty in securing any adequate appreciation of it. And yet an

---

[1] Charles Waldstein, *Essays on the Art of Pheidias* New York, 1885.

increased power of perceiving the beautiful, and greater love for beautiful objects ought to be one of the choicest fruits of study which deals with the one people who in all the history of mankind were supremely endowed with this knowledge and love of beauty, and with the power of expressing it in enduring forms of art.

This feeling for the beautiful cannot be obtained by any reading or learning of facts about beautiful objects. Beauty in sculpture is appreciated by a power Feeling necessary gained through seeing beautiful statues, not sary as well as by reading descriptions of them. The knowl Knowledge. edge of what is good in architecture comes from seeing fine and noble buildings, not from learning their dimensions, or the materials of which they are made. A love for good music comes from hearing good music, not from studying the various books about musical history or musical theory. The most exact knowledge about the syllables, the feet, and the cæsural pause of the Homeric verse will not give the student any adequate idea of what the verse really is. He must hear it read aloud, and must so read it himself, in order to know its beauty. The student, then, must get his power to appreciate the beauty of Greek art by seeing the best of its creations, or, as that is seldom possible in the United States, by seeing the best obtainable representations of them. There is no danger now, I imagine, that the student will fail to see pictures enough in his school-rooms. Rather, it seems to me, is he exposed to the risk of seeing too many. The various processes of photographic reproduction have been so developed that prints of one kind or another are very common. Confusion of ideas, lack of clear vision of the best, must be the result of too many pictures, and especially if they are cheap ones.

A careful selection of photographs should be made for the purposes of illustration, whether of the art monuments illustrating the author being read at the time, or of a systematic course of instruction in the history of **Materials for** art. If there is in the school a regular de-**Illustration.** partment of art with its own collections and with its separate teacher, then help can be obtained from this source. But this is likely to be the case in few schools, and the teacher of Greek must look out for this part of his instruction. What he can have will be entirely dependent on the money at his disposal. I believe it is best to have at least one good plaster cast of some piece of sculpture, and one such cast bronzed. The advantages of casts over pictures hardly needs to be emphasized, and a single example at least should be secured, if possible. The head of the Hermes of Praxi teles would be my choice, if no more than a bust can be bought. If a full statue can be afforded, there is a fair choice between several, but the Aphrodite of Melos would perhaps give the best satisfaction. Not too many photographs should be shown at any one time, or even hung on the walls at the same time. It is better to change the pieces, and so secure undivided attention to the one or the few in view. A great advantage in the representation of Greek sculpture is gained by showing a specimen with the colouring restored, or at least by the knowledge on the part of the teacher of something about the practice of colouring marble. There is one fine illustration in colour in Baumeister's *Denkmäler*. The teacher should watch for an opportunity to look at Hamdy-Bey and Reinach's *Nécropole royale à Sidon*, Paris, 1896, and especially at the illustrations in the accompanying atlas of plates. These are magnificent representations of the sculptured reliefs on the so-called Alexander Sarcophagus of Sidon. Interesting also is the conjectural restoration in colour of the Doric temple architecture in Fenger's *Dorische Polychromie*, with atlas of plates, Berlin, 1886. These last-mentioned are not likely to be found outside of a large library, but a chance to examine the first one, at least, should not be allowed to escape.

Some explanation and interpretation of each piece shown is necessary, and for this the teacher must make a careful preparation. The teacher must have mastered the subject quite as much, perhaps even more, in this field as in the grammar work. In grammatical matters he can give only what he *knows*, and as a guide to the beauties of Greek art he can give only what he *feels*. Colleges give some opportunity for this study of Greek art, and universities offer special courses of instruction in the field. With the aid of a book like Gardner's *Greek Sculpture* such museum collections as are now available in every city of considerable size may be made to supply what deficiencies previous training has left. Simplicity of statement is extremely desirable in all explanations. In no field is it easier to use words which convey no definite impression to the student. Enough of illustration and explanation should be given to show in some measure the historical growth and development of Greek art. This is easily done in connection with the reading of Homer, and then of an Attic author or authors. Or it may be done in connection with and as a part of the work in Greek history. Once explained, the picture or cast should be looked at long and, if possible, lovingly by each student, καὶ οὕτως αὐτὸ ποιήσει.

Most that I have said has been with regard to sculpture. The apparatus for instruction in Greek art in the wider sense must make some provision for illustrating some of the most famous temples. To the list of views given on page five of Elson's catalogue, I should add, if possible, a plaster

Architecture, Vase Paintings, Coins.

model of the Acropolis. This gives a much better idea than any number of maps can do of the Propylæa and the walled sides of the hill. How far any attention can be given to vases and to vase paintings must be a matter for individual judgment. Possibly the school library can own one of the various splendid volumes which deal with the subject and which contain fine reproductions. This field, interesting as it is, is secondary in importance to the sculpture. With Greek art as expressed in the coins the school can do little, though it may be possible sometimes to show some specimens. Possibly the interest of a young collector of coins may be made available for encouraging him to a deeper study. In that case Gardner, P., *Types of Greek Coins*, Cambridge, 1883, will be of valuable service.

It is the duty of every teacher to settle the proportionate value of the subjects presented in the previous The Question pages for his individual work and the needs of Values. of his pupils. To do this wisely he needs such a careful training for his work as has been outlined above at page 207. He needs a thorough training in the language, for no one can teach a language which he does not *know*. He needs a broad acquaintance with its literature, for no one can teach a literature which he does not *feel*. He should have a knowledge of the literature and of the social and political organization of his own country, that he may be able to illustrate the life and the thought of an ancient people. He should know the science of language for the sake of being able to illustrate the phenomena of Greek by the more familiar facts of English. A man fully equipped can rise above the petty restrictions of any method, and may say

σὺ τῇδε κρίνεις, Ἡράκλεις, κείνῃ δ᾽ ἐγώ.

APPENDIX

FOR convenience a list is here given of dealers in photographs, prints, and plaster casts of subjects connected with Grecian and Roman antiquity.

I. Addresses of Dealers in Photographs and Prints.

NEW YORK.
> The Witter Co., 503 Fifth Avenue.
> The Berlin Photographic Co., 14 East 23d Street.
> Braun & Co., 256 Fifth Avenue.
> Hegger, Inc., 37 and 39 East 28th Street.
> George Busse, 12 West 28th Street.

BOSTON.
> Soule Art Publishing Co., 500–510 Dudley Street.
> A. W. Elson & Co., 146 Oliver Street.

MALDEN, MASS.
> The Perry Pictures Co. This firm publishes the Perry Prints at one cent each, for twenty-five or more; size $5\frac{1}{2}$ x 8 inches.

SYRACUSE, N. Y.
> Thompson Publishing Co., Publishers of The Blue Prints at one cent each. The same firm publishes also a great variety of larger photographs.

II. Addresses of Dealers in Plaster Casts of Works of Architecture and Sculpture.

BOSTON.   P. P. Caproni & Bro., 1914–1920 Washington Street.

The firms in the above lists will furnish catalogues or any desired information concerning their stock upon application.

A Suggested List of Photographs of Roman Subjects.

1. The Roman Forum.
2. The Arch of Constantine
3. The Column of Trajan.
4. The Cloaca Maxima.
5. The Atrium Vestae.
6. Portrait of Vestal Virgin.
7. Pantheon — Exterior and Interior Views.
8. Reliefs from Arch of Titus.
9. View of Excavations at Pompeii.
10. A Street in Pompeii.
11. The House of Pansa.
12. House of the Tragic Poet.
13. Mosaic of ' Cave Canem.'
14. Pompeian Wall Painting.
15. The Baths of Caracalla.
16. The Aqueducts Claudia and Anio Novus.
17. The Coliseum — Exterior and Interior Views.
18. The Mausoleum of Hadrian.
19. Tomb of Caecilia Metella.
20. A Columbarium.

For a list of photographs of Greek Subjects the reader is referred to the excellent selection by Professor F. B. Tarbell, mentioned on page 322.

Index

Made in the USA
Monee, IL
12 July 2021